EROS DENIED

is a remarkable and revolutionary book
which, in the few short years since its first
publication, has already become a classic
in its field. Author Wayland Young, a
Member of the British House of Lords, a
historian, and a novelist, here demonstrates
convincingly how the Western world has
through the centuries suppressed and per-
verted the erotic instincts. The result is a
brilliant history of the sexual mores of the
West, highlighted by constant comparisons
to the erotic customs of other societies and
cultures past and present.

"[Wayland Young] strikes me as one of
the best men ever to deal with the sorry
muddle we've made of sex in the West. . . .
When the continuing revolution in our ideas
about sex finally has been accomplished,
Eros Denied will be remembered as a road-
mark along the way."
— Webster Schott, *Kansas City Star*

EROS DENIED

Sex in Western Society

Wayland Young

GROVE PRESS, INC.   NEW YORK

For Liz, Easter, Emily, Mopsa,
Thoby and Louise

ACKNOWLEDGMENTS

My thanks first for their courtesy and help to the staffs of the Library and the Prints and Drawings Department of the British Museum, the Institute for Sex Research at Indiana University, and the Warburg Institute in London University.

From among the numerous people who have generously helped me with ideas and knowledge, I would like to single out Gaetano Cozzi, Raimondo Craveri, Louis Dunand, Charles Fabri, David Foxon, John Gagnon, Milton Gendel, Hans Egon Holthusen, P. C. Koller, Umberto Limentani, Hermann Muller, V. da Sola Pinto, Wardell Pomeroy, Denis de Rougemont, Arturo Stenico, Alan Tyson, Charles Wagley, Robert W. White and Rosalind Wilkinson. Drs. Magallon and Wiener have greatly helped me with inaccessible or baffling bits of research.

And most thanks of all to my wife, through the mill of whose patience and common sense every sentence of this book has been three or four times over, and without whom it would have seemed even more cockeyed than it is.

The collection of material for this book continued over many years and the actual writing of it was mainly completed some five years ago. The text has been brought up to date where this was necessary.

—W. Y.

CONTENTS

ATTIS THE SHEPHERD

Attis the shepherd vowed chastity as the gods commanded, saying: "If I break this vow, may the love I break it for be my last." He broke it. He loved a nymph, and became in her what he had not been before.

Attis went mad; it seemed that the bedroom ceiling was falling on him, that he was being burned with torches, and whipped. He began to gash himself with a sharp stone, crying out: "This I have deserved, and I will pay my deserts in blood. Let the part that undid me perish! Let it perish!" He cut off the burden of his loins, and suddenly there was no sign of manhood left him.

The madness of Attis became an example, and still his soft followers mutilate themselves and wail.

GLAUCUS THE CHARIOTEER

Glaucus the Charioteer, thinking to turn desire to emulation, kept his mares from mating. Offended Aphrodite, having secured license for vengeance from her father Zeus, led Glaucus' mares to her well, and there gave them a herb to eat. On the next race day the mares threw Glaucus from his chariot, dragged him and devoured him.

PART I

Chapter 1

Introduction

Around the thought and the act of sex there hang a confusion and a danger, a tension and a fear which far exceed those hanging over any other normal and useful part of life in our culture. The tension harries us not only in extreme forms, whether ridiculous or horrible, but also in the dim, nagging form, so familiar that we hardly notice it, of ignorance and doubt.

Throughout the rich urban West, though most of all in the Anglo-Saxon West, many, perhaps even most, people spend their whole lives in hesitation and confusion about sex and love.

They hesitate and are confused because they are not free. For a number of reasons, some essential to human nature itself and some contingent to human nature but essential to the structure of Christian and post-Christian beliefs and attitudes, we in the Anglo-Saxon countries, and to differing degrees throughout Christendom, Islam, Jewry, and the societies influenced by them, are unfree in the faculty to love. We are unfree in two ways: as we consider the faculty, and as we exercise it. Love is neither a free object in our minds nor a free agent in our hearts.

No man is entirely free, and the things which bind him are many. Some have to do with his nature as an individual, some with the nature of the society he lives in, and some with society as such. The systems of religion, political ideology, political and economic structure, and so forth, within which each man lives, give him some freedoms and deny him others. It so happens that, for reasons some of which will be examined in this book, the system within which we in England and America live gives us many admirable freedoms, but rather conspicuously denies us one in particular. It denies us the full freedom, the *run* of ourselves and our societies, by staining, by flawing, by cutting off, demarcating, labeling with a notice saying "this is a special corner" the area where physical desire and fulfillment have their function.

Let us take an example. It is the duty of the copyright libraries in England and the United States to possess every book which is published in each country, and many books published abroad, and to show them freely to all who need them for their profession, or even for their serious and systematic interest. These libraries are the image of our national cultures; expressed through the medium proper to them, which is the printed word, and in depth as well; that is, they also express our past through the old books they keep. They are England and America; all the England and America that can be printed, now and heretofore.

But there is an exception: books describing sex are kept locked up and special permission is needed to consult them. The libraries, which are bound by law to have everything that is published and to keep it for individuals to read, are also bound by law not to publish obscene works. "Publication" can consist of showing a book or thing to one person; the latter law thus cuts across the former. Analogous situations prevail in the visual arts and the theater, in conversation and in conduct, and the chapters which follow will examine some of these modes of expression more closely.

This element of unfreedom runs through every mode of perception and action in our culture and is naturally expressed as clearly in the individual mind as it is in society, in the arts, and in custom. If one particular area of a society is demarcated as special and dangerous, then the corresponding area in the individual mind and emotions will be demarcated and labeled in the same way. We regard our sex lives, most of us, as private, important, and potentially explosive in a way we regard no other part of our lives. The conformation of society irradiates the microcosm from the macrocosm, reproducing each social valley as a personal wrinkle, each range as a minute rugosity. In the flux and reflux which binds the individual into society the microcosm irradiates back into the macrocosm so that the same man who approves a law because he personally assents to its provisions will govern his actions in accordance with that law. He will go secretly to a whore, he will keep the bawdy book in a locked drawer, and, because-and-therefore, he will agree that whores should be kept off the streets and that there should be control over the printed word in the interests of decency.

There are good and bad, necessary and unnecessary unfreedoms, but all unfreedoms, whether on balance good or on balance bad, have certain disadvantages. The political unfreedoms of the eastern European countries at the moment are held by us in the West to be bad. By some people in the East they are also held to be bad, and by some they are held to be good, or at least necessary for the moment. But all people everywhere—or at least all people of any degree of humanity and common sense, and there are some of those among the upholders of "communist tyranny"—will agree that they are there. The disadvantage is that the people are—unfree. It hurts.

The unfreedom to discuss, describe, depict—in a word, to possess—sex and love with the full resources of the individual imagination in Anglo-Saxon countries just as indisputably exists; some would justify the consequent hurt in the name of a higher good, and some would not. A long and well developed tradition of thought and expression stands behind each of these positions. This book places itself in the tradition which holds that the unfreedom to love hurts more than is justified by the countervailing gains, and I here take for its motto some sayings of one of the most forthright and intelligent exponents of that tradition: Montaigne.

> On the one hand nature drives us thither since she has attached to that desire the noblest, most useful and most pleasant of all her acts; while on the other she allows us to flee it and vilify it as insolent and of ill repute, to blush for it and commend abstinence. Are we not brutes to call the act that makes us, brutish? (*Essay on Virgil*)

And again, speaking of man:

> All flee when he is born, all follow when he dies. To destroy him, we seek a broad field and bright daylight; to build him, we grub our way into a dark and narrow nook. It is our duty to hide and blush when we make him, but it is our renown, and one from which many virtues derive, to know how to unmake him. The one is insult, the other worth; for Aristotle says that in a certain phrase of his country to *bonify* someone is to kill him. . . . *Nostri nosmet poenitet*. We count our being vice. (*Essay on Virgil*)

Thus Montaigne. More recently, Bernard Shaw made a closely related point when he said it was impossible to explain obscenity without being obscene. This observation rises like the top seventh of an iceberg into the clear air of epigram. Below the sea, six-sevenths of its truth coldly and blindly operate against warmth of life, freedom of thought, and excellence of art.

All unfreedoms can be dissolved and all the laws which express them can be rescinded. There is no political, intellectual, or spiritual freedom which *cannot* be won; so much is common ground between Christians (the redemption), Marxists (the withering away of the state), and ordinary hopeful mortals in between. Freedoms are generally won by being demanded. But here a distinction arises between freedoms which can be demanded even when you haven't got them, and freedoms which cannot be demanded unless they are already there; censorship can make it impossible to demand or even discuss freedom. Freedom of expression—perhaps even freedom of feeling and understanding—about sex is of this latter sort, as is political freedom in eastern Europe now.

Established opinion in the Anglo-Saxon countries holds that it is in the public interest to prevent the publication of "obscenity" unless it can be affirmatively proved that such and such an obscene publication is *in* the public interest. But it is difficult or even impossible to argue that the accepted limits of obscenity should themselves be redrawn without actually infringing them in the process, and having to defend one's argument against a charge of obscenity. In this case, one would have to prove affirmatively that a discussion of the public interest was in the public interest, which is a startling thing to have to prove in a democracy.

The effect is naturally that the present conception of the public interest becomes sacrosanct. If I merely say, speaking generally: "We call too many things obscene, we are too restrictive in our definitions," nobody will pay any attention, and our conception of the public good will remain unchanged. If, on the other hand, I give examples, saying: "Consider these," and give my reasons for thinking they ought not to be held obscene, my book may be suppressed for obscenity before anybody has had time to consider it, and our conception of the public good will still remain unchanged. Our society has painted itself into a corner.

The reader will find many weaknesses in this book; most are my own weaknesses as a writer, but some are the results of this dilemma; the law of obscenity has the indirect effect of perpetuating itself. *You cannot argue with it without breaking it.*

So much for the local and temporal situation. One must respect the laws of one's country, and the shape and content of this book are largely determined by the present state of law and opinion on obscenity in England and America. (Part of this shaping is conscious; I have no doubt part of it is unconscious too.) I have done what I could to keep the law and, when I was in doubt whether a point or an example which seemed to provoke established opinion was necessary for my line of thought, I have left it out. But, though law and custom are good, the free writer must be prepared, if he cannot reconcile the conflict, to recognize a higher good: fact and reason. Our law and our custom are as good as they are mainly because when, in the past, they have conflicted with fact and reason in the minds of certain free writers, those writers have chosen fact and reason.

In this book, I take the idea of *exclusion* as my guiding thread. We exclude sex from the realm of the normal, we even extrude it, so that it becomes strangulated or gangrenous, like a limb beyond a tourniquet. In the first half of the book I discuss the actual exclusions; what is it that we do exclude? First, I take the excluded *words*, and consider the phenomenon of the "words we all know but don't use." Then I consider *excluded images*, meaning erotic art and literature, including the sub-art and sub-literature we are accustomed to qualify as "pornography." Next I discuss two examples of *excluded actions*, and then the principal class of *people* who are excluded from the main flow of our culture for sexual reasons: prostitutes.

Having considered what things we exclude, I turn next to the question *why* we exclude them, how we came to feel that they ought to be excluded. The sixth section of the book is thus a fairly long *historical* excursion which seeks to find some of the reasons why we in this culture, as opposed to the people of some other cultures, do exclude certain words, images, actions and people. After a short section on one particular *means* of exclusion, namely *projection* in the psychologist's sense, and on the myths it gives rise to, I come to the end of my account of what is wrong and how it got that way. The book ends with three chapters describing some of the elements in our culture which might contribute to putting it right.

PART II

EXCLUDED WORDS

Chapter 2

Language: English

The first object of exclusion to be considered, words, is also the medium through which all must be considered. Montaigne well understood not only the consistency of feeling, but that of language as well, and the need for a consistent relationship between them. Still in the essay on Virgil, he quotes a Virgilian love-scene and goes on to discuss its language thus:

These good people needed no sharp or subtle contrasts; their language is all full and large with a natural and constant vigor; the head, the stomach and the feet as well. Nothing is forced, nothing mincing, all goes forward with an equal tenor. *Contextus totus virilis est; non sunt circa flosculos occupati.*[1] This is no soft or merely inoffensive eloquence; it is muscular and solid; it does not so much please as fill and ravish, and most ravishes the strongest minds. When I see those fine periods unfolding, so alive, so profound, I do not say it is well said, I say it is well thought. *Pectus est quod disertum facit.*[2]

---

[1] Seneca, *Letters:* 33. "The whole fabric is manly; they don't bother with fiddle-faddles."

[2] Quintilian, X, vii, 15. (Literally: "It is the breast makes the

And again:

> How is man wronged by the genital act, which is so natural, so necessary and so just, that he should not dare to speak of it but with shame, and should exclude it from serious and gentle conversation? Shall we say boldly: kill, rob, betray, but *that*—only in whispers?

The point is close to the famous one of Confucius:

> If language is not used rightly, then what is said is not what is meant. If what is said is not what is meant, then that which ought to be done is left undone; if it remains undone, morals and art will be corrupted, if morals and art are corrupted, justice will go awry, and if justice goes awry, the people will stand about in helpless confusion.

The people are indeed standing about in helpless confusion; they run to see a man killed on a broad field and in bright daylight, they accord renown and attribute virtue to the generals who are skilled in unmaking men, they proclaim loudly *kill, rob* and *betray*. Meanwhile a forced and mincing language whispers *sexual intercourse, outlet, contact, deep emotional and spiritual involvement, interplay of two mature personalities*. What is said is not what is meant, for what is meant is *fuck* and *love*.

In all languages, but in English more than most because it is a fusion of two linguistic rivers, the Latin and the Teutonic, there are usually several words for one thing. This diversity does not mean that the thing or action is multifarious, it means that our view of it is multifarious. By using a different word for the same thing one may express one's opinion of it, or throw a different light on it, or draw attention to its relation to one other thing rather than to another other thing. Very often there is a senior word, a principal or obvious word for the thing. It may be

---

eloquence." Perhaps "if the heart is large, the pen will be graceful," or even, "*l'homme c'est le style.*")

the oldest, or the commonest, or the shortest, or the first that we learn in childhood. This one senior word, more obvious than the others, may change from time to time. So *buss* has been superseded by *kiss, victuals* by *supplies,* and *wireless* by *radio.*

Let us take as an example a thing where the principal word has remained unchanged for a very long time and does not look like changing: *God.* This is a short, old Teutonic word; below it and around it cluster many longer, newer words and analogical and metaphorical usages, expressing a continual ebb and flow of meaning and feeling. There is the *deity* of nineteenth-century philosophers; the *Logos* and *Paraclete* of Hellenist theologians; the *Eternal* of Protestant hymnodists; the nonconformist *Lord*; the *Most High* and the *Ancient of Days* of those who take refuge in periphrasis from the danger of blasphemy; the *Creator* of the causally inclined; the *Father* of the filially inclined; and perhaps even the *Guard* and *Gudd* of priests who stand so far outside the reality of God that they cannot bear to pronounce his name.

Similar lists could be made for most of the main things that present themselves to our consciousness, and almost always it will be easy to identify the senior or obvious word, the word which children learn first, and by reference to which one would explain all the others to a child.

But when we come to things and actions of sex, the situation is very different. The short, old obvious words are there all right, and they are known to everyone, but they are certainly the rarest in written use, possibly not even the commonest in spoken use, and probably the last one would refer a child to in explaining the others. And yet there is no doubt that they are the senior and obvious ones, just as *God* is for what it means, and *house, love, do* and *go* are for what they mean.

I propose to use the short sex words throughout this book, whenever the context calls for them. But since this is an unusual thing to do in a book which is neither pornography nor a war novel, and might seem deliberately offensive without some explanation, it will be courteous to the reader to introduce them carefully. The whole book will be in a sense an explanation of why I have thought it necessary to use them.

At the end of his *Etymological Dictionary* (1887), Skeat gives a list of what he calls Aryan roots, and we should now call Indo-European roots. These are the single syllables which seem to underlie most of the words in the languages now spoken from Calcutta west about to Hawaii, and from Novosibirsk to Tierra del Fuego. The Indo-European group includes all the European languages except Finnish, Hungarian and Basque, most of the Indian languages, and the three great dead languages, Sanskrit, Greek and Latin.

In a sense, the whole science of distilling the Indo-European languages back to find the common sound is no more than a game; that is to say it *is* done backwards, a posteriori, and nobody supposes that at one particular moment in one particular place some infant with a sublime sense of the suitable opened his mouth and said MUT, and that the peoples of the world heard and agreed and the news went forth with the result that we all still say *mother* and *mère* and *mutter* and *madre* and *mat'* and *māe*. But the fact remains that this is what we do say, and it is quite remarkable enough to justify the drawing up of a list which gives MA or MU for the basic motherward sound, and the corresponding baby-like formulation for many hundreds of other meanings.

No. 242 in Skeat's list signifies "grow, become, be, dwell, build." It underlies, he holds, our words *future* and *felicity* and *fecund*, and also *fawn* and *bower*. It is present in the Greek word *phusis*, (nature, or suchness) which gave us our *physics* and, in the Latin *fui*, I was, and *felis*, a cat, or fruitful thing, in the still-used Latin word *fetus*, and in the German *bauen*, to build, with all its countless derivatives. Skeat's No. 243 signifies "enjoy or use," and is present in *fruit* and *fruition* and *function* and the French *froment*.

The roots as Skeat writes them are BHU and BHUG. Try making this sound; one blows it out in a sort of generous scattering, or one may feel it as a puff of contentment. It seems to be around today still uninflected in the wolf-whistle, and the exclamation written *Whew!* If indeed this noise is really the basic noise for all that is constructive, peaceful, pleasant, forward-looking—to be, to grow and to build—one may wonder that Skeat left out the most obvious manifestation of all: *fuck*. The word is central to the whole complex of meanings. It is the becoming of beings and the beginning of their growth; it happens in dwellings and builds children. We enjoy one another and bear fruit; or again, we build a fetus in felicity and become fecund. The form is perhaps as widespread as any in the Indo-European languages; you have the Greek and Latin *futueo*, French *foutre*, Italian *fottere*, German *ficken*, Russian *ibat'*, Serbo-Croat *jebati* and certainly countless others I don't know.[3]

Root 74 in Skeat's list means "to swell out, hence to take in, to contain, to be hollow, to be strong." It is present in our *cave* and *ceiling* and *celestial* from the hollow vault of heaven, and *cumulus* clouds, and the *church* that embraces all worshipers, and even perhaps *quaff*. Root 76 is present in *hug* and *hunch*, and Root 77 in *hide* and *guard*

---

[3] A conviction of my own ignorance seems to be powerless to stop me protesting against Eric Partridge's determination in several books, and most recently in *Origins,* 1958, to connect the word with the root that gives English *beat,* French *battre,* etc. The colloquial *bash* and *bang* of course are connected thus, but surely both in meaning and in shape and sound *fuck* goes with the *function-fruit-fetus* group. There is a whole string of Greek words in phut and· phit which seem to claim this sound as belonging to them: *phutueo,* to fuck, plant, beget, engender, bring about, spawn; *phituo,* to sow, plant, beget; *phuo,* to bring forth, which is allied to *phusis* itself (compare Latin *natura* and *natus,* born); *phutor* and *phitus,* a father; *phutios,* generative. Can one really doubt that a fucker is more usefully considered as a *phutor,* a father, who fucks his children into existence, than as a *batteur,* who beats them or his wife into submission? In the last resort perhaps it depends how one feels.

and *keep*. The roots as Skeat writes them are KU and KUK and KUDH. If you try these, you seem to be arching your mouth and lips into a gesture of containment and shelter, or protection and reception, which sounds the same whether you are sucking in or blowing out. We use the sound uninflected today to describe the noise made by pigeons, and we carry it over to describe people when they seem to behave in a way as receptive as that of the pigeons; "they were positively cooing at each other."

Here the word Skeat leaves out is *cunt*, Latin *cunnus*, Greek *kusthos*, French *con*, German *Kutt*, ancient Egyptian *q.efent*, Dutch *kunte*, etc., etc., and once again it is central to the whole complex of meanings. It *takes in*, it *contains*, it is *hollow*, it is *strong*; it *hides* and *guards* while a man and woman *hug* and *hunch*, and, if we allow the word to cover womb as well, it *swells out* and *keeps* the child.

A prick is of course that which pierces, but the neighboring roots in Skeat are PRAT or PLAT, to be extended or unfolded, PRI or FRI to love (giving *friend* among other words) and PRU, to spring up or jump up (giving *frolic* and *frog*.)

There they are, then, these three words, which are the main words for the main concepts of generation, as old and as basic as house or love or God, but not, apparently, as necessary. It seems unlikely that there is any adult in the English-speaking world who does not know these words, but there must be plenty of people who die without ever having uttered them; it is easy to think of women of a certain age and class who would *sooner* die *than* utter them. There have been people convicted of crime for printing them. Forty years ago I should certainly have been convicted of a crime for printing them here.

On the other hand, if I wrote f——, or f——k, or *flip*, or *muck*, or any other counter which is recognized to mean *fuck*, I should have been moderately safe from prosecution, just as anybody who wrote the M-rqu-ss of Gr-nby was safe from prosecution until we tightened our libel laws up a bit. In libeling the M-rqu-ss of Gr-nby we wronged the Marquess of Granby. In writing f——k, we wrong common sense and try patience.

Writing in Italy in the first half of the sixteenth century, Pietro Aretino said: "If you want to be understood by anyone outside the University of Rome, speak clearly and say fuck, prick, cunt and ass. You and your thread in the eye, obelisk in the Coliseum, door in the orchard, bolt on the exit, key in the lock, pestle in the mortar, nightingale in the nest, dibble in the ditch, pump in the balloon, sword in the sheath, and then your stake and your crozier, your parsnip, sparrow, "him," "her," apples, leaves of the missal, "that," *verbi gratia*, the thing, the affair, the good news, handle, arrow, carrot, root. . . . Now why don't you say yes when you mean yes and no when you mean no, or else shut up?"[4] The coy rusticity of the High Renaissance vocabulary looks absurd enough to us. Consider "he put his sword in her sheath." There is no objection on the score of clarity; if it happens in a love scene, we know exactly what we are being told. But it is absurd, because the image brings other feelings with it. Swords are sharp, dangerous; look out, don't cut yourself. Also, swords are sheathed when they are finished with, not when they are beginning to be used. Again: "She took his parsnip in her hand." Quite clear what is happening, but—*parsnip! Really!* He is immediately a rustic lout, probably malformed, and she, consequently, takes on a character of her own. We laugh in self-defense against a picture which is at best gross, and at worst perverse. Likewise pestle and mortar—grinding duty. Pump in the balloon; steady there; she may burst. And so on.

But are these periphrases really any more absurd than our own? Let us take some of the modern expressions which correspond to Aretino's list. Here is our love-scene; what shall the couple do? Shall they *copulate*? Over our

---

[4] *Ragionamenti:* "parla a la libera, e di cu, ca, po e fo, che non sarai intesa, se non dalla Sapienza Capranica . . ." etc.

picture of them slides a suggestion of two dogs in a laboratory, observed by biologists. Shall they *lie together*? They may do so in siblike companionship a night long and have nothing to show for it. They may even have a Wagnerian sword between them. Shall they *make love*? They may indeed, but what does this love look like when they have made it? It is a pretty phrase, and at least they are making something; but *love*? Is that really what they are making? When they have finished, what ontological chorus stands forth to say—here is what they have made; behold, it is love? If they have really made anything, it is not so much love as a child. Love appears as a child, as a *putto*, as infantine Cupid in our tradition, but it is at best a trope. Fifty years ago people used to say "make love to" when we would say "make up to." "Go and make love to the Deputy Director." Or shall our couple *have intercourse*? They will certainly be said to have done so if the circumstances are adulterous and if they fetch up in court afterward. But where did they find the intercourse they were going to have? There was intercourse; one minute they were not having it, the next moment they were. The same if they *have sex*. Shall *intimacy take place*? They may have been extremely intimate in the sense of being conversant with one another's most inward desires and ambitions, in the sense of being at ease with one another, without ever so much as touching little finger to little finger. Some of our most intimate friends are of the same sex as ourselves, come to think of it, and we are not homosexuals. But if the intimacy that is between us were to go one step farther and actually to *take place*, we should be understood to have behaved in quite another way. It is the police, not normally the most intimate with the rest of the population, who use this quaint phrase. Shall our couple have *carnal knowledge* of one another? The closest carnal knowledge one person may have of another is that enjoyed by the pathologist of the patient from whom the cell was scraped which he is examining under the microscope during a biopsy. Before the growth of modern medical insights, the closest carnal knowledge to subsist between people was perhaps that of a mother for her child. She grows it, she bears it, she checks millimeter by millimeter after its birth that its flesh is in order, she nourishes it flesh to flesh from her own body, she washes it, exercises it in health, pores over and tends it in sickness, she knows every turn and indent and suffusion of its flesh better than her own. But this is not what we mean.

To turn to more vernacular expression, shall he *lay* her? The layer adopts a most aggressive attitude to the laid. He tackles her, fells her, lays her out. She was upright and then suddenly, by his agency, she is horizontal. Or again she was a sort of evil specter who was exorcised by his sexuality; this shade of meaning seems to be present in the phrase *well and truly laid*. There she is, down, fixed, humbled, never more to trouble law-abiding folk. Shall they *get laid*? This form is as fatalistically passive as the last was aggressively active. Each is tackled and felled by the other, or both are simultaneously tackled and felled by some juggernaut love god.

There there are the more remote ones. Shall they *sleep together*? To read a sexual meaning into sleeping together is to suggest that people never sleep side by side except after a sexual contact. Why should we be expected to understand "sleep together" in this sense any more than we would "eat together"? What picture do we actually see if we close our eyes and think of a man and a woman sleeping together? A picture, surely, of a man and a woman sleeping together; she has her head on his shoulder, he has his arm around her; they are breathing heavily and their eyes are shut. For all we know they are fellow passengers on a long journey and, having shared their sandwiches and their life stories, are—sleeping together. Of course it may later lead to their *sleeping together*, or it may not. But language is not water to be poured away in this manner. To go yet further into the mists of circumlocution, they might *be united*. They might indeed; in a church in marriage, in a grave in death, or in a business association. He might *enjoy her*, or she him. Enjoy has two senses. It would be a pity if they did not enjoy one another, in the sense of enjoying one another's company, from the beginning of their acquaintance. But if on the other hand he enjoys her in the second sense, as he would enjoy a reversionary interest in his brother's estate, we may wish that all he had to enjoy in that sense were something which would suffer less than a woman would from her consequent inability to enjoy him in the other. Shall he *cover* her, or *serve* her? Then they are a pair of cattle- or horse-breeders so steeped in their trade that they have got to look like cattle or horses themselves; with a low or a whinny he plunges at her; she is perhaps held down by a couple of stable boys. I have even heard among car-loving English people the expression *service*. She comes into the service station every two thousand miles, is lovingly dismantled by him, and he by her, greased, oil changed, battery topped up, and returned to real life the next morning as good as new.

And there are countless others.

Now this is not meant to suggest that these expressions are invalid or to be avoided. It is only meant to point out that each one means something else as well as its main meaning. They may be doing it in a certain particular way, whether it is legalistically like enjoying, or biblically (and probably hellfire deuteronomically) like having carnal knowledge, or with a conscious well-intentioned industry, like making love, and so forth. The only word which has no other meaning whatever is *fuck*. If we wish to say what happened with neutral clarity, qualifying neither them nor their action nor ourselves as narrators, that is the only word we can use.

Similarly we may say that he admired or caressed or entered her *vagina* if we are in an anatomical frame of mind, or her *toy* or her *treasure*, her *garden*, her *gates*, her *front* or *back door*, if we are in a flowery one, or her *slit* or *slot* or *hole* or *crevice* if we are in a carpenterlike one, or her *quim* or *queint* or *twat* if we are archaic. We could even go so far as to mention her *pudenda*, if we were really pushed for a word, and wanted to tell her *en passant* that she ought to be ashamed of having such a thing at all, let alone allowing a *man* anywhere near it. But the only word which will leave our frame of mind out of account and will not qualify her as the sort of person who should properly be described in this or that special terminology, is *cunt*.

Again, we may think of his *testicles*, or as Cleland did, his *inestimable bulse of lady's jewels*, or anything in between. Or we may furnish either of them in our imaginations with *bottoms*, *bums*, *derrières* or (Cleland again) *posterior globes*. The only words which will carry us forward in precision and freedom from extraneous associations are *balls* and *ass*.

We can look in vain for *fuck* in the Shorter Oxford English Dictionary, Webster's New International Dictionary and other traditional dictionaries. Although no philologist claims that it is other than a language word, it is relegated to the dictionaries of slang and cant, and even there, until Wentworth and Flexner's Dictionary of American Slang (1960), it appeared as *fxxk*. The dictionaries may exclude it, but Anglo-American law agrees with the philologists that it is a true language word. In the case of *Edgar* v. *McCutcheon* (Missouri Supreme Court Reports, 9:768) the plaintiff complained that the defendant had slandered him in alleging that he had had carnal knowledge of a mare. The word *fuck* was used to convey the imputation. The defense claimed that since the word is not found in the dictionaries, it cannot be held to be comprehensible to those that hear it, and to utter an incomprehensibility cannot be a slander. The court upheld the judgment of a lower court; it is an English word, and it does not follow because it is not found in the dictionaries that it is not understood by those that hear it.

Again: a certain lawyer in London defended a prostitute against some quite grave charge. It appeared as he talked to her that her defense would have to turn in part on her precise relationship with a certain man. He asked her: "Did you sleep with this man?" and she answered: "No." With his social background, he was not to blame for failing to realize that she was speaking a different language from him, an older and more precise one. She meant just what she said; she had not passed the night with him or fallen asleep in his company. But they had fucked, as he later found out by chance on the morning of the hearing, and as she hastened to confirm it to him when he asked her again. The point is that when you come to something important, like the law, you cannot afford to play around with words in this way; you have to be exact.

And not only the law. In several of the fields of organized research and organized social action on which we increasingly rely in our attempts to improve things, word taboos are increasingly found to be a hindrance. In their book *Pornography and the Law*[5] the Kronhausens mention the complaints of sociologists and psychologists who have been hampered in their work by these taboos, sometimes not even being able to present reports of it to learned societies. Marriage guidance counselors too, and social workers in general, are increasingly finding that they have to talk the language of the people they deal with.

It is interesting to trace the history of the word *fuck* in Farmer and Henley's *Slang and its Analogues,* privately printed. The first example is from the Scottish writer Sir David Lindsay, where it appears in the Teutonic present participle form of *fukkand,* analogous to the German *fickend* (1540). In all the examples before the Puritan regime of the Commonwealth in the mid-seventeenth century (five in number), the word is printed out in full. After 1660, it begins to be written *f—k* and *f—.* It was during the first and shorter of the two hegemonies which Puritanism has enjoyed in England that the word fell into disfavor, that is, at a time when the action it describes came to be regarded with special misgiving and alarm.

[5] Eberhard and Phyllis Kronhausen, *Pornography and the Law,* New York, 1959.

But something very interesting happened here. The action gathered an increasing cloud of suspicion and fear around itself, and the word consequently began to be written incompletely, as though those who wrote it did not wish to commit themselves to knowing precisely what it meant, or wished to preserve the "innocence" of those who truly did not know what it meant, while yet making themselves clear to those who were hep to it. The bonds of meaning were loosened; the word strayed away from the thing. But it was a word so prodigiously well-nourished by the importance, the centrality, of the thing it meant, that it could not simply wither away and die out. It continued unabated—one may guess it became even more frequent in conversational use—but began to be used in quite a different way.

The life that was in it festered and it became destructive in revenge for its exile; it took on the pejorative sense which it still has so strongly today. For every time that it is now used in its true meaning, it must be used a hundred times to convey blame, and a thousand times to convey a neutral emphasis. For every time we say "Let's fuck," we must say, "You fucking bastard" a hundred times, and "A fucking great something or other" a thousand times. There is a rigmarole—I think it is of Australian origin—which perfectly conveys the distance the word has traveled from its original use. "I was walking along on this fucking fine morning, fucking sun fucking shining away, little country fucking lane, and I meets up with this fucking girl. Fucking lovely she was, so we gets into converfuckingsation and I takes her over a fucking gate into a fucking field and we has sexual intercourse."

The exiled word bears the marks of the disapproval with which those who first exiled it in the seventeenth century regarded the thing it meant. Few people now believe that a bastard is to blame for the circumstances of his birth, and yet the insult is still valid; "You bastard" is still an injurious thing to say. Now take "You fucking bastard." Not only, we say, did your mother and father fuck when they shouldn't have, a thing which by our tone of voice we still hold not only against them but against you too, but you yourself are also given to fucking. You are as it were double dyed in this unhallowed and deplorable activity; you positively reek of it and we will have nothing to do with you.

We also insult a man by calling him a prick, which is what he has, or by calling what he says balls. The main feeling behind these turns of phrase is the desire to liken him or his views to what we hold to be low and nasty; it would not mean anything very different if we said "Ah, shit." This feeling is of course the "puritan" one. But puritanism is a highly complicated and ambivalent thing, and once again we can find the opposite feeling coexisting with the wish to debase and defame. When we are provoked to utter a sudden obscenity we do not seek to debase what we are describing only by likening it to what we already hold base; we also take our stand alongside life itself, and from that vantage point exclaim how far short of life what we are describing falls. At one and the same time we say "What you say is as contemptible and ridiculous as a pair of balls," and "Bear in mind that there is in the world such a noble thing as a pair of balls, and compare what you are saying with that."

If this seems hard to believe, let us compare the effects of the following two scraps of dialogue.

1. *Someone*: What is lacking is a true sense of the ineffable yearning of man laboring under the curse of existence.

   You: Shit!

2. *Someone*: What is lacking is a true sense of the ineffable yearning of man laboring under the curse of existence.

   You: God!

The gap between the meanings of your two different exclamations is very narrow; if you had said: "Balls!" you would have straddled it.

The alienation and severance of these words from their true meanings and the fact that no other words have succeeded them as the undoubted and obvious senior words for what they mean—who could say *testicles* in conversation? one says nothing—is a profound linguistic revolution, and leaves the languages in which it has occurred profoundly enfeebled.

In every sphere of life except that of love and fucking, it is taken for granted that the best language is the clearest and most precise language. Consider for a moment trying to speak or write about carpentry without using the words tenon or mortise. One could probably get past by saying protuberant section and excavated section, but one would be wide open to misconstruction. It is the same situation that we are describing above; not every protuberant section is a tenon, not every excavated section is a mortise. Just so, not every fuck happens in bed, and we often go to bed with someone without fucking. Equally, the history of English poetry is usually—and to my mind rightly—taught as an oscillation between times when fresh, natural, hard and precise speech wells up in the work of a new generation, and times when speech becomes artificial and elaborate and periphrastic, bending toward an unreal currency of accepted but imprecise counters, until the next wave of hard clarity comes in from the way people talk. This is the doctrine of the preface to Wordsworth's *Lyrical Ballads,* and it would apply just as well to what certain English poets did again in the 1930's.

The principle that clear and precise language is the best language is one continually hammered home in government and politics where gobbledygook leads to injustice. The whole craft of legislation is devoted to the attempt to describe clearly what people may and may not do, and that of philosophy to saying clearly what is and what is not true, or truth.

There is no substitute for English. Denying freedom of its own language to speech and literature is the same as denying freedom of inquiry to research. If in our culture the law or a pressure group were to forbid research scientists to pursue one particular line of inquiry, there would be a justified outcry, because the whole point of research is you don't know where it's going to lead. It may turn up something good; the researcher must be allowed to scan, and to consider everything that turns up on his screen. In this book I shall be scanning in the field of sexual custom and morality, and for that I need these short words. I need them because they are precise. Fuck means fuck and nothing else. Fucking may be legal, as between consenting adults, or illegal, as in *Lolita*. It may be held by this or that religion to be virtuous, as it is held to be between married couples in our culture, or it may be held to be sinful, as between people who are not married to one another. It may bring pride after it, as when a young married couple beget their first child, or it may bring shame, as when a man fucks a whore and gets the clap. It may be pleasant, as it is in love, or unpleasant, as it is when it is done in revenge or to humiliate. It may have any number of emotional or moral qualities and bring any number of good or bad effects, but the action itself is always the same; it is *fucking*. There is no substitute for the word, and to avoid it, whether we fear prosecution or whether we are restrained by a "decent reticence," is to deprive ourselves of a necessary and precise concept, and thus render ourselves less capable of making sense. It is not surprising, therefore, to find that those who extol a "decent reticence" are usually the first to complain of the depravity of youth and the seductive titillations practiced by advertising; to complain, that is, that "the people stand about in helpless confusion." They prevent them doing anything else.

Chapter 3

Language: Our Neighbors

It would be possible to write a whole book on the degree to which "four-letter words" are excluded in different languages, and to relate this to social structure and religious beliefs. Ignorance and the wish to write some other things later combine to make me limit myself here to our three main neighbors among languages; French, Italian and German.

These languages, like English, have their four or five short words which are more or less taboo in conversation and literature. In French they are *foutre, vit, con, couilles* or *couillons,* and *cul.* On the whole they are slightly less taboo than in English. *Foutre* in its true and original sense is just as taboo as *fuck,* but in its secondary or alienated sense it is much less so. *Fous-moi le camp* means "Fuck off," but a French schoolchild who said this would receive only the mildest of rebukes, if any. *Je m'en fous* means "I don't care"; it is a much weaker expression, less angry, than 'Fuck that." It is not an obscenity, and can be used just about anywhere, although there is also a euphemism, *Je m'en fiche.* The tendency derived from it—*Je m'en fou-tise*—is a recognized political doctrine. The correct translation of *je m'en foutisme* would be "apoliticality": the Greeks would have said *idiocy.* The past participle *foutu* is also in "respectable" use. *Nous sommes foutus* means "We've had it"; it is not as emphatic as "We're fucked." Though the main secondary use is this one of defeat and indifference, there is also a merely emphatic use, as in English: *foutue bête,* "damn fool."

It is when we come to *vit* and *con* that French really differs from English. *Vit* is absolutely taboo, even more so than *prick* in English. *Con* on the other hand, though pretty well taboo in its primary sense, is quite current in its secondary sense, in which it means "silly." *Vraiment, je trouve ça assez con*—"No really, that's pretty silly." *Ne sois pas si con*—"Don't be so silly." It is an ordinary conversational word. The difference in use between *vit* and *con* suggests a feeling somewhere in the French psyche that men are secret, dangerous things, and women open, everyday ones. This impression is heightened by the really paradoxical sense of the word *déconner,* to uncunt, or discunt. It means to relax, to let one's hair down, to horse around. It is the opposite of the English *to pull one's finger out.* In English we get out of our woman when it is time to get down to work, to take life seriously, to brace ourselves and do our duty. In French they get out when it is time to finish the day's work, to laugh, to play the fool. If you put *déconner* together with the secondary meaning of the word *con,* you get a picture of woman in France as a stupid, obvious, unpleasant duty. But one can go too far in relying on language for a picture of someone's national life.

Couilles[1] suffers about the same degree of taboo as balls in English, but does not have the secondary sense of nonsense; that is provided by the female organ. *Cul* is if anything a little more taboo than *ass* in everyday speech,

---

[1] From Latin *colei.*

though in the compound *cul-de-sac* it is of course tolerated on street corners to mean dead end. Sack-ass.

At a time when there was a drive by certain pundits for the "purification" of the French language, Voltaire made fun of them by claiming that anything which even sounded like a dirty word was extremely dangerous; he cited *concupiscence* as an example.

In Italian, the linguistic situation is complicated by regional differences and dialect uses. It is a commonplace of political observation that Italy is not quite a nation in the sense that France or Britain is, and the same is true of linguistic practice. The word of common European stock is *fottere*, and this is taboo. On the other hand the derivative *sfottere*, meaning to mock, is in current conversational use. The verbs *chiavare* and *scopare*—to key and to brush—are also of nationwide application.

The senior language word for prick is still *cazzo*, as it was in the Renaissance, but the Renaissance word *potta*[2] for cunt now sounds archaic, or perhaps Tuscan. It is one of the Tuscan dialect words which have got a bit left out of the general tendency of the Tuscan dialect to become the Italian language. The main language word now is *fica*, and since the word for fig is *fico*, foreigners sometimes get into trouble about this at the market. It takes a good control of genders in the plural to be sure of asking for a kilo of figs.

The rather coy *uccello* (bird) for prick is also a nationwide usage. It gives rise to the image *uccello in gabbia* (bird in cage) and bears comparison with the German verb *vogeln*, to bird, which is familiar to readers of Freud, even in translation. There are countless dialect words, like the

---

[2] From Latin *puta*, a girl. The word is thus first cousin to *putto* and *putta*, the decorative boy and girl babies in Italian art, and life; to *pute* and *putain*, the French whore; to *puta*, the Spanish whore, second cousin to German *Fud*, and *Fotze*, cunt, distant relative to our *poop* of a ship, and all of them are descendants of the same BHU sound we discussed above, p. 11. A *prepuce* is what you find in front of a boy: *prae putum*.

Venetian *bigolo* and Genovese *belin* for prick, and for cunt the Piedmontese *ciorgna*, Lombard *fava* (bean), Venetian *mona*, Florentine *passera* (sparrow), Roman *fregna* (perhaps a corruption of *frangia*, fringe?) and *sorca* (perhaps analogous to *sorcio*, mouse, or perhaps to *solco*, furrow) and Neapolitan *fessa*, which is of course the same as the familiar *fesso* (cf. French *fesses*) for ass. In Sicily, as mainland Italians are quick to point out, there is an unparalleled wealth of discrimination; cunts, for instance, are classified according to size from little young ones, which are called *sticchio*, to big motherly ones, called *pacchio*, with different graduations in between.

Coglioni is used about the same way as the French *couillons*, but is nearer the surface of polite speech because of the common expression *rompiscatola*, or "boxbreak," meaning a great bore, which is a euphemism for *rompicoglioni* or "ballbreak"; and because of Bartolommeo Colleoni, the Venetian condottiere whose monument by Verrocchio is of such clanging and magnificent beauty that many people think it the best equestrian statue in the world. The Colleoni family were called that because their rude forefathers were proud of having big balls, or some say because their armorial device showed three balls. Likewise the noble family name of Brancaccio obscures an earlier claim to have big pricks—*gran cazzo*.

The picture in German is different again; here the taboo falls lighter as the meaning of the words passes from the genital to the excretory. *Ficken*, or North German *focken*, is completely taboo in polite conversation and literature, perhaps even more so than in England. It has no secondary sense. There is a pleasant insult, though, in which it is used in its true sense—*Lassen sie sich umficken*—"get yourself refucked," in other words, "go back to your parents and get them to make a better job of you."

The male organ does not even have a word to itself; the principal word for it is probably *Schwanz*, which also has to cover the meaning *tail*. After that there is a welter of whimsical analogues—*Pimmel*, *Schwengel*, *Prügel*, *Zipfel*, anything pointed, hanging, swinging. These words correspond to the British dong, clapper, American whang, etc.

Cunt fares better. The word which shares an origin with ours not so many generations back is the North German *Kutt.* But there are all sorts of similar sounds like *Futt, Fud, Füd,* and *Fotze.* (A dangerous one, this; in Bavaria it means just *mouth,* which continually surprises North Germans.) All these are taboo.

Like French and Italian but unlike English, German has a language word meaning balls and nothing else—*Hoden,* and it is not too terribly taboo. That is to say it is found in the official dictionaries, whereas *balls,* though it has eighteen entries in the shorter O.E.D., is not allowed to carry this meaning in any of them.

Broadly speaking, there is no language taboo whatever on the excretory, in which Germany differs sharply from England and the Latin countries we have mentioned.

A lack which is common to all these languages is that of a vernacular word for clitoris.[3] It is hard to lull the suspicion that peoples which have recourse not merely to a Latinism but even to a Hellenism for so obvious and pleasant a part of themselves may be missing something. It suggests that a clitoris is something a doctor might have to know about, but ordinary people would not wish to be assumed ever to have noticed. Why did the Greeks have a word for it, and we not? Our record in this respect is deplorable; the shorter O.E.D., for instance, having derived clitoris from the Greek *kleitoris,* goes on to derive that from *kleiein,* of all things, which means to shut. We shall return to the psychological significance of this sort of derivation later on. For the moment let us admit that it might just as well be derived from the next word along in the Greek dictionary, and one which sounds closer, too—*kleitos,* meaning renowned, famous, splendid, excellent. Meanwhile, a gap remains to be filled in the English language, as in the

---

[3] The German word *Kitzler* simply means "tickler," from *kitzeln,* tickle. It is better than nothing, but it is not self-sufficient.

others. The expression *on the spot* is coy; the expression *man in the boat,* though picturesque in its evocation of an ardent gondolier, is even coyer.

All in all, is English a good language for love? The literary tradition is poor, when you compare it with the Latin languages; a polygot would never think of making love in English or using it to write a love scene. We are, there is no doubt, weird in our feelings about the body altogether, and this colors our use of words. Arms are all right, it is a word we can use freely. Signposts, the law, coincidence, chairs, we allow them all arms without a thought. Legs are all right now, though furniture had limbs in polite circles a hundred years ago. Thighs will never do, though; nothing has thighs except people, and the word has an erotic sound in our ears. In Italian *nun's thigh* is a kind of cake. Nothing has buttocks (ridiculous word!) except people, and the fact that the bottom part of a block, the kind of block sailors use to pass ropes through, is called its *ass* fills us with giggles and doubt. In French, *angel's ass* is a color. So is *goose-shit,* come to that. The usage in the Latin languages reflects the feeling that the body and what you may do with it is far more a normal part of nature than we allow it to be.

It was of course this uncomfortable lurid glow coming off certain words which Lawrence set out to dim, and so bring the words back into the ordinary run of language. How far he succeeded is hotly disputed, but how far he could have been expected to succeed is an easier question. If a language has had a tourniquet on it for three centuries, no one can hope to restore normal circulation with one snip of the scissors. But a language is certainly better with all the concepts flowing freely through all the word-uses, just as a person is better with all the blood flowing freely through all the capillaries. Perhaps English is gangrened forever by the long tourniquet of prudery. But perhaps not; one should keep trying. It is the only language we have.

PART III

EXCLUDED IMAGES

Chapter 4

Introductory

In the last section, I described the way in which we are not at peace with ourselves about love and fucking, and the way in which our tensions and doubts are reflected in our very use of words, so that we cannot find it in us even to speak plainly of the actions and the parts of the body concerned. Periphrasis arises from anxiety and guilt, and begets them anew in each generation.

We now move on to another category of things which are excluded in rather the same way as words—images. By this I mean forthright descriptions and depictions of people fucking, or nearly fucking. Such descriptions and depictions are commonly passed round by men in the absence of women, just as the four-letter words are used by men in the absence of women. Like the four-letter words, they are regarded with more or less reserve according to the time, the nation and the class.

It is easier to find out about these images in different cultures than it is to find out about word usages; when you have said a word, it is over. When you have made an image, whether written, painted, drawn, sculpted, or whatever, the chances are that, if it is good enough, it may find its way into a museum and be seen there by later inquirers.

Chapter 5 criticizes the vagueness of present English and American law which regulates our access to these images, and which rests on the word "corrupt." If we are to have a socially meaningful law of obscenity, instead of an outward manifestation of inner doubts and fears, we must know what we mean by this word. Research questions are formulated which might help us to settle on meanings.

In Chapter 6 I mention some of the collections of erotica and the peculiarities of working in them.

In Chapters 7, 8 and 9, I discuss some of the overtly erotic images which have come down to us from various cultures as far apart as the medieval Hindu and the Victorian English. I give summary accounts of quite a number of these works, partly to correct the prevalent impression that the various cultural traditions of erotic art are small, thin, or undifferentiated, and partly as factual grounding for later discussion. I distinguish between those that were made before or outside Christendom, and those that were made within Christendom. I further distinguish among the latter various degrees of "pornographicness," and various degrees of achievement on the usual aesthetic scale with "bad art" at one end and "good art" at the other. I decry a work to the extent that it is produced by and for a masculine compulsion to masturbate, and that only, and praise it to the extent that it is produced as a true statement and a direct celebration of what people do to express the love they have for one another and to continue their kind. Images which do this, do it successfully, and do nothing else, are extremely rare in our culture.

In Chapter 10 I deny that erotic images are excluded in our culture for reasons of general aesthetics, which might be valid all over the world, and conclude that they are excluded, like the four-letter words, because of a fundamental unwillingness in our culture, which is not always shared by others, to consider and praise the action which makes us.

The section as a whole implies that our culture is too restrictive in censoring erotic images. It does not discuss the censorship of images of "perverse" sexual activity or of violence not in a sexual context (beyond calling for research), and does not imply that censorship of such images is too restrictive at present.

Chapter 5

Corruption and Depravity

In Britain for the last century the legal definition of obscenity has rested on the phrase "deprave and corrupt." In the Hicklin Judgement of 1868, which provided the law for ninety-one years, the phrase was: "corrupt and deprave those who are open to such influences,"[1] and this piece of British judge-made law has overflowed to the United States where the courts have often taken it into account in reaching their decisions. In the British Obscene Publications Act of 1959, the phrase is "corrupt and deprave those into whose hands . . . it is likely to fall." The older formulation is nonsense; "corrupt and deprave" are not "influences," they are transitive verbs. A simple correction provides: "corrupt and deprave those who are likely to be corrupted and depraved." Put like this, the only possible meaning stands out clearly: the crime is being defined by the likelihood of persons unknown to

---

[1] Hicklin was the defendant. He was condemned in a judgment by Lord Chief Justice Cockburn for having published *The Confessional Unmasked* with the Protestant Electoral Union.

fall victim to it. It would be analogous to define murder as "killing those who are likely to be killed" or theft as "stealing from those who are likely to be stolen from." It is obvious that no such nonsense could have lasted for nearly a century in any field about which people could bear to think. But obscenity was such a loaded topic that not even a judge could think clearly about it, and no legislator could bear to set it right.

Semantically, the 1959 British formulation is an improvement, it makes sense. The crime is no longer defined by the victim. The victim is no longer defined by his likeliness to become the victim, but by his likeliness to come in contact with the thing (publication) which may or may not have made him a victim. Whether it has in fact made him a victim or not is decided on other grounds. These grounds are still the words "corrupt and deprave." And in the main respect, since it still rests on these words, the new Act is no improvement on the Hicklin Judgement.

In the United States the situation is less clear-cut, but dependence on the concept of corruption was hardly less great than in Britain until recently. All states except New Mexico have laws against obscene publications, and the great majority of them define *obscene* in a pleonastic manner, as "filthy," "lewd," "impure," etc. Naturally if one suspects something is obscene one does not get much farther forward by seeking to determine whether it is lewd, and the American courts therefore quickly adopted the Hicklin Judgement as a useful definition. Probably the wiser jurists were never too satisfied with it, and already by 1913 Judge Learned Hand[2] complained of the inadequacy of the test, although he followed it. But in 1950 *Corpus Juris Secundus* still led off its discussion of obscenity with the following: "The test which determines the obscenity or indecency of a publication is the tendency of

---

[2] Quoted by Lockhart and McClure, "Obscenity in the Courts," *Law and Contemporary Problems*, Duke University, No. 20, 1955, p. 588 ff.

the matter to *deprave and corrupt* morals by inciting the lascivious thoughts or arousing the lustful desires of those whose minds are *open to such influences*." It also took as its leading case *The People versus Larsen* (5 N.Y.S. 2d 55) with this: "The gravamen of obscenity is the tendency of the matter to *corrupt morals* or to lower standards of right or wrong concerning sexual behavior."

But reliance on these concepts of corrupting and depraving, which are no more easily defined than obscenity itself, is being mitigated in American practice by an increased reliance on evidence of the author's intent in writing as he did, and on the evidence of critics and other people who are assumed to have special knowledge about the aesthetic or moral merit of the work prosecuted.

And this is to the good, since nobody knows what "corrupt and deprave" mean. In court, it is usual to read out the dictionary entries: "make morally worse," etc. Nobody is ever produced who is alleged to have been made morally worse, and no attempt to formulate standards of moral worseness is ever made.

Much of our law rests not on the proven effect of this or that on an individual produced in court, but on the judgment of a reasonable man what would be the likely effect of this or that on a hypothetical individual. But to have any value, such judgments must rest on experience, and in other spheres they commonly do so. For instance, if a man is accused of offering a financial reward for the commission of a crime, judgment based on experience may be certain that a hypothetical person would be tempted by the reward to commit the crime. We know people act for money. But we do not know people are "corrupted" by reading "obscene" books because we do not know what corruption is.

There are two ways of judging a moral condition (such as "corruption"): by actions, and by states of mind. Which should be applied? Perhaps the former. If we are to judge the condition by actions, by what actions are we to judge it? We should very soon land up with a list of "corrupt" actions, and we should have to accept this list as part of the law. What would the actions be? Fornication? Adultery? Masturbation? Flagellation? Morality would become subject to law in a most unwelcome manner, and we should be back in a sort of creeping puritan legislation at second hand. But even assuming we accept this, we must then go on to establish that our putative victim of the corrupting publication did not commit a listed action before he perused the publication in which it is described. We must next establish that his beginning to commit it was caused by his perusal. We cannot establish the first two points with much certainty, and we can hardly establish the third at all.

But perhaps we should adopt the canon of judgment by states of mind. We should then have first to decide by what means states of mind at any given moment are to be determined, second, what states of mind are corrupt or depraved and what are not, third, what increased prevalence of such states over other states in the mind of a given individual will allow us to say that he has been corrupted or depraved, and fourth, whether this critical increase was due to the perusal of the publication in question. If the other approach was difficult, this one is ridiculous.

This is not to say that sociologists could not usefully inquire into the matter. It would not be too difficult to consider one or two actions which are agreed by common consent to be depraved: if they were also crimes, the inquiry would be made easier since it could be made among those who had been convicted of those crimes. An obvious starting point would be sexual assault. The ideal inquiry would follow three lines. It would discover first what was the incidence among those convicted of sexual assault of habitual reading of matter describing sexual assault. (Having first defined "habitual.") Second, it would discover what was the incidence of the commission of sexual assault among habitual readers of matter describing sexual assault. This would be hard to do; the investigators would have to contact their sample in the shops where this matter is sold.

And third it would have to discover what is the incidence of habitual reading of matter describing sexual assault among a control group chosen at random. The incidence of the commission of sexual assault throughout the population is provided by general criminal statistics.

When these four sets of figures had been compared, it might be found that there was a positive correlation between the reading and the action, or it might not. If it were found to be so, the next step would be to determine whether it was a causal relation or not. It might be that both the reading and the action were caused by a third thing, perhaps influences and events in childhood. If it were found that there was not a positive correlation between the reading and the action, or that there was a negative one, it would be necessary to inquire whether the reading even served as a substitute for the action, and made it less likely. All these things could be discovered only through interviews conducted by psychologists, and analyzed by statisticians.

Only when a statistically valid and psychologically thorough investigation of this sort had been carried out could we begin to think about an obscenity law that might actually do what we want it to, namely, whatever it is we do want it to, since even that remains to be decided. The present law is not so much designed to affect society in this or that manner as to express our mistrust and fear of erotic images.

Chapter 6

Erotica: The Sources

All the great libraries of the Western world have a special section, more or less difficult of access, in which erotic books are kept and also, depending on the degree of freedom prevailing in these spheres, books considered blasphemous or seditious. The popular belief that the collection of erotica in the Vatican is the largest and best arranged in the world, and that the idea of segregating erotica originated in the Vatican Library, is mistaken. The Vatican Library is a large one, and naturally contains most of the erotic books published in Europe up to a certain time, just as it contains most of the others. It has a separate designation or shelf-mark for valuable books of all kinds, and slightly more attention is paid to the issuing and return of these books than to the more easily replaceable ones, as happens in all public libraries. Overtly erotic books are treated in this way, but they are listed in the general catalogue, along with all other books, whether valuable or not.

The Bibliothèque Nationale in Paris segregates erotica in a special section called *l'Enfer*, originally an abbreviation of *enfermée* "shut away," but now universally taken to mean Hell. They are listed in the general catalogue, and an independent catalogue of *l'Enfer* made by Guillaume Apollinaire was published commercially (Second Edition, 1912).

The British Museum Library in London segregates the erotic books, along with some considered blasphemous,[1] in a special section called the Private Case. They are not listed in the general catalogue, and no special catalogue is published, or even available to readers in the library. It is possible, though difficult, to obtain permission to have any book brought to one which one can name with the help of general bibliographical material—I managed to get such a permission to write this book—but it is in no circumstances possible for the reader to have access to the catalogue itself.[2]

I do not know what the procedure is for any of the American libraries except that of the Institute of Sex Research at the University of Indiana, since any student of this material would waste time going elsewhere in the U.S.A. At Bloomington, Indiana, they have one of the three biggest collections in the world, and on all counts the best arranged and the easiest to work in. You have to have a reason for working in this specialized university institute,

---

[1] For instance, there is still locked up there a pamphlet of 1854, arguing that Jesus Christ was "born of a foetal kyst, *sine concubitu*," and offering this as a compromise to those skeptical Japanese and Chinese.

[2] I used to think that this was because of a general prudery, or because of a belief that some limit had to be placed on the curiosity of characters like me, otherwise we'd want to see simply everything, which would never do. But since I discovered that the books are shelved by date of accession, and that, though the cataloguing rules are theoretically the same as for the general catalogue, yet in practice to find a book by Rochester you look not under RO for Rochester, or even under EA for Earl of Rochester, but under RI for the Right Honourable the Earl of Rochester, I have seen that there is a more human reason for it. Those who are allowed access to these books must read them at the front table, right up under the eye of the library staff. When you see how many illustrations have been torn out in the past, you understand this ruling too.

but, once your claim is made out, the full resources of American librarianship are brought to bear to help you. The feeling that the books are there to be read is a delightful one for those used to wresting them from the perplexed and embarrassed bureaucracies of the Old World.

I asked what happened at the Lenin Library in Moscow, and was told that erotica are in the general catalogue, but that the assistant who receives a request for one will have a look at the reader to see he is not too young.

The larger special collections may contain something like twenty thousand volumes. Many will be different issues and editions of hardy perennials like Cleland's *Fanny Hill* or Musset's *Gamiani*. Many will also be books that would not find themselves locked away at all if the collections were to be set up now, but which have not yet been released onto the open shelves as a result of the more relaxed feeling about sex in this century. Perhaps a thousand or so will be the first or main editions of books which could not, in the present state of law and opinion in England and America, be on the open shelves or on open sale. Of these, the great majority are works published since, say 1750, of no literary interest, and of erotic interest only until you have read two or three of them. Such books are still being published at a great rate. They follow, probably more closely than their authors realize, a pattern determined partly by the psychological need of the consumer, and partly by the traditions of the literary form itself, of which more below.

There remain perhaps fifty books whose sole or greatly predominating content is erotic, and which are well enough done to set the tone for all the rest, or to teach us something about the time and the place of their writing.

The situation in the graphic arts is different. Very few erotic works of sculpture or paintings are in public possession; the great galleries of the world by and large do not contain Hells. An exception is the National Museum in

Naples, where erotic paintings and statues discovered in Pompeii and the other destroyed Roman cities of Campania are kept. It is not difficult to see them; a word to a keeper usually suffices.[3] But the masterpieces of erotic painting and sculpture are mainly in private collections, and are extremely hard to find. At the most, there may be engravings of them in the print rooms and *cabinets* of museums and libraries.

The main characteristic of this whole field from the point of view of scholarship is the difficulty of finding out who wrote or painted what, let alone when or where. Such has generally been the weight of social disapproval of erotic literature and art in Europe that it is almost the rule to find an author or an artist has covered his tracks with same fanciful title page; "Amsterdam 1778" could mean "London 1884," "Heliopolis Anno Mirabile" could mean "Bombay 1923," and again and again "M. le Comte de" something or other rather priapic-sounding disguises some familiar writer. Equally with pictures; draftsmen masquerade as one another or as copies from the antique, many different series of engravings go under the same name, and there are certain writers and painters on whom almost anything of this sort may legitimately be fathered. Giulio Romano is the most conspicuous of these. When you find an old book of astronomy or aesthetics, it may take you an hour in a good library to find out who wrote it, and when, and probably why. But when you find an erotic book of any age, it may take you a week, or you may never find out at all. For this reason I cannot claim that any of what follows is free from mistakes of scholarship; on the other hand it is unlikely that it is all wrong throughout.

---

[3] Some of these have been reproduced in *Roma Amor,* London, 1961.

Chapter 7

Outside Christendom

The hells of the West contain two sharply different kinds of work; those produced outside or before Christendom and locked up because of Christian values, and those produced within Christendom; the extraneous and the rogue. In the present chapter we will consider those produced outside Christendom.

These are images and descriptions which it never occurred to their makers were special, or would ever be locked up and treated as inflammable. They are, very much more than the corresponding ones originating within Christendom, a normal part of art, and thus of life. It would be better, I know, if I could give an account of them in the context of a general account of how fucking was and is regarded in different cultures before and outside Christianity, but this I cannot do, because I don't know enough. The things are where they are in our world, locked up. We gain access to them through bars, and try as we will we cannot remove the bar-feeling in our minds when we look at them or read them. No doubt only a fraction of pre- and non-Christian erotic art has found its way into Western libraries; the Greek statue which was dug up as opposed to the one which wasn't; the Roman fresco which wasn't destroyed by the seventeenth-century cardinal as opposed to the one which was, the Indian text which was translated by the Victorian black sheep as opposed to the one which wasn't. These are the ones available, and these we can only avail ourselves of with our Western spectacles on.

Let us start with the *Kama Sutra*, a book which was published for the general market in England and the United States only in 1962.

It is a book of advice to young people, written in northern India by one Vatsyayana some time in the first millennium of our era. The name means the Manual of Love, and refers to the first of the three ages of man according to one of the schemes of Hindu ethics: Kama—love or pleasure; Artha—arts, skills, and industry, or work; and Dharma—enlightenment or fusion with the One. Like other Hindu texts on this or that, legend has it that it is a digest of a longer work, too extensive for human understanding, which was itself a digest of part of the Gautama's *total* work, which put down everything about everything. The *Kama Sutra* advises the youth on the best way to live the age of sensual pleasure, and it is understood that he is later to go on to be an industrious father of a family, and then a sage severed from the joys of the world, which in later life are to be seen as snares, and devoted only to the ecstatic contemplation of the One, or God. It contains sections on gaining the confidence of a virgin wife, on prostitution, on love philters and remedies for impotence, on courtship and on judging whether the girl is in love with you. It is addressed primarily to men, and assumes throughout that the woman is a socially inferior being, but never that she is emotionally, physically or spiritually an inferior one. Here is for instance some advice on courtship: "He should show her a pair of human beings cut out of the leaf of a tree, and suchlike things, at intervals. When engaged in water sports, he should dive at a distance from her, and come up close to her. He should show an increased liking for the new foliage of trees. . . ." And here is a way for a boy to judge if a girl loves him: "She remains with both hands placed on his body motionless, as if she had been surprised by something, or was overcome by fatigue." The strangest aspect to the modern Western reader is the minute regulation of what should be done when, and precisely how. "When the man, making the sound Phat, strikes the woman on the head, with the fingers of the hand a little contracted, it is called Prasritaka, which means striking with the fingers of the hand a little contracted. In this case the appropriate sounds (for the woman) are the cooing sound, the sound Phat, and the sound Phut in the interior of the mouth, and at the end of congress the sighing and weeping sounds." The tone throughout is small, cool, domesticated, open, and above all tender. The author accepts, but never labors, the basic Hindu premise that the union of man and woman is emblematic of the union of human with divine, or rather of the many with the One.

Just as the *Kama Sutra* is based on and refers to earlier books, so in turn it is taken up and revised in other books of advice, the most notable of which is the *Ananga-Ranga*.[1] The legend is that one day a shameless naked woman walked into the court of a certain Rajah, declaring that there was not a man present. Among the supposed eunuchs and fairies was the author, who is variously called Kallyana Malla and Koka Pandit; he asked the Rajah's permission to see what he could do. He took her home and laid her so well that she consented to reappear with gold pins through her arms and legs to prove it. The Rajah commanded the author to write down how he had done it.

Following the *Kama Sutra*, the book starts with tables about what part of which sort of woman you should caress in what manner on which days of the month, for how long,

---

[1] "London and Benares, 1885."

and with how much desire, adding cross tabulations for the various sizes of yoni and lingam (cunt and prick). The end result is 243 different kinds of congress. Spells and potions follow, and a list of fourteen places where one should not fuck. Numbers two, three and four are when a Brahmin, a Guru or the father of either of the parties is present, number ten is on a highway, and number thirteen is in an open field. These are the only limitations on the score of privacy. On the whole the book is more schematic and less pleasantly poetical and imaginative than the *Kama Sutra*, but it ends up with some splendid passages on the pleasures and the right ordering of marriage.

The nineteenth-century translation contains an editorial footnote describing how most of the Indian and other Asian editions contain illustrations of the manners and caresses tabulated. "At Poonah and other parts of Western India there are artists who make this the business of their lives, and sell a series of about eighty . . . at the rate of two to five rupees each. The treatment is purely conventional, and the faces, as well as the dresses, probably date from several centuries ago. A change took place when an unhappy Anglo-Indian officer, wishing to send home a portrait of his wife, applied to one of our artists with that admirably naive ignorance of everything 'native' which is a growing custom of his race. The result was that the Englishwoman's golden hair and beautiful features appear in some fifty or sixty highly compromising attitudes, and will continue to do so for many generations to come."

Another means of knowing the Hindu erotic tradition is through photographs of temple sculpture. The best examples accessible to us are those published by Mulk Raj Anand in *Kama Kala*, Geneva, 1958 (also edition with English commentary) and *Kama Shilpa* by Francis Leeson, Bombay, 1962 (published by Grove Press, Inc., in America); these are the temples of Khajuraho (tenth century) and Konarak (eleventh-twelfth centuries). They are very large temples, standing now abandoned on plains, covered all over with high reliefs of people fucking. The groups are always spirited, but some are pretty sketchy. The best, on the other hand, have a kind of melting grace, a natural attention to one another, and a modest backing in symbolism which make them very beautiful. The same photographs were published above the counter in an issue of the *Evergreen Review* in 1959. Anand's book is published in England at a "collector's price." An amusing collection of Western reactions to these statues, ranging from James Mill's "hardly conducive to chastity" to hopeful justifications (Well, you see, it's to show what you put behind you when you go into the house of God), is in Lawrence E. Gichner's mainly unreliable booklet *Erotic Aspects of Hindu Sculpture.*[2]

The illustrations of the Krishna legends—Krishna and Rada, Krishna and the cow girls—often gave rise, right down to the time of the British impact on India, to single pictures which we lock up. There are also many Persian pictures and much Persian poetry which fall under the key.

But the greatest mass of Eastern erotica in Western collections is that from China, Japan and Korea. Japan is two-thirds as populous as the United States, and China is four times as populous. In dealing with Sino-Japanese culture the Western beginner has to remember that he is dealing with something not only much bigger but also much older than his own culture. If one thinks of the difference between Germany and Italy in 1500, or the difference between France in 1780 and France in 1880, one would never dream of saying anything about "Europe" in this context. So much the less so should one say anything about "Sino-Japanese culture" if one considers the difference between say southern China in 1000 B.C. and Tokyo in 1960 A.D. There are four thousand years of history instead of two and a half, and there are and always have been three or four times as many people. Thus what the outsider may think of as a specially Sino-Japanese trait, or an abiding

---

[2] See pp. 309-310 for more about these temples.

one, or a fundamental difference between there and here, may be no more than the chance selection of what he has seen or read.

But with all these reservations, it is clear that there are things in Far Eastern erotica which there are not in any Western erotica, and that what is visible to a superficial student looks and sounds and feels different in certain respects.

To begin with, it was a custom in China and Japan and is still quite a widespread one, at least in Japan, for the parents of a bride to give her and her husband a "pillow book." These are books of pictures of people fucking and are meant to suggest ways and means, to be an auspicious sign, and generally to help things forward. They contain pictures first, then text; the Japanese pulp magazines of today still start with a series of pin-ups and then go on to the text. Single pictures of the same sort are called "spring pictures," just as a common context for erotic paintings in the Hellenic world and the Italian Renaissance was under spring in a cycle of the seasons. Nakedness is rare; usually the couple have masses of heavy clothes swirling around them. The clothing is commonly parted, though, to show the relevant parts in action, and in Japanese pictures these are often colossal, comparatively. It is an extreme example of the haptic in the visual arts; haptism[3] is the disproportionate emphasis on the part of the picture which the picture is about, as a child will draw a cowboy with a pistol the size of a small cannon, or a woman with enormous eyes because that is where you look to see if grown-ups are pleased with you.

Needless to say there is nothing childish about Japanese art. Every symbolic image is haptism carried further; who ever saw a hammer and a sickle without anybody holding them? They are meant to make you think of industry and agriculture, just as those gigantic Japanese parts are meant

---

[3] From the Greek *hapto*—I seize: by implication, to seize one thing emphatically while ignoring everything else.

to make you think of fucking. They live in a world of their own, separate from their owners, like great beasts questing, the pricks with huge veins racing over them like rivers on a map, and the cunts with the hair sparking and splashing away in all directions like a thunderstorm, all standing out in darker colors against the hieratic drapes and the small, pale other-flesh. This haptism is rarer in Korean pictures, and very rare in Chinese. It is not universal even in Japan.

Many artists used to start their careers in spring pictures —so did writers, with pillow books—because they were regarded as good training and offered a steady sale; the Western analogy would perhaps be the young painter who sold academic copies to begin with, or the young writer who got a start in the newspapers. Later, they went on to more difficult and interesting matters.

The pictures come in all degrees of merit from the quasi-machine-made output of the early nineteenth-century artist Kunisada, who is said to have done more than all the others put together, to the profound insights of Utamaro, who worked fifty years earlier. The liberty Utamaro takes to construct a visual grammar out of the way everything seems to be coming from the wrong direction enables him to see the thrust and balance of love in an emotional and spatial relationship almost unknown in the West. These are true images of the aspect of love which delights and bewilders because you don't know what's going to happen next, or where it's going to come from.

But perhaps the greatest surprise to the Occidental is the number of people about. Friends and family stand around in benign approval. Sometimes they hold the bride up in a convenient position for the husband to get at, and over and over again the child of the marriage looks on, sometimes with his tiny erection to show he's keeping up with father, sometimes watching the mechanics with awed delight.

Often balloons are used, saying things like: "How big you are," or "Shall we come now?" Sometimes also there are little satirical characters looking on called *mamesuke*:

bean men. Another of the great masters, Harunobu, used them quite often. They have balloons saying things like: "He's not doing too well," or "A bit late for that sort of thing, isn't it?" They peer over screens and from under mats.

These books and pictures take their rise from a culture where fucking was fully built into the religious and social fabric of life. There were, and I understand still are if you look for them beyond the MacArthur Belt, Shinto processions in which, as in old Greece, gigantic phalluses are carried, while children are lifted up to see what made them, and to draw benefit.

But of all the cultures where the erotic was a normal part of life and art, the one which is most important to us, because so much of it is still running in our blood, is the vanished one of Greece and Rome. Most literate people have some idea from their reading of the normalness, the unexcludedness, of the erotic in this culture. They will have read something of Aristophanes and Theocritus and Catullus and poor snarling old Martial, and above all of Ovid. They will know that at some times and in some cities an ithyphallic herm (the torso of a man with a pedestal instead of legs, and with an erection) was the normal decoration of the doorposts of private houses, that the garden god Priapus with his basket of fruit, whose wooden effigy lived in the orchard at the bottom of the garden, often had an erection on him, and they will have thought about what sort of society it was which had a religious orgy once or twice a year in the Saturnalia and the various festivals of Bacchus, Ceres, Cybele, or who not. They will have recognized that the horrors of Euripides' *Bacchae* were a distortion and explosion of part of the normal pattern, and not a mysterious tweak from the forces of evil, coming out of a blue sky. They will know that in Sparta adolescent boys and girls played and exercised naked together, that in Athens the young girls followed a tall emblematic phallus in religious processions, that educated prostitutes were held in honor, that homosexual love was subject to the same free play of social and individual forces as heterosexual love, and that, in short, loving and fucking was part of the religious, economic and emotional fabric of society on just the same terms as anything else.

Since this was so, it is not surprising that the very existence of such things as erotic books or pornography in the Greco-Roman culture is uncertain. Diogenes Laertius gives a list of erotic books, but none of them has survived, and one can't tell how he defined the category. The famous book of "positions" by the woman writer Elephantis, which Tiberius is said to have been fond of, was presumably something akin to the Japanese pillow books, and to be used in the same way. Licht[4] holds that the first book of "positions" which is mentioned in Greek literature, that of the courtesan Astyanassa, mentioned by Suidas, may be a misunderstanding of a joke. The name *Astyanassa,* he thinks, may simply be constructed from the verb *a-stuein,* not to have an erection. The joke would have been that the poor girl was so ugly she could do nothing better than write books about it.

The *Dialogues of the Whores,* by Lucian, is not an erotic book at all, but a collection of comic anecdotes with a leftwing bias showing that whores are part of the oppressed proletariat but can get along all right if they know the ropes. Some modern editions of it, however, have been locked up because of the illustrations.

Erotic passages in the course of general works in both prose and verse from the Greco-Roman culture used to cause the whole work to be locked up, or were excised from it, or left in the original in translations. This no longer happens much; Theocritus and Aristophanes and Ovid and Catullus and Martial and Petronius are now translated and published without too much ado, though often the erotic passages are still translated with kid gloves on.

A true picture of the place of fucking in Greco-Roman

---

[4] *Sittengeschichte Griechenlands,* 1928, Ergänzungsband, p. 155.

life and religion cannot, though, be got solely from the
printed word. The graphic images of this intensely visual
culture are an integral part of it, and a look at some such
collection of photographs as Licht's is necessary to even a
dimmish understanding of this, which was the closest to
ours of all the extra- or pre-Christian cultures. Licht's first
two volumes are a fairly simple-minded compendium of the
"sexy bits" from Greek writers; they have been translated
from the German and are on open sale. The third volume,
containing the illustrations, has not been translated, and is
kept locked up.

These erotic images of antiquity, which have survived
in numbers, range from mere jokes to works of great
beauty. There is a very wide spread between the coarse,
jokey image of someone paying his or her respects to a
herm and the dignified and lyrical scenes of erotic dancing
and love-making, all of which can be found on Greek or
Roman vases.

It was by no means only from the great days of Athens
that good work came; the erotic lasted as well as other sorts
of art, until Christianity arrived with its special cult of
chastity. The workshop of Marcus Perennius, for instance,
was in production from 50 B.C. to about 40 A.D.; it was
the most distinguished of all those which contributed
to the enormous industry of the "Aretine Vases." Hundreds
of thousands of fragments are at present being studied and
pieced together at Arezzo, of which thousands carry erotic
motifs from Perennius. Perennius' own work was first
found during extensions to a convent in 1882, but the
work of other potters of his time was never unknown, and
excited admiration throughout the "dark" and Middle
Ages. Ristoro d'Arezzo, describing the general nature of
the fragments which were always being turned up around
Arezzo, wrote in 1281, ". . . and there too was luxury,
shown in its every different action. . . ."[5] Everyone, Ristoro
said, was amazed by the beauty of these vases and cried

---

[5] Quoted in U. Viviani, ed., *I Vasi Aretini*, 1921.

out that they must have dropped from heaven; he does not record that anyone in his day was shocked by their explicitness. In the seventeenth and eighteenth centuries they were called "Etruscan Vases," and the Staffordshire manufacturer, Josiah Wedgwood, seeking to revive the great tradition, called his new pottery town *Etruria* after them.

Anyone who studies these vases will feel that he is in a different world from our own. If he compares in his mind's eye the comic daubs from the Greek vases with other such daubs that he has seen, the erotic dance with other dancing scenes from Attic vases, the Roman marble with other nudes from the time, and the Perennius terra sigillatas with the "Etruscan"-Wedgwood tradition in general, he will perceive that there is no difference, there is no change of gear when we go over from a dinner scene, a running or dancing scene, or a libation scene, to a fucking scene. There is the same vigor, grace, candor and balance about these images as there is about all that is best in Greco-Roman art. It would be impossible, looking at these, to derive from them any suggestion that fucking was a doubtful, dangerous or shameful thing.

This is not to say that satire was absent from the Greco-Roman tradition of erotic art, or that openness and a feeling of normality about fucking necessarily involves solemnity. There was too a whole tradition—some of the images repeat and repeat like stereotypes—of what later critics often tend to regard as low laughter but which I think could better be described as normal laughter; low laughter would be a later invention in this context. The mere existence of the faun and the satyr with their animal bottom halves make the point that man should not get above himself because he uniquely possesses reason; solemnly to elevate oneself above the animal is to get above oneself, since oneself is still half animal, and always will be.

There are countless joke pictures about hermaphrodites. The giggle at the expense of the disappointed swain who unwraps a sleeping nymph only to find she's got a prick on her as well as breasts was a regular one. There are jokes about apparatus—two pricks mounted on a wheel; Eros rocks the wheel, and they fuck one girl and bugger another —jokes about armies—phalanxes of pricks—jokes about almost anything, based on the eroticization of it. Joke shades off into charm; very many little winged phalluses survive, bronze ones, with the wings strapped onto them like the wings on Hermes' heels. These would be virility charms, to ward off the evil eye; perhaps worn round the neck. Romans today still touch their pricks when they see a cross-eyed person in the street. The charms were called *fascina,* or little bundles. The mechanism by which our *fascinate* derives from a word meaning *little bundle* is good guessing ground. So is the connection between the colloquial German *vogeln,* to bird, meaning to fuck, with these winged phalluses, and the Italian use of *uccello,* bird, for prick.

The very idea of pornography is foreign to Greco-Roman culture, the idea that the erotic could be a special subject matter in the arts, let alone a forbidden or clandestine one. Licht found the word *pornographos*—a writer about whores—once only in his reading of classical literature. For them—though for the Greeks more than the Romans—fucking, like everything else, was an action suitable for religion, for narrative, for depiction, for tragedy, for comedy, for poetry, and for satire. It was simply not a "loaded" topic. It could be right, it could be wrong, it could be ennobling or degrading, just like any other sizable chunk of human life. There was no special or dangerous area demarcated, there were no exclusion mechanisms at work. This applies to the culture as a whole; ascetic and prudish temperaments were naturally not absent, and their writings were later endorsed by Christian teaching. But they were not the culture.

The values of the culture itself are still alive under our doubts and misgivings; sometimes they are hidden very deep, as they were in nineteenth-century England and America, sometimes they partially emerge as they did in the eighteenth century and are perhaps doing again today; sometimes they have been the object of conscious pursuit, as they were for a moment in sixteenth-century Italy.

The records and evidences of these three cultures, the Hindu, the Sino-Japanese, and the Greco-Roman are there, uncomfortably there, in the locked cupboards, for us to make what we can of. They are and always have been, to those who have seen them, a gritty sort of thing. They chafe. They irritate us, we do not understand them, we wish we knew more about the people who made them. We secrete pearls of nostalgia around them, or we come up in angry weals of denunciation. They force our nature; we must feel that either we have been wrong all the time or there is some terrible penalty to pay for taking sex in one's stride like that. We examine the records of those cultures for traces of penalties paid, and find none, or none worse than we have paid in our own, and are more confused than ever. We turn again to the images, holding on to our chairs. It is all so unusual; we feel with the whole strength of our being that it is most unusual. Our culture never does that sort of thing. Pornography, yes; nasty dirty little bits for people to masturbate over; we understand that all right, and condemn it. But not this perfectly frank, perfectly insouciant celebration of something which just *isn't* celebrated like that.

When we examine the records of these cultures, we do indeed find plenty of things which we deplore, but can they possibly be the price of feeling open and normal about fucking? The Greeks were homosexual, the Romans militaristic, the Hindus uncharitable, and the Chinese and Japanese conservative. But what of it? We ourselves are militaristic and materialistic. How to compare whole cultural traditions? One cannot compare what is best in each, and see which is best of all because the best in each is always the best of that kind in all humanity, and the kind is always different. (One is best at beauty, another at law, another at peace, another at custom.) One cannot compare the whole of each with the wholes of others except in a very hazy way; they are too big and too complicated. One can only say that by and large, taking the comparison between Hinduism and Christianity as an instance, by and large the Hindus are more tolerant and we are more charitable.

They will hardly go out and massacre a man for his belief, but they will easily let him starve at their door. We will hardly let him starve at our door, but we will easily massacre him for his belief.

Perhaps there is some shadowy connection here with the freedom to represent fucking which they have and we have not, but I rather doubt it. If there were, it might run something like this. Christianity holds every man unique before God in merit and in identity. Hinduism not so; only in lumps by caste. Christianity will therefore care more than Hinduism *who* each man is, and who his parents are. It will therefore surround begetting with special screens of isolation directed partly to being sure who is whose child, and thus who is who, and thus in the long run to being sure that each who has a who-ness which is going to make all the other whos look after him if he is ill or sick, and develop the means to do so. Hinduism, caring less for who-ness and more for suchness, perhaps erects a less careful screen around the who-making bed, and certainly lets whos starve and die of disease. Conversely, the suchness of all whos is more sacred to Hindus than to us; we deprive them of it by violence more readily than they do.

Chapter 8

In Despite of Christendom

With much misgiving, I have rather arbitrarily set the erotic books and pictures which have arisen within Christendom into five categories, and shall attempt to order the material accordingly. The categories overlap; many works show the characteristics of two or more of these categories. The works I mention below are only the most interesting ones, whether because they are good of their kind, or because they are the works of writers or artists who interest us for other reasons.

The five categories are the comic, the perverse, the haptic-convulsive, the all-out pornographic, and the celebratory. In my judgment, that is also an ascending order of interest.

1. The Comic

These are not primarily works of erotic content at all, but ones which use the erotic as a vehicle for satire, or for jokes which seek to please simply by associating one thing with some other, unexpected, thing. The comic-erotic is primarily an eighteenth-century form; it took up, consciously or not, a strand present in the Greco-Roman culture. Examples are Voltaire's *Pucelle d'Orléans,* Diderot's *Les Bijoux Indiscrets* and, in the visual field, the print called *Hogarth's Cottage.*

In the *Pucelle d'Orléans,* Voltaire uses the following formula in narrative heroic couplets: take the history of Joan of Arc and her times and retell it so that whenever anything boring and historical, and especially a battle, is about to take place, they all stop and copulate instead. It is certainly very funny, not because of its sexual content but because of the *unsuitability* of everything, and because of Voltaire's familiar naive delight in the bumps and grinds of divine intervention; St. Denis is forever floating about on a small cloud and exclaiming in a shocked way at the goings-on. There are excellent lines in it: for instance, the description of the Biblical heroine Judith as *"galante et homicide."* And there is one idea which gives the full force of Voltaire's atheism in a way that nothing in *Candide* does; it is that the Apostles chose Judas by lot to do what they were all agreed had to be done. Very many eighteenth-century editions.

Diderot's novel, *Les Bijoux Indiscrets,* has been translated as "The Indiscreet Toys." The toys are the women's cunts, and they are indiscreet because they talk. It is a pseudo-Oriental hodgepodge, in which encyclopedist notions, day-to-day theatrical and musical criticism, Africa, Sultans, and "Brama" are all mixed up. The hero, a prince, obtains from a Sultan a magic ring which will make any girl's cunt prattle about what it has been up to recently. The narrative framework is provided by the thirty trials the prince makes of his ring before finally daring to try it on his own girl friend, who turns out to have been chaste all along. It is full of an exuberant and mercurial wit; though sometimes quite specific, it is not often very lascivious in effect. Here is the first appearance of the ring. "The Sultan leveled his ring at her. A loud burst of laughter, which seized Alcina at some comical saying of her husband, was suddenly cut short by the operation of the ring; and immediately a murmuring noise was heard under her petticoats." (An indiscretion.) ". . . all the ladies grew pale, looked at each other in deep silence, and grew vastly serious . . . lest the conversation should grow warm and become general."

The print "Hogarth's Cottage" shows a boathouse standing in a wood, reflected in a calm lake, while the sun sets between two hills like the Langdale Pikes. This is a visual pun. The boathouse is a cunt, the hills breasts, and the sun the chin of a woman between whose legs we are standing.

As far as I know, the comic-erotic form did not exist in Christendom much before the eighteenth century—Rabelais was not an erotic writer, but a digestive-excretory one—and did not endure long after. This is not to say there is no wit and humor in erotic works which are not primarily comic in intention.

2. The Perverse[1]

The perverse tradition in erotic art rests on the need of the writer or artist to make, and the reader or beholder to receive, descriptions and depictions of whatever sexual oddity it is that controls their desires.

There is a very great bulk of sadistic books and pictures. The work of the Marquis de Sade himself is discussed below in Chapter 24. A conspicuous modern sadistic novel is Guillaume Apollinaire's *Les Onze Milles Vierges, ou Les Amours d'un Hospodar*. It is concocted from his own

---

[1] The fact that I use the word *perverse* here and not the currently more favored *deviant* or *deviate* implies not a moral judgment or a social attitude, but linguistic caution. *Perverse* means "turned across"; *deviant* means "going off the way." I cannot see that the former is any ruder than the latter. Colored people and developing nations change their designation every so often, or have it changed for them, in the hope that justice and humanity can be introduced by synonym. What would come after *deviant*? *Paragyrist*?

reading in the tradition, efficiently enough, and contains some horrible impalements, and so forth. The same reasons which prevent the sadist from coming into a workable relationship with his environment (see Chapter 24 below) also prevent the sadistic artist from achieving anything very much. There is perhaps something to be learned from Leonor Fini's illustrations to Sade's *Justine;* it does not seem likely that one could go much further along the road of being pretty about pain and death.

Each kink has its literature. For pederasty, the first work is probably the best; this is the *Alcibiade Fanciullo a Scuola* attributed to Ferrante Pallavicino, who was born in 1616 and lived his short life as a political journalist in Venice. He incurred the wrath, as they say, of the papal family of Barberini, who sent someone to him pretending to be a messenger from Cardinal Richelieu. This man told the unworldly and exalted Pallavicino that Richelieu had invited him to go to Paris as his official historian. They set off together, and at Avignon Pallavicino was arrested, kept twenty months in prison, and then beheaded. He was twenty-eight.

The Boy Alcibiades at School was posthumously published in 1652. (Reissue, Paris, 1862.) In it the schoolmaster describes to the boy the pleasures of buggery, working up from *double entendre* of a most philosophical nature to open description, and at the end they get down to it. Pallavicino promised "more lasciviousness" in the second volume but it was never written. The style is heavy and soft, and has a certain complex majesty. His world is the private one of carefully cultivated feeling, based on Platonic philosophy and the equation of the body personal with the body cosmic; it is full of a gentle gravity which transcends the special limitation of the object of desire, and it is also quite without the terrified guilt or the jumpy awareness of hostile pressure which, understandably enough, disfigure so much later homosexual writing.

The doyen of incest writing was the eighteenth-century French novelist Restif de la Bretonne. He was a crazy individualist full of quite private beliefs and values, who thought Sade wasn't nice enough to women, and set out to put the matter right with a series of enormous novels in which he praised incest instead of cruelty. Not all of them are now locked up; in France they are fairly easy to come by. One of them, *Monsieur Nicolas,* was translated into English and published by Havelock Ellis.

Restif de la Bretonne was a shoe fetishist, by his own account, from the age of four, and calculated that he had had 217 daughters by the time he was sixty. This was because he believed that all chance encounters should result in offspring; he was never quite clear whether he had a corresponding number of sons; he was not interested in sons. The daughters he used to meet again by chance, recognize them by the voluptuous turn of their legs and feet and "by the thermometer of his heart" and start all over again. His biographer[2] has noticed that the only people he called "monster" were his wife, his son-in-law and Sade. He discovered his bent as a writer through an early compulsion to write about how his balls were feeling on the parapets of bridges over the Seine; his novels run to 194 volumes. His *Anti-Justine,* which he wrote specifically to show up the brutality of Sade, starts with the hero laying half a dozen of his sisters in quick succession, and then gets down to the serious business of life, which is father-daughter incest. There is in fact no brutality in his novels, but there is a great deal of shoe-smelling. The incest is used as a *sauce piquante;* the forbiddenness heightens the thrill.

A notable modern novel written out of a perverse compulsion is *Trois Filles de leur Mère* by Pierre Louÿs. A few hundred copies of this, in facsimile of the manuscript, were published posthumously in 1929. It narrates the adventures of a young man who finds he has taken lodgings next to a family of Italian whores who specialize in buggery; the three daughters have been trained for this work by their mother. The fantasy is deviant enough; incest, general

---

[2] See C. R. Dawes, *Restif de la Bretonne,* London, 1946.

nymphomania, little girls of ten, and so on, and it tails off in a senseless repetition which shows the obsessive character of the impulse to write it, and which Louÿs, who was a considerable writer of narrative and dialogue, would no doubt have cut if he had been writing for publication. But there is one character in it, Charlotte, the eldest daughter, who is real and touching, and the dialogue throughout is also real; that is to say it is as sharp and true and respectful of human motive as the dialogue in the overtly published novels which we usually judge to be considerable. There is a real eloquence in this girl's part (it is almost like a play, all talk). She hates everybody and everything for what has been done to her, which is every horror, and loves only her own finger. She knows the whole world can't be wrong in its values, and she alone right, but she can't see what the world holds right, is blind to it and knows her blindness, and therefore holds herself in contempt. This is one of the largest and most real presentations of the whore-character in European fiction.

3. The Haptic-Convulsive[3]

The writers and artists in the tradition of perversity are bound in a peculiar lock with their own compulsion; those in the much larger tradition of the haptic-convulsive are bound in the same lock with sexuality itself. They are mastered by it, at the mercy of that in them which cannot leave it alone. To use the word *perversion* for the former category and not for the present one is perhaps illogical; one should use it for both or neither. I put into the category of haptic-convulsive all those books and pictures which make one think: "Poor fellow; he had to." The hallmarks are a mixture of horror and delight, and a brute emphasis on the mechanical and the local, on the organs themselves, the details.

At this point it becomes hard to distinguish the cate-

---

[3] A note on the trade in "hard core" pornography, most of which falls in this category, is in Appendix 1.

gories; there is a three-dimensional continuum between this one and the next two. The statements "this is horrid but fascinating" (haptic-convulsive), "I am giving you your money's worth" (all-out pornographic) and "this is beautiful and real" (celebratory) can coexist up to a certain point in a picture, and can succeed each other very swiftly in the same written work.

I believe the first book of purely or mainly erotic content to be published in Christian Europe was the *Hermaphrodite* of Antonio Beccadelli, written in about 1426, and this is haptic-convulsive. The Latin text was reissued in 1892 with a French translation by Isidore Liseux, the copious and scholarly French publisher of erotica and the general literature of love. Beccadelli, who wrote under the name of Panormita, the man from Palermo, was one of the first generation of Italian Latinists who later got called humanists and were found to have brought about the Renaissance. At that time, the Italian writers had hardly gone beyond imitations of this or that Latin original. Beccadelli's model was Martial, and to a lesser extent the "fescennine songs" of antiquity, little bawdy rhymes which were so called either because they abounded in the Tuscan town of Fescennia or, which is perhaps more likely, because they fulfilled the same function in words that the *fascinum,* or phallic charm, fulfilled in the realm of magical objects. (See p. 52.)

Beccadelli was an excellent imitator; his verses run very smoothly and sweetly and sometimes have a musical melancholy which would have endeared them to nineteenth-century schoolmasters if they had not been surrounded by such *filth,* as they would have found it, and if Beccadelli had been born fifteen hundred years earlier.[4] He was in the mainstream of humanist learning; the hermaphrodite of the title is an emblem of that hobbyhorse of humanist philosophy, the reconciliation of opposites, and the arrangement of the book takes up the allusion. The first half is prick, the

---

[4] E.g., Morte sua lugent cantus lugentque choreae, Flet Venus, et moesto corpore moeret Amor.

second half cunt. The poems were dedicated and sent to
Cosimo de' Medici, and there is one addressed to Battista
Alberti asking him, because he is a good scholar and a good
friend, what Beccadelli should do because his girl is so de-
manding that he is quite exhausted, and then, suddenly, because she *stinks* so. Like Martial himself, which presumably
was what endeared Martial to him, he was half fascinated
and half disgusted by women and fucking. He is full of
jokes and melancholy, now savage and sparkling, now melt-
ingly sad. He is also much concerned with buggery. How,
he keeps asking, can anyone who has once discovered the
joy of buggery ever revert to that dreary business, fucking?
On the whole, the impression he makes is of one grappling
with a new idea—that the Roman writers could be adapted
to contemporary life—and making only a fairly good go of
it. He was born in Palermo in 1394, worked in the univer-
sities of Siena and Bologna, where he loved the loves he
writes about, and died in Naples at the age of eighty.

Pietro Aretino, the greatest erotic writer in Christendom,
who comes in my last and best category, the celebratory,
had two pupils who tried to handle the erotic, and succeeded enough to be locked up ever since, but not enough
to be read with any pleasure. Lorenzo Veniero wrote a
couple of long poems: *Zaffetta,* which consists mainly of
abuse of a girl who wouldn't open her bedroom door to
him, and *La Puttana Errante,*[5] the Wandering Whore.
This rather famous narrative poem is a convulsive declaration of horror and fascination, and is very different from
Aretino's cool understanding of prostitution. For 380 eight-
line stanzas the whore wanders around the cities of Italy,
usually being welcomed in triumph because her fame has
preceded her, the fame of being able to cope with more and
bigger clients than any other whore in the world. Veniero
cannot come to terms with the fact that a whore is promiscuous, he keeps repeating in horror this one fact that
she has a great many men. He is also delighted by the fact

---

[5] See p. 87 for another work of the same name.

that she is old and smelly. Aretino dignified this stuff by writing an introductory sonnet for it.

The other pupil was Niccolo Franco, who turned against Aretino. He wrote a cycle of a hundred ninety-five sonnets, which he put into the mouth of a wooden figure of Priapus in a garden. This Priapus passes his days lamenting how wet he gets, explaining to any girls who happen to pass by what a good fertility god he is (all they have to do is climb up on him), insulting Aretino as a bugger, and damply impugning clerical morals. There is an occasional flash of gloomy fun.

> Buggera il Papa, e tutti i suoi prelati,
> Con ogni altra persona religiosa . . .[6]

But what really held Franco up was the fact that his old master Aretino praised buggery and, he assures us, practiced it. When he had finished with the Priapus sonnets, he wrote a hundred and nineteen more devoted exclusively to this fact. Later in life he was imprisoned for heresy, and was finally hanged as a result of the posthumous reinstatement of a certain Cardinal Carafa, to whose downfall he had contributed in the first place.

Continuing to leapfrog chronologically through the vast collections of the haptic-convulsive: Rowlandson. Rowlandson was the most copious draftsman in the English erotic tradition, and largely determined the way it went. There are mountains of his erotic engravings and drawings in many different collections, and I imagine they cannot be hard to come by on the open market. He had tremendous dash and openhandedness, but the enormous output is obsessive. He was clearly as much repelled as pleased, though always fascinated, by the fact that men and women, incredible creatures, do this amazing thing. The men are usually caricatured, and sometimes both men and women are, and these are painful to see. Dirty old men figure a great deal, paying to peer up the cunt of a whore, gawking at a nude model, etc, etc. Often music comes in: a military

---

[6] The Pope buggers, and so do all his cardinals,
And so do all the other clerics . . .

band, a string quartet all frigging away as they play. When the satire is not simply at the expense of fucking itself, it sometimes comes off rather well. There is one on the perennial theme of loose behavior in the park, where smart couples walk up and down in their Sunday best, but these are not people, they are pricks in various stages of erection and dejection. There is one of an over-virile Latin waiter carrying a tray on his prick.

Very occasionally he breaks through the barrier of his laughing horror and comes into a sort of peace and grace. The best of these are a handful of prints in the series called *Pretty Little Games,* and one of the two called *Jolly Gypsies,* which is his shot at the Golden Age myth. (See Chapter 26).

Fragonard belongs here; his erotic pictures are strangely disappointing. He seems not to have been able to carry over his grace and balance into this field; everything comes out wrong. Clothes are rolled up and peered under, girls play with little dogs, and again and again naked virgins clutch pillows in their sleep; which is not really so much what girls do as what men like to think of them doing. Somehow his heart is not in it; he seems to have been working from a part of himself, the haptic-convulsive part, which might never have come to the actuality of canvas at all if it had not been for the fashion of the society he lived in. The effect is one of uncertainty.

Other good painters tried and failed to achieve something in the erotic; Turner (little booklets of washy water colors, obscurely voyeurish), Millet (soggy chalk drawings of lovers in fields), Degas (who could not give a whore a tenth of the attention he gave a dancer; illustrations to an edition of Lucian's *Dialogues*).

At the time of the Decadence, the draftsmen snatched and leered. Beardsley (illustrations to the *Lysistrata* and other books); effete and solipsistic, a hard struggle to get an authentic *frisson*. Franz von Bayros (many illustrated books); hectic wasted forms—the literary clichés show through the images—tiny pretty Lesbians, girl with rhino horn, girl with elephant trunk; sometimes an offhand badness in the drawing, betraying contempt for the consumer. The decorator of the Sezession movement in Vienna, Gustav Klimt (illustrations to Lucian); through the keyhole, communicating a panting lust. Bony people. None of these was an inconsiderable draftsman, but none was master of his material.

As archetypes of the haptic-convulsive, let us take one illustrator and one writer. François Bouchot (1800-1842), in a book of illustrations called *Diabolico-Foutromanie* (Diabolico-Fuckomania) carried to the farthest possible extent the feeling that fucking is a base and animal affair by simply putting animals' heads—bears and goats and pigs— on human bodies. Possible connection with witchcraft.

The literary archetype is the English Victorian pornographer Edward Sellon. His many novels are the gratification of impotent dreams; dreams of absolute power, of absolute indulgence, in castles not of this world, with girls not of this world. At crucial moments his characters say Erghhh! and Ughhh! like characters in a contemporary comic.

The makers and consumers of the haptic-convulsive fail only by partiality. Everybody has erotic fantasies, most also have erotic realities. These people could grasp nothing bigger than their dreams, and them they bottled and sold. It is the bottle which offends, not the dream; since the proper use for dreams is to flow and mix into the whole knowledge and feeling which makes a man.

This localization of perception in the arts and of feeling in life is itself an exclusion mechanism. In that it excludes the rest of the person, or the scene, or the life, it is simply the obverse of prudery. Pornography inflates what prudery has first excluded. In this sense, prudery makes pornography.

4. The All-Out Pornographic

This category differs from the former, the haptic-convulsive, in that the writer or artist does it not because he has to but because he wants to. (Of course he may "have to" from the financial point of view, but he is not emotionally compelled to.) He is in command of his material, has decided that he will turn to this particular form, and proceeds to do the reader proud. It shades off on the one hand into the former category when undigested dreams and compulsions come to the surface, and into the next category, the celebratory, when it rises above arbitrary specialization and becomes a valid synthesis of perception and execution, in other words, when it lapses into art. The hallmarks of the all-out pornographic are thus a sane but capricious gusto, a determination that the consumer shall have his money's worth, and an impression that the purpose of the whole operation is to provide male consumers with something to masturbate over.

The literature is once again enormous; but here I will discuss only a few books.

The form was only half-fledged in the Renaissance; perhaps Aretino's *Ragionamenti,* of which more below, came nearest to it, but that book is full of social and political observations, and could not qualify as "all-out." The book which first developed the form and which largely determined its future development right down to the latest paperback was the *Satyra Sotadica* of Nicholas Chorier.

It would be interesting to give a short biography of the father of Western pornography, but almost nothing is known about Chorier. He was a provincial worthy and historian of the Dauphiné. *Satyra Sotadica* was first published about 1660, that is, about the time when the prose novel as a whole first made its appearance in Europe. It claimed to be the work of a notional Spanish court lady called Aloysia Sigea, translated into Latin by a real, but recently dead, Flemish scholar called Meursius. There have been numerous editions in French since 1680.

It consists of dialogues among girls with Latin names, and repeatedly harks back to classical times as the golden age of fucking, from which the moderns have fallen off. The dialogue form was presumably chosen on the precedent of Aretino, and before him Lucian. The manner is rather heavy and boring; there is something stodgy and pedantic about it, quite unlike the vernacular fire and sparkle of Aretino. But it is an epochal work in the sense that it is the first book (I think) which contains nothing but sex from start to finish. It contains just about everything that two or more people can do in bed, and runs through the stages, which are followed in almost all later works of all-out pornography, from simple fucking through buggery and homosexuality, different forms of "contact" to use the jargon of modern sexology, orgies, flagellation, and incest. There is nothing else and, within the demarcated field, nothing is left out. It is the first work of rigid specialization, and thousands of later works have done no more than ring the changes on it.

Though the literature of this category in English is substantial, it is less so than in the preceding one, and less interesting than the literature of this category in French and Italian. The first English book is on all counts still the best; this is *Fanny Hill,* by John Cleland, first published in two volumes in 1748-49, expurgated edition, 1750, and since reissued very many times, sometimes under the original title, *The Memoirs of a Woman of Pleasure*. It is not a purely pornographic work, only about eighty per cent so. That is to say, Fanny's background is sketched in, she falls in love, she needs money to live on, her lovers have careers and positions which we are told about, even if shortly, and in the end she marries the man of her choice. But with those small intermissions, it follows pretty closely the pattern laid down by Chorier; you get a bit of everything, and lots of most things.

Cleland had a most remarkable prose style. He set himself the task of avoiding coarse words, that is, all those words which I argued in Chapter 1 should not be avoided. This drove him to extremes of flowery periphrasis; I have already quoted "his inestimable bulse of ladies' jewels." Here are some more, taken at random: "his plenipotentiary instrument," "a just concert of springy heaves," "what delicious manuals of love devotion" (breasts), "the prodigious effect the progressions of this delightful energy wrought in this delicious girl," "the baronet led the extasy, which she critically joined in," "refrain who could from such provoking enticements to it in reach?" "sometimes he took his hands from the semi-globes of her bosom and transferred the pressure of them to those larger ones, the present subjects of his soft blockade."

There are some ambitiously illustrated eighteenth-century editions of *Fanny Hill.* Some of the early illustrators tackled the job without too much fuss and guilt, but none of them was a good draftsman.

Cleland's devious and florid style, presumably because he was the only English "pornographic" writer of any interest at all, and was consequently so often republished, has affected English pornography right down to the present. A striking recent example is *Lust,*[7] by Count Palmiro Vicarion, a pseudonym which conceals, strangely, one of the tersest and most colloquial of our younger poets. Examples: ". . . she tried to avoid my outstretched arms and advanced clamour calling for satisfaction in similar regions." "The most malleable zones of my unique masculine effects," "circumlocuting their buttocks in a unified and widening orbit."

Mirabeau wrote pornographic novels, and they are a very good example of this category; one gets a clear impression of a man who could do plenty of other things, doing this simply because he has chosen to. *Erotica Biblion* adduces texts from the classics to prove that the Romans fucked too. *Ma Conversion* is a first person account of the life of a gigolo, avid for *tartufferies,* for the license behind the pious facade. There is a startling picture of an American woman with "brownish red breasts, as hard as marble." The book contains the first appearance known to me of the overt notice to the reader of its own purpose which later became commonplace in pornographic novels: *"Eh bien, lis, dévore, et branle-toi."*[8] A lot of it is written almost in note form, suggesting a hurry to get the damn thing over

---

[7] Paris, Olympia Press, 1959.
[8] "And now, read, devour, masturbate."

and done with. The following paragraph from *Ma Conversion* will give an idea of the style of a great deal of the inferior *lecture galante* of eighteenth-century France.

> Tout favorisait mes feux; la beauté du jour, dont les rayons, amollis par une gaze diaphane . . .[9]

> "Arrête, téméraire!" s'écrie la tendre Julie. "Cher amant, Dieu . . . je . . . je meurs," et la parole expire sur ses lèvres de roses. L'heure somme à Cythère; l'Amour a secoué son flambeau dans les airs; je vole sur ses ailes, je combats, les cieux s'ouvrent . . . j'ai vaincu . . . O Vénus! couvre-nous de la ceinture des Graces!" etc., etc.[10]

Another book of Mirabeau's, *Le Rideau se Lève, ou L'Education de Laure,* is a more carefully written affair. He cunningly starts off with a father-daughter incest and then reveals that he was not her father at all. But she continues to call him Papa, so you get it both ways, the forbidden thrill without the forbidden reality. It goes on through a lot of meticulous, cheerful, rather monotonous "pornography," until he suddenly changes the plan, kills off most of the characters with declines brought on by overindulgence, sends the remainder into a convent, and gets down to a long exposition of sexual morality, which, he says, ought to be tougher for women than for men.

The *Manual of Classical Erotology* of Friederich Karl Forberg appeared in many different languages throughout the nineteenth and into the twentieth century. Forberg, who wrote in the late eighteenth century, was the inventor

---

[9] "Everything favored my ardor; the beauty of the day, whose rays, softened by diaphanous drapes . . ."

[10] "Hold, rash one!" cried the tender Julie, "My dear love . . . Oh God . . . I . . . I am dying!" and the words expired on her rosy lips. The hour has struck in Cythera; Love has brandished his torch on high; I fly upon wings; I do battle; the heavens open . . . I have won . . . Oh Venus, cover us with the girdle of the Graces!" etc., etc.

and most wholehearted exponent of pornography as "science." The ostensible idea is that such things will leave the serious and scholarly unmoved, and only inflame the depraved. His *Manual* is a collation of all the "sexy bits" from the classical writers, from which he derived a tabulation of everything that two or more people can do in bed. The upshot comes by another route very close to the "nothing-but" narrative form invented by Chorier.

Fuseli did a number of erotic drawings: they are more often in his open and decorative manner than his Gothic one. In quite a number the man, the "I" of the wish-fulfill-ment, is being seen to by several girls at once, like a patient surrounded by nurses.

After the works of Sade, perhaps the most famous erotic novel in the French language is *Gamiani,* attributed to Alfred de Musset. It went through forty-one editions before 1930. A preface claims that the author wrote it in answer to a challenge that he could not write an effective erotic novel without using "coarse" words. He does in fact avoid the short ordinary words, and does so with very much less fuss than Cleland in his parallel attempt in Eng-lish. The action of *Gamiani* is largely Lesbian; the name, which comes from the surname of the heroine, an Italian countess, is to suggest the word *gamahucher.* The style is not bad, in a frenetic and exclamatory way. A young man plans to seduce the mysterious countess, hides himself in a cupboard, and finds that he is the witness of a Lesbian affair. So he comes out and joins in. Most of the book is taken up by the ensuing triangle, and later on there is a dog and a monkey as well. It belongs squarely to the romantic tradition in that love and death go together. There is a scene where Gamiani climbs onto the erection of a just-hanged man (Félicien Rops in his illustration changes this to a crucified one) and it ends when the two Lesbians take poison and experience orgasm and death simultan-eously. Gamiani's last words are: "I still had to know whether in the torture of poison, in the agony of another woman mixed with my own, there was a satisfaction of the senses. . . . It is frightful, do you hear? I die in the rage of pleasure." Romanticism in a nutshell.

Chapter 9

Transcending Christendom

With this category, we enter a rather different field. In the last chapter we were discussing specialized products; there is probably some justification in calling them "pornographic," and refraining from judging them by the best standards we know. They have all been the products of a basic alienation in the Christian and post-Christian spirit which makes us exclude and punish fucking and the idea of fucking; they were made in a dangerous special enclave, and they are meant to be consumed in it too. They were far indeed from the simple celebration of the Hindu and the Greco-Roman cultures.

But just occasionally a man formed by Christendom breaks free to do what so many could do before it and outside, to see fucking as one of the actions that make up life, to see desire and fulfillment as two conditions like others, and to judge that good. In novels it is sometimes done, more often in the French tradition than in the Anglo-American. In novels, we increasingly agree that this is a good thing to do, and the placing of the erotic scene in the normal context of life is something now generally approved by opinion, and specifically sanctioned by English law in the clause of the new Obscene Publications Act which requires the court to consider the book as a whole. A rather different situation prevails in the visual arts, since a picture or a statue cannot place the erotic moment in the context of life as a whole; it must choose one moment and stick to it. There is thus in Christendom a handful of masterpieces of open, sane celebratory erotic art which remain unknown.

The first is a series of prints to designs by Giulio Romano, and a related series of sonnets by Pietro Aretino. The prints are usually called *I Modi*, "The Ways," after a phrase of Vasari's, who said they "show the ways in which low women lie with men." (Vasari wrote later, in the full flush of the Counter-Reformation.) The sonnets are usually called *I Sonnetti Lussuriosi*, "The Lustful Sonnets." I shall introduce these at some length, since they were the first such works to arise in Christendom.

We have seen how in ancient Greece and Rome fucking was not held to be a special thing to which description and depiction were inapplicable. But in the Middle Ages the eye and ear of art were withdrawn from the meeting of man and woman. More; the eye was withdrawn from the bodies themselves of men and women, so that the Gothic nude was not a man or a woman, but a symbol of something else; of lust, perhaps, or wisdom, or folly, or plenty. All this is ably discussed in Sir Kenneth Clark's book, *The Nude*, where he puts the thing in geometrical terms. The distance between the breasts of a woman in Gothic art is half that between breast and navel. In classical and Renaissance art, the two breasts and the navel form an equilateral triangle and the distance between breast and navel is the same as the distance between navel and crotch. (It is the same with men, of course; I write of women here because I, like Sir Kenneth Clark and the artists we are talking about, am a man.) Now anybody who has looked at a woman knows that the triangle breast-breast-navel is about equilateral, and not elongated with the apex downward. It can hardly be supposed that Western woman mutated about the fourth century A.D. and mutated back again about 1500, all of Western women together in one move, so it must be that medieval artists were not painting and sculpting what they saw. To take this further and inquire whether they meant to distort their images in this way, or whether it happened without their meaning it, would be naive. They were human, and they were competent; they could do plenty of things Renaissance artists couldn't. The best way to formulate it is to say that their attention to and their liking for the human body was of a different quality from that of the ancients, the Renaissance artists, and us. All this is discussed with splendid acumen and dash by E. H. Gombrich in *Art and Illusion*.[1]

A good older account is to be found in Wölfflin's *Classic Art*[2] where he compares a fifteenth-century recumbent Venus (by Piero di Cosimo) with one of Titian's. The Piero looks like a sausage with one leg and one drainpipe attached, and somewhere in the vicinity there is a hand which it is not impossible may be hers. The Titian looks like a woman. As Wölfflin points out, it may be that Piero's model happened to take up a pose where she did look like that; if Titian's did, he moved her.

(One must avoid oversimplifying here. A walk round the Cathedral and Campo Santo of Pisa or the Cathedral at Orvieto is enough to show that this is not an adequate account; there are classically proportioned thirteenth and fourteenth-century nudes there in some quantity, and very fine and strong they are. Roman sarcophagi and the odd Hellenic marbles were never unknown in the Middle Ages; they just did not predominate as models of how to look at things. The doors of the church of San Petronio in Bologna are usually left out of the accounts of all this when we try to see a straight development. The Adam and Eve panels on

---

[1] London, 1960, pp. 9-30; New York, 2d ed., 1961.
[2] London, 1952; New York, 2d ed., 1953 (first German edition, 1899).

them were made by Jacopo della Quercia between 1425 and 1438, and you'd think not Masaccio, not even Ghiberti, but Michelangelo himself made them. In one of them jealous Adam is ruefully measuring the length of his prick while Eve caresses the serpent. Is human love not enough to cast out sin? It is a striking image for the date.)

It was not until fifty years after Jacopo's doors that painters and sculptors in general, when they were faced with a naked body, began to ask: "Yes, but how does it work?" So they went to the dissecting rooms of the hospitals and morgues. And even then they were not content; they asked: "Yes, but *why* does it look like that?" So Leonardo peered at the way the light went round a sphere, and they all sought the company of mathematicians, and many of them *were* mathematicians, and the sciences of optics and solid geometry began to move again, hand in hand with the arts, for the first time in Europe for a millennium and a half.

So much is schoolbook history; the answers they found to these questions are at the foundations of modern medicine and physics. But once you ask a question about the nature of reality, provided that you are intelligent and persevering, you are almost bound to find the answer. Did the literate population of central and northern Italy suddenly become more intelligent and persevering about the year 1450, and continue like that for the next century or so? The mystery does not lie in the fact that they found the answers; it lies in the fact that they asked the questions which had not been asked for a thousand years. And this is a matter of feeling, not knowledge. The difference between asking a question and not asking it is quite a different kind of difference from that between finding the answer and not finding it. Whether you can answer it is a matter of intelligence and perseverance. But whether you ask it in the first place is a matter of emotion.

What emotion? I would say, the feeling of being authorized to ask it, the feeling that one is allowed to inquire, and that things and people will not bite if you look closely at them. This was the new feeling in the Renaissance, and it opened gates behind which answers had been piling up for years. To be more exact; it was not so much a new feeling as a new extension of an old one. Medieval thinkers had felt authorized to inquire very closely into the nature of God, and so did Renaissance thinkers. (The theological roots of thought in the Italian Renaissance are easily neglected if you think too much of the Humanism and the sensuality. Michelangelo and Alberti, to take only two of the greatest innovators, had no doubt that they were expressing the nature of God in their work; Michelangelo of God as redemption and healing. Alberti of God as Platonic harmony of proportion.) But they did not feel that the study of God excluded the study of things and people, and it was this sudden extension of what may be inquired into that made the Renaissance. For the first time in all those centuries, these people burst through the pusillanimous rigors of the medieval church and tumbled into awareness of the fact that God is not jealous, not exclusive, not dangerous. We may even say they came to a fuller understanding of the basic truth of all religion, that God is Love, which can be otherwise put: God is license to inquire.

And so they had a damn good look. And among the things these men had a damn good look at were women. Leonardo did, and he got that equilateral triangle right. So did Bellini in Venice, though it's probable he was only pushed into it late in life by his young pupil Giorgione. And it is with Giorgione that we take up again our proper study, the erotic. The great inquirer Leonardo did not happen to like women; circumstances saw to that.[3] Fucking was to him an object of scientific inquiry only, not feeling. There is an anatomical section drawing of his showing a man and woman fucking; it is the fruit of his hours at the dissecting table, not of the terrible ambiguities of spirit which still shake us in his pictures. It is Leonardo the

---

[3] See Freud's famous essay, and Giuseppina Fumagalli, *L'Eros di Leonardo*, Milan, 1952.

engineer, not Leonardo the artist. But Giorgione broke
through into new seas of feeling, as well as of permissible
inquiry, with his "Dresden Venus" of 1500. For the
first time in Christendom he painted a stark naked woman,
lying down, and inviting desire. In two respects he broke
right through to an expression of what men really do
feel about women, and in two he failed to. The two
breakthrough points are first that she is a classical woman,
or very nearly; that is to say she has the equilateral triangle, not the long gothic one. The second is that she
has her fingers over her cunt in a gesture which overtly
provokes desire in the men who see her. The two points
of non-breakthrough are first that she is lying in a piece
of landscape, which puts quotation marks round her; we
are not yet invited to perceive and enjoy her simply as a
woman, but a comment is made on woman-as-living-
nature; and second that she is asleep. We can see her all
right, we have a damn good look, as Giorgione did. But
she cannot see us, or anything else. The voluntary blindness,
the feeling "but I haven't got a license," which Giorgione
conquered in his own spirit, is not yet entirely abolished.
It has taken refuge in the woman he painted. She is the
last sleeper of the Middle Ages.

She awoke. Through the door Giorgione opened there
poured two armies of painters: one was Titian and the
other was everyone else. Italy, and after Italy, Europe, were
flooded with naked Venuses. Titian poured them out; the
best and most famous is his Urbino Venus, painted thirty
years after Giorgione's and, since she is lying in precisely
the same position, precisely achieving what Giorgione began. She too is stark naked, lying down, overtly inviting
desire. But the breakthrough is complete in that she is no
longer in a green landscape, but in bed—exactly, as Sir
Kenneth Clark says, where you would expect her to be—
and she has her eyes wide open. She is having a damn good
look back at Titian and at us. And, in Browning's words,
"God has not spoken yet." Titian lived to ninety, and his
pictures continue to embody the main truth of all religion,

of all binding together; that perception is piety, inquiry righteousness, and knowledge love.

But long before Titian achieved the culmination of the woman-as-woman pictures, others had pressed Giorgione's advantage through in other directions. There began a tradition of pictures which edged toward the extreme and most equivocal breakthrough of all in showing girls being fucked by gods disguised as this or that. Leonardo started it with his Leda, though, as you would expect with Leonardo, they were just going for a walk together, and the main impression she gives is of saying to the beholder: "No thanks; as you see, I've got a swan." Michelangelo put the swan between her legs, where he had seen it on a Roman sarcophagus, and there it has stayed, a smooth, feathered token of masculinity, in a thousand versions since.

Europa is embroiled with the Bull, Io yields to the Cloud, Danae receives the shower of gold. Some of these pictures hark back to the old Christian iconography of Eve and the serpent, where the naked woman desiring an animal did heavy duty as an emblem of original sin. Those that do, do not belong to the Renaissance tradition, but to the patristic and medieval tradition of fucking as guilt, as treason to God; a tradition still vividly alive to us, which will be examined later on. But others, for all that they were sometimes held to stand for the union of the Virgin Mary and the Holy Ghost, are manifestly humming and hawing on the brink of what perhaps seemed the final audacity; that of showing a man and a woman fucking and enjoying it. Correggio in his Io and his Danae and above all in his arcadian scene of a whole lot of little Ledas dallying with a whole lot of swans (Berlin) took the thing farthest of this group.

And then in 1524, in Rome, under the very nose of the Papacy, it was done. In the basilicas the candles flickered as Cupid and Priapus and Venus stirred in their tombs beneath the altars. From India and China to Japan's vermilion temples, live gods pricked their ears. Africans who knew neither Christ nor plantation paused in their dances, as the stirring became a rumbling, the rumbling a heaving, the heaving a cracking and the whole vault of Christendom groaned and settled into a different shape.

That sort of paragraph doesn't mean a thing, but this I do know: that when we think of the founders of modern Europe and America, of Luther and Copernicus and Galileo and Newton and Michelangelo and Calvin and St. Ignatius and Locke and Hobbes, we should count Giulio Romano, Marcantonio Raimondi and Pietro Aretino with them.

Giulio Pippi, usually known as Giulio Romano, or Julius the Roman, was Raphael's star pupil. He was the first of the Renaissance artists who had passed his childhood among the remains of imperial Rome, so many more then than now. The others had come to Rome to emulate the Romans; Giulio *was* one. At the time when he rocked Christendom he was in his late twenties and unmarried. He came from the artisan class, and was the best of the contingent of assistants and pupils who worked under Raphael, often with a very free hand, to decorate the Vatican for Pope Leo X. In him, the license to inquire is absolute, and the mandate to glorify and celebrate the level eye of inquiry is binding. And with the inquiry and the celebration goes also a devotion to effect, to the histrionic, to an almost arrogant show of technique. Where in the Vatican and the Farnesina the Olympian lucidity and grave balance of Raphael is gathered into a flash of theater, into a nuder nude, into a humanity that seems to leap out into your arms like a child jumping off the top step, so that you can *feel* the weight and structure of it, there the documents often confirm that it is the assistant Giulio's work.

Frederick Hartt, in his *Giulio Romano*,[4] which is the principal study, argues convincingly from his work that though he loved ancient Rome, he was also afraid of it. There is a dark terror in some of his paintings of Roman ruins; in his early picture, "The Martyrdom of St. Stephen,"

---

[4] New Haven, Yale University Press, 1958, 2 vols.

they are pulling a Roman vault to pieces to get stones to stone the martyr with. But for every one of these tenebrous, almost neurotic, images, there are ten of joy in humanity, and especially of joy in the bodies of women. Many years later Giulio was invited to be the architect of the new St. Peter's in succession to Bramante, but he died before he could return in triumph to the city of his birth.

Aretino, in a letter[5] which later formed the basis of Vasari's life of Giulio, described him thus: "He was always *anticamente moderno e modernamente antico.*" This "always anciently modern and modernly ancient" is one of Aretino's best phrases, and the fact that he chose to apply it to Giulio Romano when he could just as well have applied it to half a dozen other contemporaries, may be an indication of how well he understood the centrality of Giulio's work to the whole thing we now call the Renaissance. Vasari, having plagiarized this, goes on: "There was never anyone to equal him in the drawing of helmets, saddles, sword gear and strange masks, and with such ease and dispatch that drawing in him was more like writing in a copious and practiced writer. . . . Nor could anyone think of a fancy but he understood it as soon as they opened their mouths, and immediately expressed the mind of others with his brush. He was so full of every kind of good quality that painting appeared the least accomplishment he had."

Shakespeare thought of him thus: "The Princess hearing of her mother's statue . . . —a piece many years in doing and now newly performed by the rare Italian master, Giulio Romano, who, had he himself eternity and could put breath into his work, would beguile nature of her custom, so perfectly he is her ape; he so near to Hermione hath done Hermione, that they say one would speak to her and stand in hope of an answer. . . ."[6]

---

[5] Quoted in Hartt, *op. cit.*, p. xvi.

[6] *Winter's Tale:* V. 2. Hartt (p. 193, n. 1) says this is not Giulio Romano at all but someone else of the same name. He has in fact discovered another G.R., who kept a shop in Bologna at which he

After the publication of the erotic prints and the ensuing scandal, which we shall come to in a moment, Giulio
Romano went to Mantua, where he spent the rest of his
life. There he built and decorated many splendid palaces
and churches for the ducal family, the Gonzagas. The
architecture is always heavy and complex; often the col-
umns or the pilasters stand together in a noisy crowd
nervously interacting and shouting, like people at a party,
and in his great fresco cycles at the Palazzo Te the people
are all in parties too. The giants are destroyed by Jupiter
Tonans in one of the most terrible and ambiguous schemes
of all European art; the Hall of the Giants is the womb of
old night itself. Who is destroying whom? The Hall of
Pysche on the other hand is all laughter and Eros, ceiling
of mild silver and walls of furious gold. On the ceiling there
are silver people in blue night; on the walls, hot golden
people in green fields. The character and achievement of
this artist are wrongly overshadowed in the tradition by
those of his master. He does not calmly ravish like Raphael,
but fiercely, abruptly, and equivocally.

Pietro Aretino is a tough bit for modern stomachs. Most
admirers of the Italian Renaissance definitely draw the line
at him; in the judgment of the nineteenth- and twentieth-
century scholars through whose spectacles much of our
knowledge of that time inevitably comes, there is always
an implicit reservation to their historical nostalgia—"except
for Aretino." It is like the account of Magna Carta in *1066
and All That*—"except the lower classes." Sensible students
turn aside with their handkerchiefs over their noses at the

---

sold stucco reliefs. Hartt says that because Shakespeare's G.R.
made a statue, this must be the one. This seems farfetched. Why
should Shakespeare write so glowingly of an obscure shopkeeper-
craftsman, who lived in Bologna (which was not one of Shakespeare's cities), and has not been heard of from that day to this,
rather than the builder of all the palaces and churches of Mantua
(which was very much one of Shakespeare's cities), whose name
was familiar all over Europe and has stayed so?

mention of the name. He called himself "the divine Aretino"; they usually call him "the infamous Aretino." The fellow was an obvious blackguard; a blackmailer, a pornographer, a sycophant, malicious, a megalomaniac, a lunatic with nothing but a good prose style to commend him.

Some of this is true; he was in many ways odious. But he was important, and one can't understand the Renaissance without him, which means one can't understand modern Europe without him. He was the first journalist of the modern world, the first writer to live by comment alone. In a world where the prince, often himself a writer, struck bargains with this or that professional to write what he wanted written for political reasons, or because he liked that sort of writing, Aretino was the first to set up shop alone with his pen, and to apply his vision of the world sometimes where he thought it needed applying, sometimes where it would earn him a square meal. But the choice and the judgment were always his alone. Decade after decade he poured out his pamphlets and dialogues—articles they would be, now—using himself as a weathervane of political and social and aesthetic change, and showing loyalty to no one but himself. He was the first writer in Europe to offer himself for sale as an independent eye, an independent judgment; he sold nothing but the statement "Aretino says ———." He was the forerunner of the syndicated columnist and the television personality, making a contract now with this potentate, now with that, and twisting all of their tails.

Blackmail he did, but when one comes across blackmail it is not enough to condemn it outright; one has to ask who is blackmailed. Aretino blackmailed tyrants, and blackmail, like revolution, is something tyrants cannot object to. He was in the main line of Humanism because he lived on the output of his individual mind seen as the self-sufficient spirit of man, of one man. "The world itself," he said, "of whose simplicity I am the secretary, dictates what I write." License to inquire was already established in Aretino's day; he moved over into license to declare the omnipotence of the descriptive paragraph, and fell slap into the aesthetic pit which awaits declarations of omnipotence: caprice.

He soon discovered his own special gift of writing panegyrics on one potentate and diatribes against another, and then screwing the first potentate for a year's maintenance against the promise not to insult him as he had the second. He set up house in Venice later in life, and affirmed the equality of professional intellectuals with princes by leading a life of what he called equal "satrappery." The steps of his house, he said, were worn down by the humble who came to him seeking redress for their wrongs; it was pure egalitarian journalism.

He may have been apprenticed to a painter in Perugia when he was young; his writing is full of sudden bursts of description where words seem to be standing in for color and form and composition, almost for pigment. You can see the frame around them. Some of his descriptions of the Venetian light—sunset and pink clouds—are among the usual set pieces of Italian prose still in use in the schoolbooks.

When he was quite elderly he begot a daughter, and one paragraph he wrote about her will serve to nail the myth of the "monster," of the atrocious Aretino. It is from a letter to the painter Sebastiano del Piombo. "Each smallest tear they shed, each murmur, each sigh that comes from their mouth or their breast shakes our souls. Not a leaf falls nor thistledown turns in the air but seems to us lead to fall on their heads and kill them; nor can nature break their sleep or sate their appetite but we fear for their health. . . . May God keep me my daughter." No writer can be dismissed who speaks to us like that across four centuries, and if literature means anything it means that those writers who are not dismissed altogether must be listened to across the whole band of their perception, not just where we find it easy to listen. If they can teach us what we already know, they may also teach us what we do not.

Now Aretino's name is almost synonymous with erotic

writing and to this day commercial pornography tends in Italy to the sonnet form which he used. His most famous work is not the sonnets he wrote for Giulio's prints, but the *Ragionamenti*, or *Discussions*, which take up the form of Lucian's *Dialogues of the Whores*. These are conversations between an older woman and a younger in which the mother describes what goes on among whores, among wives, and among nuns. It is very much the same; that is to say all fuck. The dialogues show in the main the tradition of classical writing which I described earlier as taking fucking as one thing among others, as a topic which he happens to be writing about this time. Next time, and often next paragraph within the discussion, it will be aesthetics, or history, or proto-Jacobin polemics. The *Discussions* are not strictly pornographic in that they are not deliberately designed to provoke desire for its own sake; they are not mere aids to masturbation.

I quoted above one of the manifestos of a character in the *Discussions*.[7] Here is another, to the same effect. "But I'm me, you see, and I speak as I think fit, not with a hot potato in my mouth. I walk on my own feet and not like a crane, and I say the words as they come; I don't dig them out of my mouth with a fork. Because they're words, not candy; and when I talk I sound like a woman, not a jackdaw."

She speaks for Aretino himself. Walking on his own feet, then, he combines the ephemeral with the permanent. He insists that a good whore should avoid petrarchisms in her speech; she should avoid all that he sums up under the word *conciossiacosadissecatochè* (rough translation: never-themurderedtodissectwhichsoever). There was in fact a rash of words like *conciossiacchè* and *unquanco* and *gnaffè* out of Petrarch and Boccaccio among the literate at that time; the worst sort of what R.L. Stevenson called *tushery* —we suffered from it in the nineteenth century—and Aretino did largely succeed in nailing it and proclaiming the

---

[7] P. 13.

propriety of Italian as she was spoke. It was another phase of taking license; *taking* license to speak, instead of applying to Petrarch for it. He also advised the whore to be nice to scholars and writers, else they would write rude articles about her. She should accept their custom at a low rate for this reason.

But besides these ephemera he had some strong insights into the permanent nature of whoring. The whore, he says, "laughs with one eye and weeps with the other." He notes that she has a choice in her clientele between the gentleman who pays more but takes longer because he undresses and does various interesting things, and the artisan or servant who pays less but gets out quicker because he doesn't bother to undress. Kinsey noted that the same class pattern holds in the sex life of Americans today.

Above all his view of the whore is unsentimental; he never suggests that she enjoys her work, or generally comes when her client does. His whores are no more golden-hearted than they are fascinating and irresistible gates to hell. They are women, thus employed, and thus conditioned.

The same painter's eye which he used in his often quoted descriptions of glass on a table, of the Venetian sunset, of a hermit's garden, of a crucifix, of a triumph, he used also in his erotic scenes. "All the limbs of that nun were so smooth that a hand placed on her loins would have slid down her leg as quick as a foot slips on ice, and hair no more dared grow on her than it would on the shell of an egg." And just as his descriptions of fucking are on a level with descriptions of anything else, so is his view of whoring part of his general view of society. "The whore," he says, "is like the soldier. Both are paid to do evil." That sentence makes him the ancestor of Voltaire, Marx and Brecht. It is the fruit of his dissociation from principalities and powers, of his writerly independence; it comes from the heart of Humanism.

Later in life, trying to keep up with the Counter-Reformation, Aretino thought it would be a good thing if he

became a cardinal. He began to write devotional works, to
which his genius was unsuited. These are painful to read
now; the painter's eye is reduced to describing in terms of
complaisant symmetry all sorts of horrible massacres and
martyrdoms, and the genial rushing humor to mere sniggering puns. Giulio, doggedly building away in Mantua,
fared better; he never tried to keep up with the times.

The third man is Marcantonio Raimondi, who engraved
Giulio's drawings on copperplates. He was engraver in
ordinary to the High Renaissance. He engraved the Greek
works for the Venetians and Romans, and the Venetians
and Romans for the rest of the world. When the Renaissance, both the Italian one and its ancient catalyst, hit
France and Germany and England and Scotland and
Bohemia and Poland and Russia and Sweden and Spain
and Mexico and Brazil and Barbary it was not only the
traveling Italians, Torrigiani to England, others elsewhere,
it was also the stay-at-home engraver who conveyed it. Not
only were Giulio Romano and Aretino central figures in
the purposes and perceptions of the humanistic High
Renaissance, but Giulio's engraver Marcantonio was a central figure in the way it was transmitted to all the corners
of the world.

It is usual among writers and scholars who may or may
not have seen them—and they are not easy to see—to take
a pretty haughty view of Giulio's designs and Aretino's
sonnets. Three sample judgments will make the point. Frederick Hartt in his (otherwise excellent) *Giulio Romano*
describes the engravings as "funny" and interest in them
as "symptomatic"; he does not say of what. Their "special
emphasis," he writes, "on abnormal and spectacular attitudes, on acute physical strain, and on frustration, is surely
significant for the psychology of early mannerism."[8] Mar-
guerite Yourcenar, who is often a most sensitive writer,
speaks of the "manuals of Aretino" and contemptuously

uses the word "gymnastics."[9] She is in an old tradition here. Eldred Everett wrote in his poems, published in 1657:

> As they from Pasture into Posture grew,
> Their bodies in all Aretines they threw.

Richard Lewinsohn in his *A History of Sexual Customs*,[10] which is a cut above the usual potboilers having this sort of title, calls the *Sonnets* "ineffably crude obscenities" and a "coarse enumeration and interminable repetition of the most vulgar expressions for the genitals and the sexual act."

All these are condemnations of the works on the grounds of obscenity. Whether they are nervous like Hartt or fulminating like Lewinsohn, the critics seem at first sight to be condemning something trivial, stupid and nasty. But are they not in fact condemning more than they think? Listen now to Bernard Berenson. "No wonder we have given over Giulio Romano, Perino del Vaga, Giovan Franceschi Penni, Polidoro da Caravaggio, and their ignoble fellows to oblivion. It is all they deserve. Let not these names come to our minds when we think of the artists of Central Italy."[11] (The names that should come to our mind start with Duccio di Buoninsegna and Simone Martini; Berenson's taste was unquestioned for a generation, and is not dead yet.) Now of course Berenson was not thinking especially of the *Modi* when he wrote that; he was thinking of a whole school of painters, a whole approach to life and society and technique, the vision of a certain generation, the one very roughly and not too meaningfully called the "early mannerists." He hated it, and he loved the Middle Ages and the Renaissance, up to but not including the Mannerists. This kind of distinction naturally made him a second-rate critic; first-rate critics hate nothing that they cannot demonstrate to be evil. But at least he went the whole hog; he threw out a whole generation, lock stock

---

[9] In *Encounter*, December, 1959.
[10] Translated from the German, London, 1958; New York, 1959.
[11] *Italian Painters of the Renaissance*, London, 1952, pp. 133-134; New York, 1957 (first published between 1894 and 1907).

and barrel. The other critics throw out what we usually think of as obscenity, but they do not notice that in so doing they also throw out the whole approach to life of Giulio and Aretino and Marcantonio Raimondi. You cannot pick and choose; if the level eye, the licensed eye, leads to something that makes us cry "shame!" we must either, like Berenson, take refuge in a safer time, or we must go on and examine the extreme, the strange, the *outré* which comes as the terminal product of that licensed eye.

And now let us consider the terminal product itself. Giulio's prints show different couples before, during and after fucking. They are indoors, usually on a bed, and all of them quite naked; in this they belong to the Giorgione-Titian tradition. They go closely with the rest of Giulio's work; that is, they are heroic, fiery, energetic, giving off a feeling of nobility and prowess. The décor and trappings are Roman. There is no feeling of shame or guilt; they are an equal celebration of one of the activities of that marvelous being, man. Opinions about this differ with habits and prejudices, but I cannot for my part see any of the "strain" or "abnormality" in them that Hartt sees. They are sometimes known in English as "the Positions"; this is part of the great bug-collectors tradition of calling anything like this "positions," as if a man and a woman were to say to each other—"I think we'll use number fourteen tonight," were to adopt it, ask each other if everything was all set, and then *perform* that number as if it were the scale of G minor, and if you go up harmonic or come down melodic you've made a mistake. They look to me more like moments seized by Giulio during the usual course of what people actually do, since it takes a scholar to miss the fact that fucking is more like dancing than anything else. Or vice versa. Dancing and fucking are not a series of positions, but a flow of movement; the use of the word "position" in this context is a product of the blocked imagination.[12]

---

[12] The actual phrases "Aretine's postures" or "Aretino's manuals" no doubt derive historically from a short book first published over Aretino's name about 1650, called *La Puttana Errante*, which has

Most of the prints are serious, noble, balanced, open. But two make comic points. In one of them someone has popped up and looks through a window; the couple are unaware of this. Just one of those things that may happen. In another Giulio has given way to his own individual form of the temptation to put quotation marks round humanity, to frame art, to cut off his utterance and make it special, to vaticinate a bit. He has one of his couples on a small trolley, being pulled along by a harnessed cupid. (As we shall see, Aretino seized on this with a guffaw; he would be bound to have.) Giulio takes this one out of his series and refers it to the gods-and-chariots approach of his more solemn public works; perhaps there is self-derision in it. It is still within the tradition of treating fucking as an equal thing; only in this case he treats it not as equal with the rest of human activity in general but as equal with the rest of his own activity as a painter in particular. The statement is: everybody is used to fucking, and I, for what that's worth, am also used to painting gods in chariots. So just for once we will not only have people-as-usual, but also Giulio-as-usual.

The sonnets Aretino "ran up" for these prints—it is his own word: "*ci sciorinai sopra*"—are more or less in keeping. That is to say, they talk about fucking without shame or guilt or coyness, and treat it with the same direct and unweighted celebration as one might treat a flower or a dance. They also adhere strictly to the Aretinesque rule of saying exactly what you mean in the shortest, most vivid and most colloquial language, a canon of writing which springs directly from the nominalist position in ontology— "words are the shadows of things" is the formulation that Aretino, following others, chose—from the feeling that a thing is too proper and too precious to be betrayed by a remote or inexact word, and from a religious attitude to

no more to do with the narrative poem of that name written by Aretino's pupil Lorenzo Venier (see p. 62) than with Aretino himself. It describes and tabulates thirty-five "positions" and accords each a pedantic title. The writing is wooden and uninteresting.

life, using the word in its original and wider sense, as *binding-in.*

> Fottiamci, anima mia, fottiamci presto,
> Poichè tutti per fotter nati siamo;
> E se tu'l cazzo adori, io la potta amo
> E sarà'l mondo cazzo senza questo.
> E se post mortem fotter fosse honesto,
> Direi: Tanto fottiam, che ci moiamo:
> E di là fotterem Eva ed Adamo,
> Che trovarno il morto si disonesto.
> —Veramente egli è ver, che se i furfanti
> Non mangiavan quel frutto traditore,
> Io so che si sfoiavano gli amanti.
> Ma lasciam ir le ciancie, e sino al core
> Ficcami il cazzo, e fa che mi si schianti
> L'anima, ch'in sul cazzo hor nasce, hor muore;
>   E se possibil fore
> Non mi tener dalla potta anche i coglioni,
> D'ogni piacer fortuni testimoni.[13]

This is actually one of the less direct ones; in few of the sonnets do the lovers take time off to discuss theology.

> Questo è pur un bel cazzo lungo e grosso.
> Deh: se l'hai caro, lasciamelo vedere.

---

[13] Come, let us fuck, my soul, let's fuck at once,
Since fucking is what man was fashioned for,
And since you worship pricks as I do cunts,
Without which life would be a fucking bore.
Could man but fuck *post mortem*, I would cry:
Let's fuck ourselves to death, and wake to fuck
With Eve and Adam, who were doomed to die
By that fuck apple and their rotten luck.
What if some craven rascals are nonplussed
By Adam's fate, and shun the treacherous tree?
We lovers know the way to quench our lust.
But come, less chit-chat: fuck me instantly,
Transfixing heart and soul with one long thrust
Of that great prick that's life and death to me;
And while you're at it, see
If those twin witnesses of every pleasure,
Your balls, can't be included for good measure.

This translation is by Richard Wilbur.

—Vogliam provare se potete tenere
Questo cazzo in la potta, e me adosso?
—Come, s'io vo provar? Come, s'io posso?
Piuttosto questo che mangiare o bere!
—Ma s'io v'infrango poi, stando a giacere,
Farovi mal.—Tu hai'l pensier del Rosso.
Gettati pure in letto e nello spazio
Sopra di me, che se Marforio fosse,
O un gigante, io n'havero solazzo,
Purche mi tocchi le midolla e l'osse
Con questo divinissimo cazzo
Che guarisce le potte della tosse.
   —Aprite ben le coscie
Che potrian delle donne esser vedute
Di voi meglio vestite, ma non fottute.

Most of the sonnets are by no means heavyweight pieces
of Italian prosody, but there is one where Aretino has a go
at a technical difficulty; that of handling extreme simplicity.
(An abacus is harder than log tables.) In it he restricts his
rhyme words to *cazzo* and *potta*, prick and cunt. The discipline of form it imposes on him seems to bring out a
greater density and truth of feeling. The sonnet is full of
tenderness, of regard for the other, in a word, of love.

Perch'io prov'or un si solenne cazzo,
Chè mi rovescia l'orlo della potta,
Io vorrei esser tutta quanta potta,
Ma vorrei che tu fossi tutto cazzo.
Perchè s'io fossi potta, e tu cazzo,
Io sfamerei per un tratto la potta,
E tu haveresti anche dalla potta
Tutto il piacer che può haver un cazzo.
Ricevi il buon voler da questa potta.
   —E voi, pigliate del mio poco cazzo
La Buona voluntà; in giu la potta
Ficcate, ed io in su ficcherò il cazzo;
      E dipoi su il mio cazzo
Lasciatevi andar tutta con la potta;
E sarò cazzo, e voi sarete potta.

Again:

Io farò adesso, e voi, quando farete?
—Adesso! Dammi tutta la linguina,
Ch'io muoio.—Et io, e voi cagion ne siete.
          Adunque voi compirete?
—Adesso, adesso faccio, Signor mio:
Adesso ho fatto.—Et io; oimè! O Dio!

There is one of these sonnets where he breaks through
into an integration of feeling, into an at-homeness between
man and his environment which is something quite peculiar
to him alone—it is interesting that this sonnet did not match
one of Giulio's prints or, if it did, the print has been
entirely lost. Here he is taking off into an image of the
interrelation of things, which one may accept or reject, but
which is certainly fecund. Probably most people in England or America now will reject it, but there it is. It is a
way of seeing family life, and by implication all human
life, which as far as I know has not been shared by any
other poet in Christendom.

Sta cheto, bambin mio; ninna nanna!
Spingi, meastro Andrea, spingi, ch'ei c'è.
Dammi tutta la lingua; ai! oimè!
Che'l tuo gran cazzo all' anima mi va.
—Signora, adesso, adesso v'entrerà;
Cullate ben il fanciullin col piè,
E farete servigi a tutti tre:
Perchè noi compiremo, ei dormirà.
—Io son contenta; io cullo, io meno, io fo:
Culla, mena e travagliati anche tu.
—Mammina, a vostra posta compirò.
—Non far; fermati, aspetta un poco più.
Che tal dolcezza in questo fotter ho
Ch'io non vorrei ch'ei finisca mai più.
          —Madonna mia, hor su,
Fate, di gratia—Hor, da che voi così,
Io faccio: e tu, farai?—Signor, si.[14]

[14] Lie quiet, my child; lullaby. Push, Master Andrew, I'm there.
Give me your tongue; ah, God! Your great prick goes to my soul.
—Lady, now it's coming, now; rock the baby well with your foot
and you will do a service to all three of us; because we come, he'll

The image of rocking the baby with the movements of
fucking comes up again in a poem by Carducci three and
a half centuries later, and the change it has undergone is
quite interesting. To Aretino it seemed a natural and convenient thing to do: "Because we come, he'll sleep." It is
an emblem of family life in general, where if you do something for one person it usually helps the others too. Perhaps
of all human life. But Carducci uses it in a context of knowing blame, and makes it adulterous.[15]

In William Faulkner's play, *Requiem for a Nun*, the
husband accuses his wife of not having bothered to put
the baby out of her bed before the lover got in. I saw this
play once in Paris; the actress playing the wife *crumpled*
at the accusation, and a rustle of pure horror went round
the theatre. It just depends on the context and the handling.

But to return to Aretino. When he saw Giulio's print
of the lovers being dragged along on the trolley by Cupid,
he immediately identified himself with the man and with
what would actually happen.

> Non tirar, fottutelo di Cupido,
> La cariola, firmati bismulo,
> Ch'io vo fotter in potta, e non in culo . . .

On that occasion the jerking of the trolley put Aretino
in mind of what was to him then and would to most of us
be always a comic predicament, that of the golf club stories
about "the wrong hole." But in some of the sonnets he
writes of buggery as something like a rather special change,
a pleasant holiday which can be arranged from time to
time. This is in accordance with much of the writing of
that age, and of the Greco-Roman culture. I cannot see

sleep.—I'm happy; I'm rocking, I'm fucking, I'm coming; you rock
and fuck and come too.—Mammina, I'll come when you do—
Don't come; stop; wait a little. There's such sweetness in this fucking I wish it could last forever.—Now, girl, come on; come now,
please, now.—If that's how you are, let's go. And you? There?—
Ah, yes.
[15] In the poem *A proposito del Processo Fadda*.

that Giulio felt the same way; all his figures seem to be in the usual place, except perhaps one.

The Raimondi prints, and probably also the Aretino sonnets, fell into the hands of the Pope himself, as they were bound to, and the Pope reacted strongly. Vasari wrote a pretty dramatic account of what happened, but that was fifty years later, and one may doubt it was quite as bad as that, let alone as bad as legend built it up to be in the eighteenth century. If we leave aside the death sentences, the pleas to spare the life, the burning in effigy, and probably even a good deal of the languishing in dungeons, we do still find that Giulio and Aretino left Rome and Raimondi was imprisoned for a while. Giulio, as we have seen, went to Mantua; Aretino went first to Milan, and then to Venice. Three years later, in 1527, came the Sack of Rome, and the afternoon clouds came up over Humanism.

What Giulio and Aretino did has been repeated from time to time; the achievement was not unique, and perhaps it was not, on the visual side, even the best. Later artists did as well or even better, though I doubt later writers have done better than Aretino. I write at length about them because they were the first such works in Christendom, and but for them there would probably never have been any others. The thing could only have been done first at the high-water mark of Humanism, at the moment when it was really in doubt for a few years whether Christianity might not prove a mere interlude in the history of Hellenic religion.[16]

There remains a handful of later masterpieces of sane and open celebration. Perhaps some of the early pastoral verse of Giambattista Marino may be counted. In particular one could admire his poem, *Pastorella*, which was only published posthumously. The freedom he allowed himself in his youth gave him a direct simplicity which is almost comically at variance with his mature work, the enormous poem, *Adone*. In this, one of the most notable surfeits of

---

[16] An account of the later history of these works is in Appendix 2.

European literature, they are forever hovering dilutely in grottoes and exchanging kisses which may last anything up to a page. In the *Pastorella* they fuck once and for all; firmly, simply and contentedly.

Marino was Poussin's patron, and Poussin himself, since his vision of mankind was not partial but total, handled the erotic as grandly and surely as any other part of life.

Rembrandt had a line in little engravings of monks and peasants pissing and shitting out of doors, and there is one rather huddled one in which the monk is tumbling a peasant girl. He took up the same attitude in a more famous and more successful print called "The Great Bed," or "The French Bed," in which a young boy and girl are making love. It is one of the most comfortable and simple in the whole corpus of erotic art: a perfect expression of youthful *Gemütlichkeit*. A puzzle: why has the girl got three arms? Rembrandt has drawn her right arm in two alternative positions, and I understand it is unique that he should have allowed a run to be taken from a plate in an unfinished state. At other times, as for instance in the "Christ Before Pilate," he went so far as to burnish out whole portions, which did not satisfy him, actually on the plate. Why not here? Perhaps someone whipped the plate off him before it was finished—this kind of thing is always happening with erotic works. But surprisingly few people notice the third arm at all. It is perhaps thinkable that Rembrandt left it for this very reason, simply as a joke about the way the erotic dulls our observation.

A French book, author unknown, called *l'Ecole des Filles*, which was first published in 1655[17] stands quite apart from the great tradition of all-out pornography which started five years later with *Satyra Sotadica*. It has the usual form of dialogues between a girl (of sixteen) and a more experienced young woman; the latter tells the former what to expect with her first lover, and the former than tells the

[17] For a bibliographical account, see David Foxon; *Libertine Literature in England, 1660–1745*, II, in *The Book Collector*, London, Summer 1963.

latter how it is going. Neither is a whore, there are no kinks, no incest, not even an orgy; only a cheerful, zestful, witty and realistic account of young people fucking in love. The author was clearly quite a young man. He triumphantly overcomes the difficulties of the Christian tradition in setting down what it actually feels like to be totally and happily obsessed in physical love. If this book were ever to be republished (a seventeenth-century translation into English exists) and a trial were to result, it would be a clear confrontation of the spirit of life and its enemies.

There is a fine fiery painting by Géricault, and perhaps some Picasso drawings belong here, although with him the erotic, at least in the last forty years, has had even more quotation marks around it than the rest of his work.

There is a book of drawings by the forgotten Hungarian liberal romantic painter Michael Zichy[18] which sometimes breaks clean through into unweighted celebration. Some of them are not free from perversity, but there are one or two of children looking forward to the joys they can't yet encompass, in which Zichy sees and states what does happen, without comment or complaisance, but with simple understanding. It is interesting that they come out of the same Viennese culture where Freud for the first time in the bourgeois age was considering the fact that children are not asexual creatures. But better than these is a series of four in the book of a husband and wife; they are to my mind some of the finest in the whole history. There is a rounded calm and contentment about them, and also a sense that what is happening is that the people are consciously and deliberately building a child, which make them one of the few real statements to have arisen in our culture about the means by which the people who carry it, and all other cultures, perpetuate themselves.

Most of the celebrations which I have been praising here have been pictures, and this is natural. We are looking for

[18] *Liebe*, Vienna, 1911, posthumously published. Zichy lived from 1827 to 1906.

celebrations of what goes right. There is much to say when love goes wrong; but little when it goes right. All we can *say* when it goes right is perhaps "yes," perhaps not even that. When we are loving, "speech is not our language," as George Sand put it. It is natural then that we should think and work in pictures.

Perhaps the finest image of all those which have been made in celebrations of love in our civilization is a picture, and, perhaps strangely, perhaps comprehensibly, it is not a picture of two people making love, but of one person; it is a picture of a woman. We shall discuss in a later chapter the difficulty a painter may have in saying what he himself feels when he represents two people fucking. When he represents one woman about to be fucked, there is no such difficulty.

The picture is a portrait by Courbet. Most portraits are face portraits: this is a cunt portrait, and that's most of what there is to be said about it. Courbet painted it in 1865 for a Turkish diplomat called Khalil Bey, then retired and living in Paris. It was kept in a kind of tabernacle with doors, on the outside of which was painted a landscape. Three years later Khalil Bey went bankrupt, and sold both this picture and the more famous Courbet, "The Sleepers," which had also been painted especially for him.[19] The former passed to the Hungarian family of Hatvany, and was sold, I believe in America, in 1958.

In this portrait, Courbet did something which ought to have been impossible; he looked where a millennium and a half of Christianity should have conditioned him to avert his eyes. Just as in his landscapes you can feel the coolness or the warmth of the air under the trees, so in this you can feel the weight of the girl on your hands as you look at it. It is not pornographic, for the following reason. A good head portrait does not just put you in mind of conversation, it makes you want to talk to that particular person. This picture does not just put you in mind of fucking

---

[19] Gerstle Mack, *Gustave Courbet*, London, New York, 1951.

in general, which is what pornography does; it makes you want to fuck that particular person, whoever she was. Painting has been mostly a man's game so far, but there seems no basic reason why a woman should not be able to paint a prick portrait as fine as this.

The great merit of the old socialist's achievement is its complete absence of comment. It is natural joy in natural beauty naturally shared with the beholder. It would be absurd to comment further on that which is beautiful because free of comment.

And the same is true of love itself. When we have pared away the blind prohibitions of a partial religion and their gray train of guilt, the unargued assertions and floating concepts of psychological dogma, and the thrashing compulsions of pride, there is not much to say about what remains. But it is there all right.

Traherne said: "To see, love, covet, have, enjoy, and praise in one." Traherne said that, and Courbet painted it.

Chapter 10

Exempt from Art?

The ancient Egyptians represented people in profile, but with one exception; slave girls and foreign prisoners of war were sometimes represented full face, "as if certain taboos did not apply to such low creatures."[1] Rabbinical commentators allowed that negative casts, as on seals, need not count as graven images, and certain families of Polish Jews are said to have gone so far as to allow incomplete statues, e.g. with a finger or an ear missing. The Eastern Church permitted painting and reliefs, but not fully three-dimensional sculpture; the test was whether you could take it by the nose.

In the last case, they were obviously worried that children and very simple people might think the statue *was* Jesus or the saint, and pray directly to the image. But in the Jewish and even more the Egyptian examples, there seems to be a general feeling that the more important a thing is, the more dangerous it is to represent it. To the

[1] Gombrich, *op. cit.*, pp. 112-113, from which this whole paragraph is digested.

Egyptians, a free man was so important that it was better only to observe him from the side. To the Moslems any sort of man has often been too important to represent at all, though abstract patterns like ropes and tendrils and scaffolding have been safe. To represent someone or something is to re-create it, and therefore to claim power over it, and you ought not to claim power over the important. Respect and honor are due to an important man, and worship to God, therefore a representation which may be respected, honored, or even worshiped, risks robbing him of his due. To claim power over a king is treason, over God blasphemy. The upshot is a feeling of danger, a taboo.

What can this teach us about the taboo on representations of fucking? There may be and have been in some people at different times a feeling that this was an important action, and should therefore be exempt from the claim to power over it inherent in re-creating it; such a feeling would suggest that it was something wild, free and holy. There may equally be—there certainly is today—a feeling that the honor in which the action should be held may be diverted by the representation, that the beholder may get stuck in his beholding and never go on to the action, which would fulfill him. I take it that some such feeling is among the reasons why we are worried about children and adolescents seeing "obscene" pictures; "you don't want to look at that, you want to do it, later." The fear of addiction is not too far removed from the fear of idolatry.

There is also the simpler feeling, arising straight out of the cultural taboo with which this book is mainly concerned, that fucking is "mysterious," that the pleasure of it depends on the mystery, and that, in a word, "knowledge casteth out love."

But there are certainly other elements too. There are technical difficulties about representing two people making love, and in a culture where the arts are considered largely as techniques—think how much more we at the moment dwell on the *how* of the arts than on the *what* or the *why*, how we explain "the creative process," how we unearth in our biographies what the artist actually saw, how we praise him for being a "real craftsman," how we feel we gain in understanding if we can watch him at work, talk to him in the coffee break—in such a culture, technical problems will be important.

I want to leave aside here all the mountains of representations of the guilty aspects of the erotic, all the "peering" images stolen through the keyhole, all the images of humiliation (called *"après"*), all the grotesque and the sniggering, all the sly, the furtive, the crazy and the damned, in short, all those in the first four categories of Chapter 5, and concentrate on the simple image of two young adults fucking and, even more, coming; those of my "celebratory" category. It is men who have made them; there are very few by women, and this is presumably so for the same reasons, whatever they are, that make men the consumers of erotic art and sub-art.

Can the image of love in action be validly set down at all? Think of the difficulties. If the artist observes two other people making love, he will be excited and his excitement will cause both his pencil to wobble and his models to feel differently; their desire for each other will be distorted by his desire. If he is not excited, his sinister calm will distort their feelings even more, and in any case it is most doubtful if he could be much good as an artist if he were not excited. Again, what sort of people will be happy to fuck for him to draw them? Exhibitionists. And what sort of artist will want to do it? A voyeur. It is certainly possible for a voyeur to draw two exhibitionists, but the chances are that he will not be a very good artist, and that they will not be very much in love. I draw attention to the wording: "the chances are." There are few voyeurs and even fewer good artists; it is only very improbable, not impossible, that one man should be both.

On the other hand the artist works not from what he sees, but also from what he knows in his own body of balance and the way things go. He will draw a man on horseback half from what his eyes tell him and half from what his knees do. When he is making love he will be able to see his wife or girl, and he will be able to feel himself, but he will not be able to see himself unless he turns his head to look in the mirror, in which case he will see himself thinking about himself, and it will not be the image of love in action. Even more so at the moment of coming. He will know what she looks like when she comes (Bernini's "St. Teresa" is the *locus classicus*) but he won't know what he looks like himself.

The Renaissance poet Johannes Secundus (see p. 316 below) wrote a poem about this. It is the eighth of his *Basia,* or kisses. (Echo of Catullus at the beginning.)

Centum basia centies,	A hundred hundred kisses,
Centum basia millies,	A hundred thousand kisses,
Mille basia millies,	A thousand thousand kisses,
Et tot milia millies	And as many thousand thousand
Quot guttae Siculo Mari,	As the drops in the Sicilian Sea
Quot sunt sidera caelo.	Or the stars in the sky.
Istis purpureis genis,	At those rosy cheeks
Istis turgidulis labris	At those swelling lips,
Ocellisque loquaculis	At those expressive eyes
Ferrem continuo impetu,	I will go with continual energy
O formosa Neaera.	O lovely Neaera.
Sed dum totus inhaereo	But while I am close attached
Conchatim roseis genis,	Against your rosy cheeks
Conchatim rutilis labris	Against your red lips
Ocellisque loquaculis,	And your expressive eyes,
Non datur tua cernere	I cannot see your lips,
Labra, non roseas genas	Nor your rosy cheeks
Ocellosque loquaculos.	Nor your expressive eyes.
Heu, quae sunt oculis meis	Alas how has strife arisen
Nata proelia cum labris?	Between my eyes and my lips?
Ergo ego mihi vel Jovem	Could I bear even Jove
Rivalem potero pati?	As a rival?
Rivales oculi mei	My eyes will not brook
Non ferunt mea labra.	My lips as rivals.

The greater part of that section of European erotic art which has to do with simple love and desire does not show two people fucking at all. It shows, over and over, a naked woman, an excited woman, a masturbating woman, because this is what the artist sees. These are images of half a couple; what is left when the artist takes himself away. (There is a fine series of little bronzes by Epstein, which are half couples.) But love is two people, and so, to show a couple loving, the artist has often turned to two women; he sets down two of what he does know and can see doing what he does know but can't see. I guess that for every representation of a man and woman making love in the European tradition, there is one of two women making love. This does not reflect the proportions of common experience; it does not reflect what the artist saw, nor what he wanted; it is simply the nearest he could come with technical certainty to the image of love. This is not to deny that many men like to think of two women making love, because it makes them think of joining in; and they like that idea partly because it makes them feel superior— they would be what both the women really wanted—and partly because if one woman is fun, two would be twice as much fun. But I am thinking here of artists and pictures which are beyond the realm of wish-fulfillment, and in that where you seek to make true statements; in this case true images of love.

Moreover it strikes the eye that the pictures of this tradition are not really pictures of Lesbians, of homosexual women, where one leads the other, but of two heterosexual women, both equal, both the sort of women that the artist knows and has fucked. Neither, typically, is a bull-dike, a stand-in for the artist himself; both are objects of his own past experience, put together for the occasion. Two examples of this long tradition will serve, they are Rodin's "Bacchantes" and Courbet's "The Sleepers." Both are on open exhibition in Paris. There also exists a series of wash drawings by Rodin.

Are these technical difficulties surmountable? Can the artist, out of the corner of his eye or the corner of his *Körpergefühl*, gather the memory trace or the experience trace which he needs in order to make a valid image of a man and a woman together? There is so much in the erotic art of Christian Europe which fails, that one often doubts it. But some of the Greek and Roman pieces show that it can be done: perhaps, for instance, the Perennius vase figures. And if the difficulty was a technical one, one to do with the limitations of human perception itself, it would work as strongly in one culture as in another. The Romans were physically like us.

They were physically like, but spiritually and emotionally unlike. Any artist in Christendom and post-Christendom will be well aware, when he broaches the possibility of representing fucking, that he is doing something extraordinary. He will know for one thing that his work will sell, if at all, at a high price and through clandestine channels. It will be a separate and special part; it will not be in the book of photographs of his life's work, or the retrospective exhibition. It will be talked about more than seen; he will perhaps not offer it for sale at all, but keep it in a special folder and only show it to those he wants to show it to, instead of exhibiting it in general hopefulness to all comers.

It is not so much technical difficulties which impose this limitation on him as the feelings in our culture about the subject represented. If an action is regarded with doubt and disapproval, so will representations of it be regarded. The fact that there are other actions which are regarded with doubt and disapproval, such as murder, and are yet represented in the graphic arts without inhibition, leads us on to the odd nature of the whole taboo on the erotic which we will discuss later.

It is hard for the visual artist to avoid the chilling taint of voyeurism, the half-comic, half-disgusting suggestion of the keyhole. We seldom see two other people fucking in our ordinary lives, and if the scene is presented to us in a picture our immediate reaction is, as it would be in life, to recoil; to feel a mistake has been made. We have opened the wrong door; we must close it again quietly. A few, a very few, artists have been good enough to convince us that these are not two other people whom we have come upon by mistake, but are on the other hand a true image of common humanity, which includes ourselves. Then, we will stay and not recoil. To bring off such an image is a feat of feeling and of ability to project statements about the individual and the general as great as or greater than the technical feat of observation.

Literature on the other hand is subject only to the cultural difficulties, not the technical ones. The writer is not so ready a prey to the chilling suggestion of the keyhole, because he can banish it in so many words. He can simply *tell* the reader that this is not a love scene come upon by accident or to satisfy the voyeur's need; he can make it clear in a few sentences, which require only moderate skill to devise, that it is on the contrary an image of the general. In any week one can read or hear a dozen stories or plays in magazines or on radio and television where the writer handles these old gambits with ease, putting the reader or viewer in and out of identification as his purpose demands. In the visual arts on the other hand, it takes a considerable master to handle our identification process with comparable certainty, to tell us whether we are the people in the picture, or the artist himself, or neither. He cannot order us about in so many words, as the writer can. A writer can be private with his reader; a painter never. This may be why, by common consent, an action which is "obscene" when it is shown in a picture or a photograph or a movie, is not when it is described in a book or a story, and why, therefore, the writer is allowed greater freedom than the visual artist.

Music is another matter again. You can put sex into music as well as you can put anything else, and better than most things. Bits of Stravinsky's *The Marriage* are as overtly erotic as anything printed or drawn, I think, and a lot of jazz and Caribbean and Latin American music hovers on the border between dance and fuck. (In fact most music outside the European tradition sometimes does this.)

Jazz is fucking; that is what the word means. It comes from the French *jaser,* which has, or had, two meanings: first, to chatter or gossip, which gives rise to the English verb to jazz, meaning to waste time, to deceive, to jive; and second to fuck, which gives rise to *jazz* music. When it first emerged from French-speaking New Orleans, it was called simply "the jass music," meaning the fuck music, because it was played in brothels and at parties. The connection between the two uses of the word takes us straight to the doubt and contempt of fucking which lie at the heart of Christian culture, and which we shall discuss later.

In music we tolerate a much greater erotic content than in the other arts; this is because born squares don't see it's there. A person who will suffer outrage and agonies of embarrassment looking at Rodin's "The Kiss" or reading *Lady Chatterley's Lover* will listen to Caribbean carnival music or the relevant bits of Stravinsky or Ray Charles with a happy smile. It takes a Tolstoy to see and disapprove the erotic force in music; it takes someone who has been blinded by conversion, not the born sex-blind. Luckily, there are not enough of them to do what the born squares do with their interminable and innumerable protests to hurt the other arts, which is why ordinary people can go on listening and dancing to erotic music in peace, and why Christendom has fallen so ravenously on jazz, with so much gratitude to its inventors, whose forefathers were not Christians in the seventeenth century.

Music is not for an audience of two people; it is for one, or many. Consider a musician playing for one person alone; it is an act of friendship, or of love. It is a gift, or it is part of a conversation. The musician has been talking, then he goes and plays, which is another statement, then he comes back and goes on talking to you. Or again, consider a musician at a party. He has been part of the party, then he goes and plays. The party meanwhile listens to him, or perhaps dances or sings to his music. He lifts and informs the whole party, becoming for a while its servant and its king.

But now consider a musician alone with two other

people, whether they are lovers or friends or even businessmen doing a deal. The situation is horrible; he is no more than a hired or servile adjunct to their contact. When he has finished playing, there is nothing for him to do but bow low and go out, after receiving a few forced compliments.

The fact that music is good for one person, and good for many, but bad for two, is true whether it is erotic music or not. If it is erotic music, and if the audience is thus one person in love with the musician, or a sexy party, which are both good, or two people in love with each other, which is bad from the point of view of the musician's function, then we can see how music too, by its very nature, is more or less exempt from the chilling suggestion of the keyhole. One to one, no keyhole; it is particular. One to a party, no keyhole; it is general. But one to two is keyhole, which is why we tend to avoid it, and to get so depressed when the palm court violinist plays round the tea tables.

To sum up this section: fucking is not automatically exempt from art. The nature neither of fucking nor of art demands that the two should be kept apart, that the eye of art should be averted from this subject matter alone of all subject matters. When we find a culture in which this exemption is the rule, and we in Europe and America live in such a culture, the exemption teaches us nothing about either love or art, it only teaches us about the culture. It teaches us that our culture holds fucking to be either too disgraceful or too holy to be included in art, and, which is another way of saying the same thing, holds art to be too feeble to include fucking. That there should nevertheless be a trade in erotic art, whether good or bad by the usual canons of judgment, tells us no more than that, though European or American, we are still human. Human beings are fucking animals and art-making animals. That the trade of erotic art should be a clandestine one, with artificially high prices, subject to legal penalties, tells us that whatever else our culture may be, it is not an integrated one.

It is a feeble, blind, and tense culture that withdraws its vision, which is art, from anything. When that from which art is withdrawn is that which continues life, and therefore culture, the culture wills its own extinction. When we call sex a "blind force" we are saying that we will not look at tomorrow. We deny ourselves. We deny our children, casting them off from the chain of existence which justifies us and defines them, by denying their origin. And we have externalized the denial, the withdrawal, the exclusion, through our favorite medium; technology. We have built weapons which threaten to do in the flesh what our taboo does in the spirit, to discontinue human life, and with it our culture. How could we not? It was possible. Will a thing long enough, and you find the means to do it. Meanwhile black and brown and yellow peoples, without Christianity and its attendant technology, stand amazed and slowly understand that the final message of the Christian and post-Christian West, from the Urals to the Pacific coast, is despair, is severance, is an ending, is No.

Christian and post-Christian and Communist culture is a eunuch; pornography is his severed balls; thermonuclear weapons are his staff of office. If there is anything sadder than a eunuch it is his balls; if there is anything more deadly than impotence it is murder.

PART IV

EXCLUDED ACTIONS

Chapter 11

Introductory

Unlike the Boy Scout, men and women are sexual in thought, word and deed. We have discussed how the words are excluded from the realm of the normal, and how the thoughts or images are; now it is time for the deeds.

What sexual actions are right, wrong, permissible, criminal, ought to be criminal, are pleasant, are ignoble: such questions are much discussed among us. The established opinion of our culture has in the last hundred years become much more permissive toward the particular actions of sexuality. A hundred years ago it held that homosexual love both of men and of women was an action of dreadful and willful depravity, an abomination and a shame to the species. Fifty years ago it held that masturbation was a very great evil and a danger to health (see Chapter 20 below). As I write this, it is just on the turn about premarital intercourse. And so on and so on.

We know now that every actual thing we can do in an erotic context is also done by our nearest relatives among the mammalian animals and has always been done in every human culture from which records survive. This, and a general swing in our own culture away from puritanism, from asceticism, from "spirituality," and toward a warmer and more bodily way of being, has loosened the tourniquet which used to strangle many pleasant loves and caresses.

We may be grateful for this. Much aimless suffering used to arise from the tourniquet, and no longer does; people, especially young people, now breathe a freer and a kinder air. But it is not enough merely to observe that such a general shift of opinion has taken place, and to applaud. What factors made us in the first place exclude certain actions, putting them beyond the tourniquet, and make us still exclude others? Should the swing of opinion go farther as it is going, or is it time for a halt?

In this section I consider two particular actions which are still excluded: incest and orgies. I could have chosen actions which used to be excluded and no longer are—for instance *soixante-neuf* or masturbation—but it seemed to me more interesting to choose two which are still definitely excluded, firstly because the very fact that they are so excluded has prevented them being very much considered, and secondly because we ought to be more interested in what actions may be permitted next by a changing opinion, than in those which have become permitted in the past.

In Chapter 12 I discuss incest, and the almost universal taboo under which it lies. I conclude that this taboo is probably determined by evolution itself and, unlike most of the manifestations of unfreedom in sex which we have been considering in this book, is appropriate to mankind as a whole.

In Chapter 13 I discuss orgies, and find a contrasting situation. Many cultures have regular orgies which are built into the seasonal and religious framework of life. Ours does not. There is a continuum stretching between the two sorts of culture, and I suggest that the place occupied in it by a given culture will be determined by the nature of that culture as a whole, including its basic feelings of identity and religion.

Chapter 12

Incest

I recently came across a paperback novel[1] which carried on the cover an extract from a review in the Manchester *Guardian*. The extract read: "The treatment is realistic and rational, and the tragic climax is one of those endings which are most moving but at the same time devoutly to be wished." I opened it at the end to see what this tragic climax was; a young woman drove her car over a cliff in icy weather and was killed. It was half accident and half suicide. For what character in a novel, for what person in life, would one devoutly wish such an ending? I supposed she was suffering from an incurable disease. I was wrong, of course; she had committed incest with her brother.

Now the *Guardian* is a liberal paper; the people who write for it would usually rather see things patiently put right than canceled in bloody cataclysms of expiation. But the *Guardian* reviewer felt like that about incest, and I

---
[1] Clara Winston, *The Closest Kin There Is*, New York, 1952, London, 1958.

expect many people in our society also feel like that about it. The taboo on the action is so strong that the man or woman who commits it is felt to be tainted, as by a mortal disease, is marked out for a death which may be tragic, but is deserved.

There is no need to run through the literature, from the Oedipus plays to Byron and Shelley and Ibsen and the most recent infusion of vigor into the tradition from Freud's lifelong study of its starting point, the Oedipus situation. Nor are Europe and Christendom alone in this taboo, as they are in so many of the other matters we have been considering. Studies have been published[2] which claim that as far as anthropology is able to say, the taboo is almost universal. Among the Incas and certain other pre-literate societies, and at times in ancient Egypt, sibling marriage was permitted or even encouraged among royalty, and in certain bellicose tribes intercourse between brothers and sisters was (and still is) encouraged before battle; it makes the soldiers braver. Again; at different times and places in the Hellenic culture, half-brothers and half-sisters of the same father were allowed to marry, though never those of the same mother.

But with these small exceptions, the rule appears to hold good over all societies, both now and heretofore; it is as nearly conterminous with mankind itself as any custom ever has been. When we seek to call up what is common to mankind, we could first say: "After all, we're all human." If this did not carry enough weight (as it clearly does not for practical purposes) we could not find anything else to say which would be quite as true as that. But the next truest thing would probably be: "After all, we're all against incest."

The taboo has been exceptionally strong at some times and in some places, just as it has been exceptionally weak in the examples I mentioned above. In the tenth and elev-

---

[2] E.g., George Murdock, *Social Structure*, New York, 1949, and S. Kirson Weinberg, *Incest Behavior*, New York, 1955.

enth centuries in Europe, marriage was prohibited by canon law between anything up to sixth cousins; in other words, as far as, and perhaps sometimes farther than, the family records could reach.[3] It was only in 1918 that Roman Catholic canon law got round to allowing third cousins to marry, and it still does not allow first cousins to. It has always been easy to get dispensation from these provisions, but they were, and are, there. The penalty for incest has been death at various times and places, and is still prison, though in most civilized countries now, the forces of law and order are as quick to send offenders to a psychiatrist as to exact the full rigor. Brother-sister incest was, oddly enough, not a criminal offense in England between 1660 and 1908, only an offense at Canon Law.

Just as incest provides something reaching toward a definition of humanity—the species which is against incest—so it also provides something reaching toward a starting point in sexual morality—the action which is definitely wrong. The temperamentally anti-sex will start a consideration of sexual morality from the question: is anything right? Which they will answer: yes, not castrating oneself. That will be their first step. The temperamentally pro-sex will start from the other end and ask: is anything wrong? And will answer: yes, incest. And that will be their first step.

Why is the taboo so strong and so universal? There is our own picture of the dire results of "inbreeding." We mention the Hapsburgs, and tell of villages where incest prevails and nobody is quite sane, or everybody has too many teeth and can't chew properly. We vaguely recall tales of gloomy castles with crazy heiresses leaning out of the upper windows on moonlit nights. "Taint," we think, and the word goes with "genetic" just as well as with "moral." Similarly, the Zulus believed that the spirits of their ancestors would turn the offspring of incest into monsters; the Mohave Indians held that incest was an omen of the extinction of the line, they felt it was like suicide; and the Tikopians of

[3] Weinberg, *op. cit.*

Polynesia believed incestuous marriages would be barren, or the offspring would die; the ancestors would kill them because the other ancestors laughed.

But many other reasons have been advanced for the taboo on incest, and these have perhaps been held by more people in the history of mankind than those which seem to connect it with genetic ill effects. Xenophon's Socrates, for instance, was against sibling marriages because they would tend to mating between the sexually immature. (If a brother and sister are going to marry, they might as well marry sooner as later.) St. Thomas Aquinas held that if sexual love were added to the love which already exists between a brother and sister, there would be so much human love that the love of God would not be able to get a look in. Jeremy Bentham was against incest because love needs surprise: "Individuals accustomed to see each other and to know each other from an age which is neither capable of conceiving the desire nor of inspiring it will see each other with the same eyes to the end of life." This is an account of what usually happens. It tells us nothing about why it does not always happen, nor about why we care so much that it should always happen.

There are countless other explanations. If they are not based on a belief in the ill effects on the offspring, they are usually no more than accounts of the reasons why most people do not commit incest, and contain no more moral or injunctive force than accounts of why most people do not wear fur coats in hot weather.

My own favorite is an explanation recorded by Margaret Mead from the Arapesh. "What is the matter with you anyway?" said the elder to the young man Margaret Mead had sent to inquire. "Don't you want a brother-in-law? Don't you realize that if you marry another man's sister and another man marries your sister, you will have at least two brothers-in-law, while if you marry your own sister you will have none? Who will you go to visit?"[4]

The evidence from anthropology about the incest taboo

---

[4] Quoted by Weinberg, *op. cit.*, p. 240.

is that it is nearly universal, that it is broken with varying frequencies in different cultures, and justified by varying reasons or myths. The evidence from genetics is extremely complicated, and still uncertain. The theoretical genetics of consanguinity can be set out clearly enough: the interested reader might refer to Chapter 19 of Curt Stern's *Principles of Human Genetics*.[5] Put with ineffable crudity, it is this. We are all consanguineous; if we were not, the population of the world a thousand years ago would have had to be a thousand times what it is now in order to give us enough ancestors. We therefore often marry relatives without knowing it, and the likelihood of our meeting up with a deleterious recessive gene which matches our own increases in a straight line from our twentieth cousin eight times removed, to our sister. But it is a slight increase only. What has much more effect is the amount of inbreeding in earlier generations of our family, tribe, or people. If cousin marriage, or even incest, is pretty common, and has been for some time, we run no greater risk of having infertile or sickly offspring by our cousin or our sister than by anyone else. But if we live in a highly exogamous society like the U. S. and Britain, where even cousin marriage is slightly frowned on, then our chances of having below-par children by our cousin or our sister will be sensibly higher. This is the theory, and various researchers are now accumulating results which do indeed seem to show it reflected in reality.[6]

But none of this can have been visible to the naked eye, against the background of environmentally caused disease and death which prevailed when we were learning our present customs. The taboo, whether instinct or tradition, must have another origin than this. The best cattle and the best racehorses are produced by continuous incest over tens of generations.

This observation itself suggests an answer. "Best" in a cow or a racehorse is *most reliable*: a stock which will stay

[5] 2nd ed. San Francisco and London, 1960.
[6] E.g., C. D. Darlington; *Cousin Marriages* in *Triangle*, Nov., 1958.

fat or swift, and will not risk its owner's profits by suddenly changing its shape or weight. Stockbreeding consists of selecting until you have a strain adapted to the circumstances you have chosen for it, and then seeing that it never gets unadapted. Incest is a fixative.

No animal which it has been possible to study (and this includes the apes) recognizes its own kin once they are grown up. At a certain point, therefore, the human race must have learned to do this. Once we formed up the concepts of sister, mother, daughter, brother, father and son, we were bound to distinguish, and endogamy and exogamy began. As soon as you spot the difference between two things, you treat them differently. Some tribes or peoples, or whatever it would be correct to call the groups of that stage, would have felt: "Sister—good—mate," and others would have felt: "Sister—bad—not mate." The former groups, selectively preferring what we now call incest, would have developed in time a homogeneous genetic pool; all would have looked and been rather alike, and so when the environment changed,—when the ice came down—the solitary genius who would have been quite useless in an ice-free world, but had dreamed mad dreams of ice, was lacking. In the latter group, with a heterogeneous genetic pool, there would have been a constant turnover of geniuses or fantastics who were usually quite useless but one of whom, when the environment changed, was to hand and proved useful. The former groups did not survive, the latter did. The chance reaction "Sister—bad—not mate" therefore became perpetuated as instinct or tradition.

The fact that incest is excluded from the realm of the normal and permissible for good reasons (if indeed these are the reasons) may have something to do with the way we exclude other things for such bad ones. For instance, Weinberg, whom I have quoted already, is clear that brother-sister incest happens mainly in families where no one has got around to telling the children they shouldn't do it. If one can imagine a family where no one tells the children anything at all about what they should and shouldn't do, and where the school does not either, and where by some freak they are not taken away to remand homes (Weinberg found some such families in Chicago), it is easy to imagine that there would be little against incest. It has to be prohibited, not necessarily explicitly, but through the pores. In all families of brothers and sisters the first young person of the opposite sex who comes over the horizon of adolescence is someone to be loved but not to be fucked. It may be that this one fact determined by evolution accounts for the small degree of doubt and misgiving about fucking which is to be found in all cultures, and that the culturally determined monotheism of Christianity accounts for the remainder of the large degree which is to be found in ours; of which more later.

Chapter 13

Orgies

Let us start with a couple of visual images. This will help us to remember we are speaking about something which may be a normal part of life, which may be cool and voluntary, as opposed to apocalyptic, satanic, vicious, and probably lethal. To find such images, we must naturally turn once again to the Italian Renaissance. Both are pictures of the moment when an orgy begins; the moment of the first overtly erotic gesture, when it becomes clear that the party is changing gear. The first is a fresco by Francesco del Cossa in the Palazzo Schifanoia at Ferrara. It is part of the month of April in a series of the twelve months, painted in 1469. Each month represents a goddess and a virtue; for April, the goddess was Venus, and the virtue probably *piacevolezza* or *dolcezza* (pleasantness, or sweetness). The ideologist behind the scheme was probably the humanist Pellegrino Prisciani.[1]

So much for the iconography. What is happening, is that a party of very young people are out in a garden some-

---

[1] Eberhard Ruhmer, *Francesco del Cossa*, Munich, 1959.

where; apparently they have just stopped playing in a concert of lutes and recorders, and one of them makes what used to be called an audacious gesture. (Why audacious? Will she bite?) Two couples immediately turn to kiss each other; the remainder stand watching and smiling, watching precisely the hand of the young man which is causing their party to change gear. Their expressions say: "Yes, that's a good idea." They had been making music together; then they went for a walk together. The next thing is that they are going to make love together; it is time for that now, time for the next part of life. Christian morality is represented by the very plain girl in the bottom right hand corner who has begun to tell her beads.

The other is a print by the engraver called "The Master of the Die" after one of the Raphael-Giulio Romano ceilings in the Farnesina at Rome. (The engraver has adapted the design a good deal.) The people are in a state of dynamic contact; they are tacitly settling who is to fuck whom first. They are looking at one another to see that no one is offended or left odd man out, they are assessing one another's bodies, or wondering whether they themselves are up to it tonight. Like the Cossa fresco, it is a picture of a moment of social contact according to the usual rules, carrying them over into what is to our time and place an unusual situation.

In Christendom, an orgy in a religious context is a very terrible thought. Such things have been known among the sects we shall be discussing later, the followers of the Free Spirit (see Chapter 22), and in diabolist cults, but the practice was always immediately and ruthlessly extirpated. An orgy even in a non-religious context is still considered a very unusual thing, a very shocking thing.

But if we are to understand Christendom, and thus ourselves, we have to remember that our attitude is not a necessary product of our humanity, only of our Christianity. Many other cultures had regular orgies at certain times of year, at the time of sowing or the time of reaping, or both.

The ancient Greeks did.[2] There is a remarkable account of a fertility rite in a contemporary African tribe in Laurens Van der Post's *Venture to the Interior*.[3] Orgies are common in Japanese and Chinese art, and were common enough in the traditional Japanese pattern of life to have given rise to a game called "Crossing the Valley." The girls lay down on the floor and the boys had to fuck them all in turn, from one end of the room to the other. The winner was the boy who "crossed the valley" without coming. There is a print called "Crossing the Valley"[4] which shows that the game was well enough known to have allowed games-manship ploys to form, even if only in the imagination. It shows a boy fucking the girl in the middle himself, and seeing to all the others at the same time with a series of dildoes fixed to a pole which is strapped across his waist.

Hindu literature and art of the eleventh and twelfth centuries is full of orgies, re-enactments of the legend of Krishna and the cowgirls. The *Kama Sutra* and *Ananga Ranga* have notes on what they call "the congress of many cows," that is, how to satisfy several women at once.

It has often enough been remarked that the Eucharist itself is an emblematic feast of love, and that a feast of love is a feast of love. St. Paul warned his readers against allow-ing the older interpretation to prevail over the new em-blematic one. Christianity did not grow up in a vacuum, it grew up in the Hellenic world, and Hellenic religion, like most others, included an orgy or two each year. The

---

[2] Commenting on a scene in Aristophanes where young virgins are carrying the emblematic phallus in a religious procession, Vil-fredo Pareto has a nice footnote: (*Le Mythe Vertuiste*, Paris, 1911). He describes attempts which were being made in his own day to legislate for the purity of youth and goes on: "Unfortunate young Athenians who had no such saviors! What became of them when they grew up? Nothing worthy of note. In fact it is only with difficulty that a few learned men in our day can remember the name of their Fatherland!"

[3] New York, 1951, London, 1952.

[4] Reproduced in Lawrence E. Gichner, *Erotic Aspects of Japa-nese Life*.

habit could not go nowhere; it was partly, but only partly, sublimated at the communion rail. The rest carried on unsublimated in various sects and pagan survivals in southern Europe, in Carnivals and Mi-Carême and Fasching, and in witches' sabbaths in northern Europe (see the works of Margaret Murray, *passim*). The American petting party is a sort of Catharized or yogi-ized orgy for adolescents, based on the ritual retention of semen.

More interesting perhaps to speculate on what the presence or absence of orgies in a society can tell us about the society itself. The first and most obvious fact is that if a society is doubtful or disapproving about all sexual activity, it will be even more so about orgies, because there's so much of it there. This is what happens in Christendom. But one can distinguish further. Take a husband and wife. If they live in a non-orgy society, their sense of identity is continuously buttressed by their monogamy; they both know who they are and are reminded of it by the fact that they are married to each other. The identity which is thus buttressed by the singleness of human love is the more likely to feel single in its relation to God. Such a person will feel: God loves me, because I am me. He also loves everyone else, of course, but he loves them singly and individually because they are themselves. My relation with God is a one-to-one thing. Equally, I love God as I, and as no one else. Of course everyone else loves him too, but as themselves individually. It is therefore more important to me to say "I love God" than to say "God is loved." And the structure of feeling continues long after the religious motivation has dissolved.

But if our husband and wife live in an orgy society, things will work rather differently. Once or twice a year they will go out and eat and dance and get drunk and fuck absolutely anybody, without even knowing who they are. The whole point of an orgy is not to know who one's partner is. (Otherwise one starts thinking "Do I love this person? If I do, would I not rather be alone with them? If I don't, what the hell am I doing here?") At an orgy, their own identity as individuals gets no buttressing from the identity of the unknown other. It therefore begins to weaken, to blur, to dissolve, to fuse. If, at a moment of total openness, the other has no identity, one has none oneself. Identity needs reflecting and confirming; when one is fucking an unknown person, there is no reflection, no confirmation, and the identity of each one runs out to meet the identity of each other in a common pool. In northern Europe the bonfire was not simply for warmth; it was there to burn down the barriers of selfhood. The water and fire symbolism of initiation rites is as much dissolving and melting as tempering and smelting.

And the people do this for the god, which is as much as to say that the god does it for the people. What then, under this aspect, are the god and the people? They are not one and many ones, as god and people are in Christendom; they are the one and the many as they were in Plato and the Renaissance; they are even one and one. The lower case, the human end of the reaction which is god and man, becomes unitary not diverse, compound not mixed, glass not sand.

But orgies mean babies. What happens to the resultant babies we think, from our non-orgy culture; where do they go?[5] Don't their "parents" mind? The answer, of course, is: no. They don't mind. In such cultures, and that does not only mean Pondoland and New Guinea, but sections of most warmish countries, they are brought up by their mothers, or whatever female relation is to hand. Cultures, it sometimes seems, can be divided into two classes: those which, when they see a baby, say, "Let's bring it up," and those which say, "Whose baby is that?"

The very same elements in the make-up of individuals

---

[5] The French writer, Guibert of Nogent (1053-1124), had an interesting solution to the problem. According to him, the followers of a certain Manichee, a French peasant called Clementius, used to burn the babies as soon as they were born, and bake communion-bread out of their bodies. As we shall see below, the charge of having orgies was a stock one against Manichees.

which cause orgies, or, a fortiori, adultery, to be part of
the scene, cause the family, the extended family including
grandmothers and aunts and all those other possible sources
of care and affection for children, to be a more real and
vigorous unit than the monogamous union of husband and
wife. Again, it is a continuum or scale. The more monogamy in feeling and practice, the more pride in paternity
and the restricted family unit. The more orgies or adultery
in feeling and practice, the more inclusive extended-family
feeling when it comes to rearing children. Divorce is found
mainly in countries tending toward the monogamous, nu-
clear-family end of the scale. It cancels adultery, and restores monogamy.

The continuum is basic to man in society. Some societies
feel that individuals are like iron filings, which can be
grouped and regrouped by this or that magnetic field, according to the time of year. The individual is less important than the field; he is merely something through which
the spirit flows. Such societies will tend to sing, eat, drink,
dance and fuck together at appropriate times in honor of
God or gods, and to be careless of human life—who cares
what happens to an iron filing?

Others feel on the contrary that the individual is sufficient unto himself and his God, and will hold that he
may change the fields which bind man to man and man to
woman, in accordance with what he is able to work out
as an individual. The iron filing in these societies is more
important than the magnetic field, and conscious of it, even
critical. This critical consciousness is the mechanism of
social change. Such societies will tend to do no more than
pray and sing together in honor of God, to be careful of
human life, and to aim at an uninterrupted monogamy
in their customs.

Orgies are excluded *de jure* in all of Christendom because of the basic objection of anthropomorphic monotheism to fucking in any circumstances but the one licensed
exception of permanent monogamy. They are excluded
de facto as well in the "northern" or Protestant bits of

Christendom, because of the greater sense there of the value and importance of the individual. The technology which arises out of Protestant individualism reinforces the mechanism; it gives rise on the one hand to big industrial cities where there are no longer natural units for any form of collective observance and a fortiori for the periodical observance of a night of licensed dematrimonialization, and gives rise on the other through advanced medicine to a longer average life span, and consequently a heavier weighting of accepted morality in favor of what the old want to do; and the old don't want orgies.

PART V

EXCLUDED PEOPLE

Chapter 14

Prostitution

> *All women are sitting on a fortune,*
> *if only they realized it.*
>
> —*Prostitute's saying*

There are in our society now two great classes of people excluded from the web of the normal because of their sex lives: whores and homosexuals. Of these the whore will better repay study in the context of this book because she is wholly excluded, all round the clock, whereas the homosexual is only excluded *as* a homosexual; he is accepted in working hours, the whore is not.

There are societies without prostitution; one of them is described in Verrier Elwin's book, *The Muria and their Ghotul.*[1] But they are very rare. It flourishes almost everywhere, and certainly in all Christian and post-Christian societies. In the Hellenic world it was part of the slavery-pederasty-prostitution triangle, the unruffled toleration of which so sharply distinguishes that world from ours, and so sharply contrasts, in our view, with the philosophic and artistic excellence we find in it. In other cultures, prosti-

---

[1] Oxford University Press, 1947.

tution has been religious in motivation, or at least ritual. In some cultures there have been prostitutes by profession, who are set apart for that work. In others, the occasional act of prostitution has been something permitted to any woman; the function is not localized in this or that person but spread throughout society. Only five hundred years ago, Anglo-Saxon society was one of the latter sort. When Pope Pius II was in Berwick on Tweed as a young man, he was surprised to find that all the Englishmen locked themselves up in a tower at night, for fear of Scottish robbers, but left the women outside, thinking no wrong would befall them, and "counting outrage no wrong." Two young women showed Aeneas Silvius, as the future Pope was then called, "to a chamber strewn with straw, planning to sleep with him, as was the custom of the country, if they were asked." But he ignored them, "thinking less about women than about robbers," and took the fact that no robber came in the night as a reward for his continence.[2]

The custom whereby a man lends his wife or daughter to a guest is a form of prostitution; in return for her kindness the family or the clan expect to receive his good will, or even sometimes the good will of the gods, expressed in fertility of crop and of people. But the wife or daughter does not thereby become a prostitute.

In our society now, prostitution is specialized, mercenary, and reprobated. We confine the function to individual women who become a class apart, and whose characters become formed by their condition and experience. We pay them for exercising their function. We also despise them and penalize them. They are extruded from the body of society, as we like to conceive it, and live a life of their own according to their own values and customs. We know little of what these values and customs are, because we fear the prostitute. We fear her because we fear our own need for her, which conflicts with our formu-

---

[2] *The Commentaries of Pius II*, "Memoirs of a Renaissance Pope," London, 1960 (New York, 1961), p. 35.

lated ideal of the relation between the sexes. We also project onto her our own guilty desires; because our accepted values declare us low and beastly when we go to her, we feel that she is herself low and beastly. Because we desire her when we go to her, we also feel that she desires us. We punish and blame her with one hand, and pay her handsomely with the other; we see her with one eye as a baited trap, and with the other as a golden haven of rest and warmth. Meanwhile, as Aretino said, she laughs with one eye and weeps with the other.

A whore is a woman who fucks for money. If you pay her enough, she pretends to come.

Let us take, as texts for this chapter, first the words of a seventeenth-century pornographer (using the word in the strict sense :: a writer about whores), and second those of a London whore today.

Writing in Venice in the 1630's, Ferrante Pallavicino advised the whore to handle her clients as follows:

Let her go along with the humor of these people, and speak as they wish, even though she hold them in scorn. Let her expressions be in general common ones, as my dear, my own heart, my soul, I am dying, let us die together, and such like, which will show a feigned sentiment, if not a true one. Let her add panting, and sighing, and the interrupting of her own words, and other such gallantries, which will give her out to be melting, to be swooning, to be totally consumed, whereas in fact she is not even moved, but more as if she were made of wood or of marble than of flesh. It is certain that the whore cannot take pleasure in all comers. . . . She must nevertheless give pleasure through her words, if not her deeds, and let her put into operation what she can, authenticating her words by closing her eyes, by abandoning herself as if lifeless, and by then rising up again in full strength with a vehement sigh as if she were panting in the oppression of extreme joy, though in fact she be reduced and languid. These lies can be singularly useful, although they are discredited by too common feigning, and often obtain little credence.[3]

---

[3] *La Retorica delle Puttane*, Cambrai, 1642, pp. 115–116.

And here is a London prostitute of today:

There's some of them lies still as stones, they think it's more ladylike or something, but I say they don't know which side their bread's buttered. Listen, if you lie still the bloke may take half the night sweating away. But if you bash it about a bit he'll come all the quicker and get out and away and leave you in peace. Stupid to spin it out longer than you need, isn't it? I learned that from Margaret. Wonderful actress, that girl. I learned from her in exhibitions when I first was on the game. She wasn't the first girl I did an exhibition with, that was a coloured girl who used to pitch near me. I was dead scared of any of that at first, and then one night this coloured pallone comes up to me and says: "Bloke here wants an exhibition; will you help me out? Three pounds each." I was scared, but she said do it just to help her, so I said, "Do we have to go turn and turn about?" but she said she'd lead all the time. Was I grateful! Anyhow, like I say, this Margaret and I used to do exhibitions after that; wonderful actress. Of course you know they're all faked, exhibitions are. We keep our hands down there all the time, which is why I used to shit myself laughing when I saw her pretending to pull hairs out from between her teeth afterwards. It was her I learned to grunt and groan from.

And another thing; when I'm with a client I always put the rubber on him very gently, you know, stroking him and spinning it out as long as I can. "You ought to have been a nurse," they say. That's always what it makes them think of. And then with a bit of luck they come before they even get into me. When they do I look ever so loving and gentle and say: "Traitor!" Well, I'm not paid just to be a bag, am I? I'm paid to make them feel good. It's easy for me, so why not? That's how I see it.

Mark that she learned to "grunt and groan" not from herself, not from a man, but from another whore. And that one word "Traitor!" sums up the whole structure of pretense which is whoring.

The pictures on the wall? I cut them out of a German phornographic book. I don't use photos much. There's some likes them and occasionally it helps to get a bashful client started. I don't know much about who makes them. I did a

day's photographic work yesterday, but that wasn't phornographic. I've been asked to, though. Bloke rang up once and
offered me fifty pounds for an afternoon's work. Said he'd find
the male model. Said he'd take my head out too and put someone else's in, but I didn't believe him. And anyhow, I don't
do that.

Here is a poem by a London prostitute.

The Game

Last night
A rather trite
Thought occurred to me. Exactly what pleasure
Is there in being a "Lady of Leisure?"
One has to submit (and grit one's teeth) to a great many men
    who, when the "fun" is at an end
Pretend
They've "never done this before."
And it's really such a bore
To listen enthralled
As they tell you about having called
At the furriers to buy coats for their spouses
(Made from mouses)
And, while wrapped in gorilla-like embraces,
You lie making faces
At your big toe over a beefy shoulder,
And he becomes colder
Because you do not respond as he breathes garlic,
Or worse, alcoholic
Fumes over your pretty neck
And you fervently wish that he'd break his . . .
There are of course so many different types:
Like the one who wipes
His hands all over your bedspread, and though you are very
    sweet to him
And entreat him
Not to do it again, he does—when you turn your back.
And you're just dying to whack
The man who is so "thoughtful" and feels he really ought to
    give you "pleasure" too because you're really far too "good"
For this life. (As if he could!)

And have you ever met the one who is just longing for sex,
But only ever pays with perfectly good cheques?
So when you're fool enough to agree—
(If you wish, he'll meet you at the bank next day, long before
    three)
You find he's hopped it—
And stopped it!
And how about the pound-of-flesher who insists
On being kissed
All over the place, and wants you to remove every bit of your
    clothes, including those nylons you spent your last pound
    on this afternoon,
Which will so soon
Be in shreds.
I'm forgetting the "slave":
On bended knee he'll crave
To be allowed to clean your lavatory,
And when you've stripped him
And whipped him
Mercilessly,
Asks: "Do you get many like me?"

What is the pattern of the whore's own desires and
pleasures? Here are several glimpses from different London
girls:

I think I have come; I'm not sure. Twice in my life I've
thought to myself, now maybe this is what they talk about.
That was before I was on the game. I couldn't bear the sight
of the man afterwards. He couldn't get out quick enough
for me.

I get my kicks from dancing, Latin American dancing
mostly. I don't know, there's something about the movements.
My first man was after a dance; I didn't know where I was.
And the father of my child was after a dance too. It's always
dancing with me.

I'm rather abnormally built. You see, my clitoris is very
high—I'm not embarrassing you by talking like this?—it's a
long way round, and so it gets a bit left out in a straight fuck.
My womb's high up too; I guess everything's a bit far apart
with me. I can only come if the man goes down. Well, there's

only one man in ten that I even want to go down, and only one in ten of those that thinks of it. I can't ask them, can I? They're not there for my pleasure, I'm there for theirs. That's how the game is. I tell you, it's not all ninepins.

I don't know why I like girls. It feels safer, somehow. And I'm not talking about pregnancy. I think everybody agrees now—take Kinsey—that the clitoris is where women get their pleasure.

The Man in the Boat's my mascot. As a matter of fact it's every woman's mascot, though there's not many men'll recognize it.

You know, the young men's pricks seem to be getting bigger and bigger. It must be the Welfare State. I hate it, though; it splits me.

Sandra would be no good on the game. She likes men and she enjoys fucking.

Perhaps what is most striking about these casual remarks is the feeling they all give of "I'm different; I'm not so well off as some; I can't; I don't; I can't." They suggest a temperament which is already in some way reduced, depleted, disabled, lacking, and that this temperament is a condition of being able to be a whore at all.

It is very difficult to discover how whores become whores. It is difficult to do from a sociological or criminological standpoint, or by observing certain cafés or night clubs, because it is not a thing you *see* anyone doing. They don't enroll through an employment agency, and you don't see thousands of them trooping to work when the whistle blows. It's also difficult to do by asking prostitutes at firsthand. If a whore feels guilty about her trade, feels that the majority society is right to condemn her for it, as many do, then she will naturally have surrounded the memory of how she commenced with a cloud of inhibitions, and may even have suppressed it altogether. On the other hand if she stands up for herself she is likely to have put in some hard thought on what prostitution really is, and to take off into Shavian arguments to the effect that there is no dividing line anyhow, no hard and fast occasion, no key moment. She may throw the question back; Is fucking for pity prostitution? For a job? For an apartment? And then of course—for three pounds. Whether she feels guilty or whether she feels defensive or even defiant, she has every interest in slurring over the moment of change. Her present way of life demands it; she could hardly continue to function if she was to admit to herself that at one moment she was one sort of creature, morally speaking, and at the next another.

One of the best of a very small number of good books on prostitution is *Women of the Streets,* by Rosalind Wilkinson.[4] In her account of how girls get on to the game, she lays stress on a preliminary period of vague, floating promiscuity, of what she calls elsewhere "increasing irrelation to society." This is something different from maladjustment, which she sees as a deformed relationship, a warped and impracticable relationship, but one which may be as strong as any other. "Irrelation" is an absence of all relationship. The girl comes to London—most London whores come from provincial industrial cities—and bums around, living with this man or that, and perhaps frequenting one of the drinking clubs the easy establishment of which has recently caused new regulations to be brought in. Or perhaps she finds work as a "hostess" in a night club. There are one or two night clubs which seem to be simply highroads into the game. This intermediate phase is the one when the girl is called a *mystery*: is she going to take to the game or not? Generally speaking, nobody pushes her. This is an important point; the popular conception of well-organized recruiting agencies is a mistaken one. The motive for entertaining the illusion is fairly clear; the more a respectable man idealizes women, and the higher the value he sets on the merits of conventional society, the less will he be willing to believe any girl capable of abandoning it except

---

[4] London, 1955.

under pressure or devious corruption. To such a man, all whores will be "poor unfortunate girls," and his imagination will people Soho and Paddington, the main prostitute districts of London, with dope-pushers, razor-slashers, and so forth.

One way on to the game is often open before the girl comes to London. A girl who has been an "easy lay" at school—not usually so much because she likes fucking as because she wants to find out if it isn't possible to like it more—takes work as a waitress or chambermaid at a provincial hotel. She sleeps with the odd traveling salesman, and one day one of them gives her a pair of nylons. The next one gives her a pound to buy her own, and the penny drops. She has been paid for it. Next stop London and the big money.

Here is the commencement of a prostitute, as seen by the man in the story:

I met this girl at a party one night; she'd been sleeping around for some time with all sorts of people. I gave her a lift home after the party and as she was getting out of the car I asked her to have dinner with me a day or two later. She kind of paused, and then she said:—Look that dinner's going to cost you about three pounds. Why don't you just give me the three pounds and come along in and do me now? —So I did.

One does not often hear of the penny dropping so clearly.

But perhaps the commonest way on to the game is by the urging of a friend or elder sister. "Wake up, girl; how much longer are you going to *exist* on eight pounds a week? Why don't you come on out and *live?* You leave things to me, and I'll see you're getting a hundred a week before you know where you are."

Here is a fairly usual "life story." Until the recent law, which cleared most of the prostitutes off the London streets, Dorothy was a streetwalker; she charged three pounds. A pound more for stripping, but she'll do it all the same if the client can't raise the extra. Hates kissing. Undertakes most kinks if she's feeling like it, but no buggery. Buggery is grounds for money back and throw them out. She was illegitimate, and brought up without a father. When she came home after school she would find her mum smooching away in the corner with some man. When she was twelve and thirteen the neighborhood kids used to say to her: "Had your R.C. yet?" She did not know what it meant, but shook her head, and they said: "All right, you can stay with us." R.C. meant "red change," or first period. She had her R.C. one day during an exam at school. She fainted, and was carried by the invigilator to the Headmistress, who said "Are you ill?" "I don't think so." "Well, I mean, er, have you eaten anything?" Yes, she had steadied her nerves by guzzling Rowntrees Clear Gums, and to this day feels sick at the sight of them. So much for sex education.

At sixteen she had her first man, and at nineteen bore a child to an American soldier. While she was carrying the child she took up with a medical student and learned for the first time that she had a thing called a womb. He also taught her hygiene.

And I may say most of the girls don't know a thing about it. They just put some soap on their fingers and tickle themselves. But he taught me to use a douche, and not more than once a week, otherwise it hurts your insides.

She believes masturbation gives you a bellyache. When her mother asked her who the child's father was, she said she really didn't know. She had passed out at a party and didn't know what had happened to her. Her mother legally adopted the child, a girl, and Dorothy never sees either of them. She blames her mother for her own upbringing, and fears her own child may be brought up the same way, but it's nothing to do with her, it's miles away now.

After the birth of the child she went to London and took work as a barmaid. She went concurrently with a well-off married man every third Sunday, and with the manager of the hotel in the afternoons. One night in a clipjoint she got drunk and started telling the manager of the joint what was wrong with the place; the pattern of the wallpaper was too small, the place was dirty, the girls were badly dressed. This manager took her on the spot as his girl friend and co-manager, and she lived with him for four years. Then it broke up, and she was underfed and began hitting the bottle. (This is the "period of increasing irrelation.") She had a taste for "pretty things and bright lights," as well as for liquor; one night she got drunk at a party and the next morning found she'd been laid and paid for it. (The same story she'd told her mother about the baby.) So there she was, a whore. She began walking the street, though she didn't stand yet.

Before the law virtually put an end to the street trade in London, standing was the end of irrelation; the mystery was accepted. Some older whore invites the walker to share her pitch and makes friends with her. There might be a Lesbian arrangement, and there would probably be something of a team about it. "With your looks and youth you could earn well, that is if you consent to profit by my experience." Perhaps they would do exhibitions together. The older woman might get a rake-off in return for her patronage. The arrangement would be a fleeting one, like everything in the underworld.

Here is another life story, one from the other end of the social scale; prostitution, like everything else in England, is shot through with class values. Mary was a successful call girl, and occasionally reached the maximum possible earnings, up to fifty pounds for an all night fix. When she was twelve, she was "the only girl without a title" at a snobbish Roman Catholic boarding school run by nuns. Her parents were kindly, but cold. The father was blind, and the mother, having had a total hysterectomy, cut out love not only from her bed but from her whole life. Then, within a year, three things happened. She found papers on her mother's desk which taught her she was the illegitimate daughter of the illegitimate daughter of a housemaid; her true mother had put her in an orphanage when she was three years old, and she had been adopted by the people she thought were her parents on medical advice to compensate for the death of their own, physically irreplaceable, son. She had her first period at school, didn't know what was happening, feared disease, and was told to take an aspirin and think about the Virgin Mary. And thirdly, perhaps not surprisingly, she created a scandal at school by refusing to believe in the Virgin Birth. Her adoptive parents were sent for and she was told to have faith.

At seventeen she wanted to go to a university, but was taken to Cyprus instead by a relative of her adoptive parents. She was not allowed to learn Greek, or to take a job there. She quarreled with the relative, returned to London and took work as a hotel receptionist. Her adoptive parents died, and she set to work to trace her true family. She found her grandmother first, herself the illegitimate daughter of an illegitimate woman; there hadn't been a marriage in the family for generations. The grandmother was not interested. Later she found her mother. This last door slammed in her face with a particularly horrible twist when she learned that her mother had put her away when she was three because she was pregnant again. She had preferred the unborn child to the child of three, and had in fact brought the second child up.

Mary killed herself at the age of thirty.

A staple of conversation among whores is the "kinkies." Until recently you could see the ads in Soho shop windows: Miss Du Sade; Miss Du Cane; Miss De Belting (Flagellation). Strict governess: Corrective Training; Corr. and Disc. (the sado-masochistic procedures in general). Miss Kiki This and Kiki That (anything). Lady's black mackintosh for sale. Boots, high-heeled shoes, plastic raincoats for sale (all with the girls inside them). Fifi of Froufrou gives French lessons; recently back from France, French and English conversation (which means *gamming*, from the French *gamahucher*, or *blowing*, or *plating*, or *noshing,* from the Yiddish *nosh,* to nibble, or eat between meals. I discuss the significance of the word *French* in this context in Chapter 27 below.).

The code for kinks is well known to those who need to know it; not many people apply to these girls for French lessons. The code for prostitution itself is more fluid, and it depends what medium is used for the ad. No London newspaper would take an ad for a photographic model, followed by her measurements, but many will take ads for fur coats, and that naturally means that the whore has to contend with a lot of people who really want fur coats. From time to time some paper or other will carry the biggest chestnut of them all: "Demolition agent for temporary erections," until a startled building contractor calls back.

The whole topic of unusual requirements, of perversions, or kinks, is a repulsive one to many people. When the "normal citizen" reads or hears kink stories he may be tempted to consider them as myths, as products of an inflamed imagination which keep on going the rounds out of some sort of unhealthy fascination, but which don't actually happen. Or he may think that all that is old hat; it is all in Krafft-Ebing, and that is where it should stay. But it is a determining condition of the whore's life that she is engaged day by day in enacting the myth, in living through the silly dream, in assuaging the unusual desire. These are not amazing, disgusting or funny stories to her; they are part of her day-to-day work, as real and as normal as dressing wounds is to a nurse; something for which she is paid, and in which she takes a wry pride.

Blowing generally counts as a kink, or a sort of semi-kink, and costs a bit extra. Some girls confine themselves to blowing when they have the curse. Others let the curse make no difference; they plug themselves up and bash right ahead, draining between clients.

Well, as for kinkies, it depends on what I'm feeling like. If I'm feeling cheeky, all right, and good luck to them. But you can't do it every day. When I was working ————'s [a restaurant] the manager said to me one night: "See that fellow over there? He's a member of parliament. Go and see what you can do for him." So I went over and he said: "Listen, have you got manacles and anklets?" I said: "No darling, but I can get them." So I arranged to meet him there a week that day. What he wanted me to do was manacle him and all and then drop candlegrease on his prick. Course I never did it. There he was next week, but I wasn't feeling the same, and I didn't even go over to him.

Beatings are usually a pound a stroke, either way.

Client came to me one night and offered me three quid for three. Fine, said I. So he got into the drag—had it with him in a suitcase, and for me too: black nylons and high wedge shoes and all. He said he was a servant girl called Millie and I was his mistress. They often want that. I had to say: "Where were you last night, Millie?" And he said he'd been out with a boy. And I had to say: "Now it was clearly understood between us when you came to work for me, Millie, that there was to be none of that." He was licking my shoes all the time. "And I think you deserve a beating, don't you, Millie?" "Oh yes, Madam, I do, I do." So then I gave him the three he'd paid for. But I don't know what it was; I was just feeling like it, I suppose, but I suddenly lost my temper, oh, not only with him, with everything and everybody. So I gave him four more and took another four quid off him and chucked him out. I really lit into him; he loved it. And yet people ask me why I like cats.

And then another time there was a client took me back to his place. I had to tie him up, you know all the girls have to know how to tie a bloke up to a chair properly. I did him really well, couldn't move an inch. And then I had to strap his prick up against his belly with elastoplast. I was feeling the same way that night, I suppose, because there was some elastoplast over so I put one piece across his mouth and another across his eyes. "There's for you, you bastard," I thought. "You asked to be strapped up, and you get strapped up." He'd told me earlier he had a cleaner come in every second morning. I hope she did, that's all I can say. That was two months ago.

Quite a common one is the client who gets the whore to dress up as a nurse, powder his bottom, put diapers on him and tuck him up with a bottle.

After all, every man has had his first orgasm somewhere or other, hasn't he? But most of them don't get like that. I often wonder about it. And what about women, anyhow?

I was taken back to his place by this bloke. And as soon as I got inside the door he gave me thirty pounds. Ah-ah, I thought; what's coming? But in those days thirty pounds was quite a lot—as a matter of fact it still is. He made me undress and sat me right across the room from him. I had to open my legs, and he took a lot of cream buns from a paper bag and threw them at me. Not a bad shot, he was, either, once he'd got his aim. Then he put marmalade on my breasts and stuffed iced cherries up my cunt and licked the whole lot off. It *was* embarrassing; I didn't know whether I was allowed to wash afterwards.

A variant of this from another girl.

A client used to come to me quite regularly. I had to undress and stand with my arms above my head. He took six kippers—he had them in pairs wrapped in cellophane, you know the things—and threw them at me one by one. If one of them missed he came trotting across the room and picked it up and tried again. Afterwards there was a pine scented foambath waiting for me. He went back to South Africa in the end. I was quite sorry. I used to get fourteen pounds a time.

And again:

A client took me back to his place, and as soon as I got in the door there was a dirty great coffin standing open. He put me in a white nightie with a rosary in one hand and a Bible in the other and a wreath of roses on my head. Then I had to lie down in the coffin. I thought: "Is this a gag to get my money?" But I had my bag in the coffin with me. Then he started nailing the lid down and all the time he was shouting out: "You're dead now, God damn you to hell." He'd told me his wife had died. He'd given me a big spanner to knock the lid up with, but I tell you I was wondering whether I'd ever get out again. I did though, and when I looked round he'd gone.

The Street Offences Act of 1959 cleared the girls off the London streets overnight, as it had been meant to. They went indoors into pubs and clubs, and on to the telephone. Some put up fluorescent red bell-pushes; some hustled by standing at open doors and windows. So much as a nose or a finger in the air space of the street was illegal. Some advertised in the press, and many in shop windows. One put up a neon sign saying: "French Lessons."

Before the Act, the penalty for soliciting in the streets had been two pounds. There was a working agreement with the police that it should not be exacted more than fortnightly, and often a girl could go six months or a year without being booked. There was sometimes a rota system, and the greatest grievance against the police was: "It's not my turn." The routine appearance in the Magistrate's Court and the routine branding as a "common prostitute" played some part in forming the underworld-like pseudo-criminal personality of the prostitute, but the fine itself was fiscal in effect, not punitive or deterrent.

The new Act raised the fine to thirty pounds, with prison on third conviction. Nevertheless, within a year the girls began to come back on the streets. They were forced to by the prosecution of the clubs they used, and of a magazine called *The Lady's Directory*, in which they published their telephone numbers. (The title took up that of a similar publication in the eighteenth century.) The £30 fine works both ways. The girls defend themselves in court, which they had not done against the £2 fine, and this means the policemen who book them have to spend a whole day there instead of half an hour. They, and their superiors, can think of better things for an undermanned police force to do, and so the girls are back on many of the streets. They simply come out later, and close the bargain with less haggling, so as to be less conspicuous.

Among the call girls, one is in a different world. Take

the word *whore*. The street and club girls use it quite naturally. It is the simple, obvious word for what they are. The phrase, almost a signature tune, "whoring it along the Dilly" [Piccadilly] has a fine generous ring to it. An occasional highbrow whore who quotes Proust and keeps up with the sexual oddities of the eminent will use the word about herself with a conscious, open-eyed feeling, in the same way that Bernard Shaw used to call himself "an old entertainer." But the call girl uses it to imply all that she is not. She uses it as synonymous with *slack*, which is the call girl's word for a street girl.

I don't look like one, do I? You wouldn't ever know, would you? Not ever? Would you? Would you?

The call girl is tremendously nice. The flat where she lives, and also her gaff where she works, if she has a separate place, are spotless; dusted, shiny, warm, welcoming. The taste will be contemporary, aware of fashion.

The first thing you must realise is that I'm not a whore. I have my friends, but I don't take just anybody. Like for instance if a man rings up and says he's been given my number by so and so, I don't just leave it at that. I put him through it. When did you last see so and so? How was he? Where did you meet? Has he shaved his beard off? He said he was going to. Oh, there are all sorts of ways to find out if they're on the square. All right, then he comes round. Maybe I don't like the look of him. "Ooooh, I'm so sorry. It's really too bad. She's just gone out. Would you believe it; isn't that just too bad." And even afterwards, if I haven't liked him I tell him I'm going off the game, or I'm going away on holiday; he'd better not come again.

You know, half my work's what we call social work. That is, say some friend of mine has someone come to London to visit his firm, and he gives him my number. I have connections with a lot of good firms. All right, he takes me out; dinner, a show, perhaps a party. I go down on his expense account, or something. It may lead to sex, it may not. Often it doesn't. I don't mind. In fact, I'm pleased.

Again:

It's a hell of a life. You know, I imagine the slack is afraid of disease, and afraid of the sex maniac who thinks it'd be fun to strangle her. Well, that's not what we're afraid of. The trouble in this game is when you're afraid you're slipping. Some days you sit and sit by the telephone smoking and smoking, and nobody rings, and you think: "Look out, kid, you're slipping. What have I done? WHAT HAVE I DONE? Are they telling each other I'm no good?"

The London prostitute comes in all colors and sizes of temperament, but there is enough in common to make it worth saying something about the not so obvious ways in which she differs from other women. She has no sense of time, because her life is without routine. Time is divided into day and night and that's all. She has a sense of obligation, but it is shakier than other people's. It works in an immediate way, because she is used to payment on the spot. If she says she will meet you somewhere in half an hour, she will. Tomorrow, or next Tuesday, is another matter. If you take her to a public place, say a restaurant, she is a little awkward or embarrassed, or by contrast flamboyant, coming in and going out; everybody is looking at her, but can they tell? Once settled, she relaxes at once. She is an excellent listener; listening, next to fucking, is the thing she does most of. Her own favorite topics are the wealth and eminence of her clients, the sexual hypocrisy of our culture, kink stories, money, clothes, interior decoration, bars, coffee bars, night clubs. She prefers the pageant of life to vicarious involvement through the arts, but she is blind to politics and the organization of society in general. She notices and comments on the women round her more than the men, partly because she is comparing herself to this mysterious competitor the wife, but often also out of straight Lesbian interest. She is probably a fairly heavy drinker. When she is watching her words and thinking what she should say next, she will tell you that she went on the game with a conscious decision, for the loot. She realized she was sitting on a fortune, and made up her mind. She continues on the game because it's interesting, and she's used to it.

When she is relaxed and talking without care or discretion, the picture changes. She is afraid, like all outlaws. She is afraid of disease. Few whores go to a doctor or a V.D. clinic for a regular check-up. On the other hand many seem to believe they are gifted with second sight about their clients' health.

Well, I have a good look at him, and if he looks a bit poxy or anything, out he goes.

This particular bit of professional vanity often coexists with a perfectly sound knowledge of the fact that infectiousness is not related to visible signs. She is also afraid of infecting a client's wife, or even his unborn child, a running, uncheckable fear which she may allow to prey on her and to carry other guilts on its back. She is afraid of the sex maniac who may want to kill her; that is why she may keep a dog or, if she can afford it, a maid. If she has no ponce,[5] she may take care to live in a house where the neighbors will accept her and her occupation, then she can shout for them in an emergency. She is afraid of being nicked; however often it has happened (and Mrs. Wilkinson cites a Belgian woman who was arrested 219 times), the appearance at Marlborough Street or Bow Street is always a humiliation. Now, under the new Act, she is afraid of prison.

Above all, she is afraid of old age. The older whores will say quite simply: "There is no way out." The younger ones will keep their chins up and pretend to themselves they're not like the rest. Nobody ever went on the game for keeps.

Of course I'm only in it for five years.
For a few years.
Until I'm bored with it.
For five years.

---

[5] See note, p. 146.

For five years. I've got it all worked out.
Then I'll—
Buy a shop.
Go into partnership with a friend who has a garage.
Buy house property and let rooms.
Buy a coffee bar.
Buy a restaurant.
Club together with one or two other girls and buy a hotel.
Get some old sucker to marry me.
Put my savings into. Put my savings into.
Put my savings into.

Not one in a hundred can save. The ability to save goes with a retentive personality, with foresight, caution, affective momentum, narrow affections. The whore is all on the surface, mercurial, shortsighted, chaotic, frigid.

What often happens is that they go on and on, into their fifties and even sixties. They pass downward into a class called the four-to-sixers, who go on the streets and into the joints before dawn, when the clients are so drunk they don't care what they're getting. Some become maids to younger women, which is probably the happiest conclusion. Then there is a saying, "End up drinking red biddy in the Docks."

The elderly whore, the old-timer, often has delusions of social grandeur. She has missed the few possible escape lines, and gets attached in a half-light of unreality to the idea of what she might have been. She cannot deny that she is a whore, so she may sideslip into denying that she is something else that she is. If she is Jewish, she may take pleasure in proving that she is not, and in looking down on the Jewish client. If she is poor she may try to prove that she is rich; if Irish, English; and, over and over again, if she is dark she will pretend to be fair. Conversely, she may try to prove that the innocent little woman in the flat above *is* a whore.

One of these old-timers asked me to tea the other day. I went along, and there were just the two of us. She poured out the tea with her little finger crooked and told me how she'd been asked to Buckingham Palace. Afterwards she entertained me by playing Gounod's *Ave Maria* on the piano.

Some whores do get married, or set up what is meant to be a permanent liaison with a man. He may be a former client or not. If he does not even know his wife has been a whore, the situation is emotionally hopeless. If he does know, it may last, conceivably. But if a woman is capable of sustaining a regular relationship, why didn't she do it at first instead of going on the game? They usually come back, the ones who marry; not because of the attractions of whoring, but because the marriages don't work. When they do come back, they are naturally welcomed with open arms; their return justifies the others.

Consider what it is like for a whore to try to construct a marriage, even in favorable circumstances. Wherever they go together—street, pub, parties, job-hunting, home-hunting—the slightest flicker of interest, of attention, from some man brings back that which has to be forgotten. The man might simply be thinking: "Now where have I seen that girl before?" It might even have been waiting in a movie line. But she knows her husband does not know where it was. If anything goes wrong—some people who are coming to dinner cry off at the last moment, a job falls through—have they found out? There is no defense against the suspicion. Laughter at one's own groundless suspicions is the most mirthless there is.

All right, one may say: London is a great big easygoing metropolis, who cares? Why don't they publish and be damned? Surely so many people would be on their side. . . . But picture turning up at someone's house who *knows*.

I shall probably be the first tart they've ever had in their house. They'll be so damned nice, they'll be curious, with that terrible curiosity of conscious liberalism. They only want to know. They'll observe my dress, my turns of speech, my gait.

That is what the whore who gets married has to face with other people. What she has to face in bed with her husband is easily imagined. It can be done, and it is done, but it's no wonder it is not often done.

The way off the game is feet first.

In 1959 a committee of inquiry chaired by Sir John Wolfenden reported on prostitution in Britain and recommended changes in the law. During the parliamentary debates on the Wolfenden Report, which did in fact lead to the new and more restrictive law, Mr. R. A. Butler, then Home Secretary, promised stiffer penalties against living on immoral earnings as a "consolation." It was not clear what for. Mr. Edwards, the Member for Stepney, a prostitute area, referred to ponces[6] as the "dirtiest, filthiest lot in creation." Another member spoke of "monarchs of the industry." Until 1948, ponces could be flogged. Whenever there is a discussion on prostitution in the press many people write saying this or that about the prostitutes, but end up: ". . . and reserve the really heavy penalties for the ruffians who batten on these unfortunate girls."

The very word *ponce* suggests *pounce;* fifty years ago ponces were called *bullies,* which sounds even fiercer. Try consulting your own feelings about the ponce. There he is, this unspeakably debased male, lurking in doorways and pouncing on his unsuspecting prey, tearing her hard-earned three pounds out of her pathetic clutch, and roaring away in his gangster-type limousine to the next girl, whom he threatens with a razor. He spends the night going round twenty or thirty of his hundred and fifty girls, or perhaps his section of the big syndicate administered by his superboss, slashing his girls, doling out shots to the junkies, coshing a client or two, and squaring four or five detective inspectors. Toward dawn he goes, surrounded by hench-

---

[6] In England a distinction is made between the *ponce* who runs the girl's life in general, and the much rarer *pimp* who actively solicits men to go to her. In America the word *pimp* covers both classes. Perhaps the American *sweet daddy* is the closest to British ponce, but it is more colloquial.

men, to the girl he has chosen for himself that night and, little recking that her flaccid flesh is still reeking from the forty or fifty slavering lechers who have been before him, enjoys her.

It is quite rare for a London prostitute to have a ponce at all. If she does, it is because she feels she needs someone to kick her out on the street at nightfall, to make sure she has the rent ready on rent day, to keep her off the bottle, to tell her what clothes she looks nice in and, perhaps most important of all, to help her see if she can't build up some sort of a sex life of her own.

The ponce in London today is usually neither more nor less than the whore's husband. He provides stability for her, a bit of discipline, someone to listen to her adventures. He fucks her as much for her sake as for his own, and takes trouble over it. He is also a gauge of her prestige. If she keeps him well in handmade shoes and black silk shirts, then her credit goes up among the whores, and his among the ponces.

"Mine's a good earner. Just look at this shirt."

Economically and in prestige values, he corresponds to the wife of the normal citizen, and the fact that he is living on her earnings and not she on his is only of secondary importance to either of them.

It often arises like this. A man is earning fifteen pounds a week, and he takes up with a girl who is earning a hundred. His self-respect may lead him to keep his own job for a bit, but then one day she is ill, or perhaps her child is ill, or she is picked up and he wants to go to court with her. He stays off work and loses his job. Their earnings drop from a hundred and fifteen to a hundred a week. So what the hell? He's a ponce: all right, so he's a ponce. There are plenty of others.

Mrs. Wilkinson published figures showing that about forty per cent of those *convicted* of poncing in England have also been convicted of other crimes. It cannot of course be known what proportion of ponces are never convicted either of poncing or of anything else. But the whore is herself usually a criminal—we make her one with our laws—and she develops a modified form of the criminal personality. It is not surprising that she takes up with others for company. Moreover, minorities against whom the majority discriminates will also seek each other out, and this is the main reason for the apparently disproportionate number of colored men among ponces in London.

I used to live in Knightsbridge when I first went on the game. It was terrible. I didn't seem to be real; you know, it was as if nobody could see me. But since I moved over here among the colored people I'm—well, you know—I feel kind of at home. I don't have to pretend any more.

Some share a ponce with another whore, or even with two others, but this arrangement is exceptional in London. It does not arise because the ponce is able to subject two or three reluctant but silly women for his own gain; it arises because in the world of prostitution, as in all other minority worlds which are at once defined and discriminated against by the majority world, like the criminal world proper, the Negro world, the world of the arts and, in former days, the worse-off working class—in such worlds monogamy is not the rule. Add to this that in the world of prostitution chastity is by definition something which does not come in, and that many whores are at least a bit Lesbian, and the multiple ponce becomes comprehensible.

Then there are the call house madams, or switch-bawds. These, in London, are women with a two- or three-bedroom flat, and a list of twenty or thirty telephone numbers. The client gives his order; she calls the most suitable girl, he meets her at the flat. He pays the madam, and the madam passes on a proportion—always alleged by the girls to be too low—to the girl. Or she allows the client to go to the girl's flat, and the girl passes on the rake-off. The call house madam is of course just as criminal as the male ponce, but society is not somehow so angry with her. After all, she's a woman, she's probably a superannuated whore herself, and women are never so frightening anyhow.

There has only been one large organization in London since the war, the famous Messina Organization. I cannot vouch for the truth of the following account of it, but it is what is generally believed among the whores.

The five Messina brothers used to buy the best girls out of the then legal brothels in France, Belgium and Italy for a down sum, marry them to sailors for fifty pounds, and bring them to London. This was, of course, a white slave traffic, and sounds terrible. But for the girls themselves it was a merciful deliverance. In the closed houses of the Continent, they would be taking fifty men a day and getting anything down to twenty cents a go for it. How they got there is another matter, but once there, there is no doubt that the Messina brothers were so many St. Georges. To come to London was the dream of all of them. In London they were set up two by two in shared flats and provided with "gaffs" (apartments) elsewhere to work in. They were run on Service lines. They paid over their entire earnings each week, and were given spending money. What was left of the earnings after the organization rake-off was then banked for them in a deposit account. They were supplied with an issue of the most destructible clothing, nylons and so on, and with food, and a bottle of wine a day would be sent to their living flats. One of the brothers or their agents would inspect their pitch nightly to see that standards of dress were satisfactory. Other girls who reached this standard were allowed to pitch there too, but anybody who did not was rushed off by the Messina girls themselves. If any girl earned outstandingly well she was given a bonus, typically a mink coat. Medical inspection was provided weekly and hospital treatment when necessary. They were given a return ticket home each year, but, naturally, were not allowed to take any of their savings with them. When they were finally judged unemployable, their savings were released to them and they were sent home. If a girl wanted to get off the game while she was still employable, it was made extremely difficult for her, but she could do it at the expense of a large proportion of her savings. The Messinas would never have English girls in the organization, and the English girls looked at it all between envy and contempt. Envy for the safety and regularity, contempt for the discipline and spoon-feeding; the same mixed feelings that they have for the idea of licensed brothels. The brothers were mostly imprisoned or deported in 1951, but a remnant of their girls remained for some years. Their price dropped from five pounds to three, and badly dressed slacks were no longer hustled off.

Apart from this, allegations in London that so and so is "running a string of girls," generally turn out to mean only that he gives them a cut rate on his string of taxis, or lets rooms to them, but in no sense controls them.

So why then are we so hot against the ponce? To begin an answer to this, we must first ask what we feel about the whore herself. We are all in touch with her, or in touch with her image in our own minds. She has been around for millennia. Every man has thought of going to her, even if he hasn't been. Every woman has thought of her husband or her son going to her. It is enough to ask yourself if you're a man, or your closest man if you're a woman, under what circumstances you would go to her. You go to her when you want sex. But if there was a woman by you who loved you and was going to come when you came, you could not possibly go to a whore. Even if there was a woman by you who did not love you, but was still going to come, out of animal spirits and general good will, you could not go to a whore. Even if she was a complete stranger, at a party say, and you didn't know whether it was going to be a good lay or not, you still could not prefer a whore, because if you did you would be paying for the certainty of pretense instead of taking the chance of reality free. By now we are pretty low down the scale, if a complete stranger at a party, whom you think about in terms of "a good lay" is still preferable; we are pretty far away from love. Perhaps the only circumstance in which a man who has experienced love, or even a casual fuck in friendship, could go to a whore would be if he was completely alone in a strange city and had the most terrible stone-ache, like millions of men every day, on military service or traveling one way or another.

So who does go, apart from soldiers and travelers? Kinkies, first. Men who can only come if they're allowed to dress up as this or that, or use the cat, or throw cream buns about; men who have associated the experience of orgasm with something which most people find irrelevant to it. If any moralist wanted to reduce prostitution and the flagellation market in England he could do it by breaking the chain of corporal punishment in the schools. Kinks are infectious; if the teacher likes it, the child will too.

Then the physically deformed; not directly because they are deformed, but because the shyness born of deformity may prevent them ever learning the experience of love. If the whore has a useful social function, as many people say she has, it is with the kinkies and the deformed.

If I have a hunchbacked client, I always keep my eyes on his face while he's undressing. I can't look at his hump, and I can't look away from him; he'd notice it at once and feel it. I keep my eyes fixed on his. I had one the other day, and we turned the light out. Afterwards he said: "Would you mind not turning the light on?" I said: "Of course not, darling. I never do." He said, as quick as lightning: "Why's that?" I said: "I don't like it. I always like to get at least into my bra and pants first."

I had one with an amputated leg, too. There he was unstrapping his wooden leg; I kept my eyes on his face, in the same way. Can you imagine what it's like to feel a man's stump going against your thigh? I don't know what I felt. I think I loved him, or something. I tell you, it takes it out of you.

Then there are the men who want to avoid trouble and complication, who simply want the "sneeze in the loins" without any responsibility, emotional contact, give-and-take, or indeed any involvement whatever; the duckers.

They know *I'm* not going to ring up and tell them I'm lonely, or write them long letters or go whining to them with this or that.

Lastly there are all the men, all the millions of men in England and America, who feel that sex is something apart from the society they live in, and wrong. They may be simply burning for a blow, or to do it dog-fashion, and daren't turn their wives round. They may be unmarried, and terrified by the thought of having a girl friend. They may never have found out that women come too. All these will end up with the whores, because they have been twisted out of sight of their own natures by the society they grew up in. If once you get to believe it's dirty, regrettable, unmentionable, something you wish to spare a refined woman, then there's not much reason why you shouldn't buy it. And if you've never found out that women come, you may find the whore's pretense of coming quite irresistible, and it may make you feel a hell of a fellow. She hopes it will.

And so back to the ponce. The whore has done her little turn, and you have paid her for it. It probably does not cross your mind that you could have something ten times as good with a real girl if you got up and took it, so you don't worry too much about the money. But the thought that the first thing she does when your back is turned is to hand the money over to someone else, and that someone else a man, and that man laying her for free, and for all you know sneering with her at your peculiarities—why, it's absolutely revolting. It makes you bust with rage. If ever you laid hands on such a man, you'd beat the life out of him, because he is living proof that what you've had was counterfeit. He is your disillusionment. Into prison with him, and let the illusions flourish. And if two years isn't enough, let him have seven, and that will be some consolation to us all.

In unpublished evidence for the Wolfenden Committee,

Mrs. Wilkinson wrote (and kindly allows me to quote):

The society formed by prostitutes and their associates, though not hereditary, is continuous; it has a fairly permanent structure and composition. It exists because it absorbs asocial or antisocial personalities; it is economically dependent on the expression of an antisocial tendency in members of ordinary society. Its cohesion is strengthened by the attitudes of the general public towards the prostitute, her guilt feelings which prevent her return to ordinary life by causing her to exaggerate and anticipate critical attitudes towards her, and by attitudes within the society itself towards its members who try to break away.

The whore world is like a little gearwheel meshing with a big one; it goes round faster, and in the opposite direction. You could see it until recently on the pavements of Piccadilly; the whores standing still and the men pouring past, looking, considering, pausing to haggle, passing on to the next. The countersociety or underworld, like the society or overworld from which it is excluded, is classridden, intolerant, but free from oppression. As to the rest of us, we cherish and pay it with one hand and belabor it with the other. That's how it gets as it is. When we cherish the whore, she feels like a necessary safety valve, warm, trustworthy and useful. When we belabor her, she feels like a criminal.

If that's how it is, I thought, I'll bloody well live up to the image—I'll buy a Rolls and get a Nubian chauffeur in a leopard-skin jockstrap and hustle with all the lights on and a cigarette-holder a mile long. And three Afghan wolfhounds on golden leashes trotting behind. And scythes on the wheels.

The overworld views the whore as a social problem or a social service, according to the amount of use it makes of her. The whore judges the overworld by what she sees. First, she sees the client, whom she holds in contempt for his gullibility and in respect for his purse. Through him she sees his wife who, he inevitably tells her, is cold. To the English whore, England is a country of women as frigid as she is, or more so, but who don't even try to pretend.

Ask me, the only difference between me and some of these wives is that they don't keep the bargain and I do.

The overworld and the underworld depend on each other, their characters are complementary, and yet ignorance prevails. If it did not, the two worlds would probably fuse, and that would be an end of prostitution. The ignorance itself is preserved by the fear, and the fear is the result of the exclusion of fucking from the realm of the normal. The whore incarnates the Extruded.

PART VI

HISTORICAL

Chapter 15

Introductory

And that is how we are; our language is depleted and gangrenous, our arts are vapid and cold, our lives are furtive and thwarted, and there's one in every village.

How did we get this way? What makes English and American people in the middle of the twentieth century feel and act as they do about love and sex? What determines the statistical spread of feelings and actions, and our judgments of what sector on this spread is normal, or right, and what sectors abnormal, or wrong?

Questions not easily answered, mainly because questions only recently asked. The very ideas of statistical spread and of "normal" (as opposed to "natural") are quite new, but few could now think without them. To arrive at a comprehensive handling of these problems, one would have to take into account evidence from anthropology, from biology—including the behavior of other species and evolutionary and genetic theory—from the history of ideas, from statistical sociology, from psychology, and from other fields. The problem is that of our attitude to what makes us, and therefore of our attitude to ourselves. It is, as far as we ourselves are concerned, total.

Nobody has yet undertaken such a comprehensive handling, and I certainly cannot. Indeed, the intellectual tradition within which we live is obviously still many generations away from breeding a mind capable of it, if it ever does. But everyone undertakes what he feels he can, and in the remaining chapters I shall attempt a sketch in one dimension only, that of the historical experience of Christianity.

The map of ways in which people have felt about fucking even within our culture is infinitely complex. The feeling, whether hostile, fearful, friendly or hectic, never exists alone. It is always tied up with feelings about other things, and most of all in Christendom with feeling about sin and, therefore, grace. One can dimly recognize two poles; one pole feels that fucking is all right on the whole, though it can be wrong; the other feels that it is wrong on the whole, though it can be right. There can hardly be any doubt in the mind of the reader who has come this far, or indeed who has lived in this culture of ours, that, in it, the latter pole predominates. The whole burden of Christian teaching about fucking is that it is usually wrong but can, in the word of Pope Gregory the Great (*ca.* 600) be "excused" in marriage.

In what follows I first mention two heretical traditions within Christendom, and their disputes with orthodoxy, and see what the parties concerned thought about it. After that I go back and discuss orthodox Christianity itself, the relation between its beliefs about the nature of God and its teaching on sexual conduct, and the traces which this teaching has left in the minds of many people who reject the beliefs about the nature of God. After that, I discuss various reactions against this teaching which have arisen since the Reformation. The implication of the section is that the "anti-fucking" values of orthodox Christianity should not be allowed to outlast the increased knowledge of other cultures, of the animal man, and of evolution, which we have attained in the last four centuries; and that the "anti-anti-fucking" values of libertinism were hardly more than a reaction against those values.

Chapter 16

Augustine Between Pelagius and Mani

In the polytheism of the Greco-Roman culture, gods were many, and did not particularly love us. They presided over this or that activity, and were invoked when it was time for that activity. Montaigne found there were fifty gods assigned to fucking; St. Augustine, with amusement, had mentioned among others Jugatinus to preside over wedding, Domiducus to lead the bride home, Domitius to keep her there, Virginensis to loosen her virgin girdle, Subigus to subject her to her husband, and Prema to press her down in a convenient way.[1] These are simply the Latin words for the actions in question, personified and made into deities arising without more ado from common speech. If a thing was done, it was as natural to have a god for it as to have a word; gods grew out of the language as grass grows between paving stones. The more familiar gods, Venus, Priapus, Cupid, and so on, though grander, were still only individuals among a crowd of equals; they too

---

[1] *City of God*, VI, 9.

came on the scene when they were needed and retired when they were not.

Fucking was one thing among others which was commonly done, and it was better and more piously done, done more in accordance with the nature of things, if it was accompanied by a libation or at least a thought for the correct god, so as, in the phrase which is still with us, "to enter into the spirit of the thing." All of human activity was regulated thus; only crime and pride were displeasing to the gods, and the gods were equally present in every thought and act, helping it forward, sanctioning it, in a word, presiding.

Then the religions of Asia Minor surged and poured round the Mediterranean; of these Christianity quickly prevailed and remained there and in all Europe until the present, losing only the southern shore and for a time Spain to its close variant, Islam. Christianity, at first with Islam, made Europe and America. If one can speak of a religion as an active agent, then Christianity dismantled man wherever it went and reassembled him afresh. Every feeling, every belief, every image of himself and of his fellows, every duty, every right, every impulse and reaction and reflection, every sentiment of community and of distinction, was changed through and through.

But the eschatological claims of Jesus were not dropped into a calm pond; they were dropped into a world already creased and weighted with religious and philosophical speculation. Around was Jewry, Old Testament and Essene. To the west was the Hellenic world, polytheist and Platonic and Aristotelian. To the east was Zoroastrianism, dualist. Farther east, Hinduism, quietist, transmigrationist, "sensual." To the north and south, various other polytheisms and animisms. All these mixed with Christianity and colored it.

It is difficult for the average educated person of today, so steeped is he in the history of the victorious strand, to imagine the chaotic and splendid wealth of doctrine and practice of the early years of Christianity. The mixture took centuries to shake down; indeed, it had not finished shaking down when it started to break up again.

In the first millennium of our era, many hundreds of sects, some great and powerful, some obscure, unorganized, even of doubtful existence, contested the truth with one another. We shall never unravel why the Western Church became "Catholic" and the Eastern "Orthodox" instead of something else. Instead, for instance, of becoming Gnostic, believing in grades of initiation, and that it was not God himself who made the world, but a fairly remote dependent of his called the Demiurge. Instead of Marcionite, believing that the just God of the Old Testament was quite different from the merciful God of the New Testament. Instead of Ophite or Naassite, believing that Jahweh was a cruel and evil God, and that therefore his adversary the Serpent was good. Instead of Cainite, believing that the mortal adversaries of the Old Testament God, Cain, Esau and others, were also good. Instead of Abelite, practicing abstinence in marriage and adopting children. Instead of Docetist, believing that Jesus only seemed to live and be crucified on earth, having passed through his mother like water through a tube. Instead of Adoptionist, believing that Jesus was God's adopted son. Instead of Arian (touch and go, this one), believing that Jesus was created by God out of nothing, and not of shared substance. Instead of Montanist, believing the second coming was imminent. Instead of Psilanthropist, believing that Jesus was just a specially good man. Instead of Manichean, believing that matter was evil and not God's creation, while only spirit was good and was God's creation. Instead of Carpocratian, believing that matter was so far from God that there was no distinction between good and evil in this life, and one could thus behave as one liked. Instead of Messalian, believing that the best way to achieve this liberty was to spend three years blowing sin out through the nose, and hating the cross as the instrument of Jesus' suffering. Instead of Helvidian, believing that marriage is as good as virginity and thankful eating as fasting. Instead of Pelagian, believing that when Adam sinned he cooked his own goose only. Instead of Mandaean, baptizing people over and over. Instead of believing that some of Eve's children were the serpent's and some Adam's, that Jesus entered his mother by her ear and was born out of it again, or indeed something else. Almost anything else.

Out of this welter of possibilities there arose, slowly, brick by brick, in dispute and struggle and persecution and power-politics, the two bodies of doctrine which made medieval Europe, the Catholic and the Orthodox. But there arose also two heretical traditions which throw great light on our attitudes to love and sex now, one of which died as peacefully as it had lived in a mere century or so, and the other of which lasted for a thousand years, dogging the church like a *Doppelgänger,* and was suppressed with terrible savagery only in the thirteenth century. They were the Pelagian tradition, and the Dualist or Manichean tradition.

In the piping days around 400 there were many doctrinal disputes and many condemnations for heresy, and they affect us now to an extent few recognize through the impact they had on the mind of that engine of faith and formulation, St. Augustine. And none affects our lives so much as the dispute he conducted with Pelagius; indeed, it often seems as though it is still being fought out.

Pelagius was an English or Irish layman; his enemy St. Jerome said he was all weighted down with Irish porridge. His contemporaries described him as a big man, and jovial. His very appearance and manners were insults to the melancholy asceticism of the other party, and his doctrines were deplorably optimistic. When first he came to Rome, he heard St. Augustine's prayer: "Grant what Thou commandest, and command what Thou wilt."[2] Against such fatalism the forefather of British radicalism spent his life expostulating. It left nothing for man to do; it degraded man to the status of a passive little parcel waiting for God to tickle him with grace. It also degraded God to imagine

---

[2] Da quod jubes, et jube quod vis.

he could have created anything so ignoble as this view of man supposed. St. Augustine—it has often been held against him, and we shall return to it later—could not imagine that man's love of God could ever be anything like as important as God's grace to man. Pelagius insisted on the importance of the human response in love to his creator.

The argument came to rest round sin. Augustine held that sin was indeed original; that death came into the world in direct punishment of Adam's sin; that when Adam sinned he condemned all of us, his sons, to sin until the end of the world, and that sin was transmitted by the act of generation, which was ineradicably sinful. Not so Pelagius. To him, Adam sinned for himself alone, and died first simply because he lived first. His effect on us is only that of bad example. Sometimes Pelagius tended, conversely, to hold that Jesus' effect is only that of good example. If a man sins, that is his own responsibility alone. Therefore sinlessness is theoretically possible to all men, though none except Christ has in fact achieved it. And what prevents me achieving it?

"Nothing," he burst out: "nothing except my own most grievous fault."

We *can* keep God's commandments, and there is no excuse for us in original sin if we do not.

"We contradict the Lord to his face when we say: 'It is hard! It is difficult, we cannot, we are men; we are encompassed in fragile flesh.' O blind madness! O unholy audacity! We charge the God of all knowledge with a two-fold igngorance, that he seems to know neither what he has made nor what he has commanded."[3]

This genial optimist, who also preached economic egalitarianism, was condemned as a heretic for the usual mixture of political and doctrinal reasons, and his teaching survived only in a watered-down form.

---

[3] John Ferguson, *Pelagius*, New York and Cambridge, 1956, p. 167.

Now Pelagius did not specifically teach that fucking was all right, though he was for a time attracted to the doctrines of another unorthodox teacher, Jovinian, who held that marriage was as good as virginity and thankful eating as fasting, and whose teaching was condemned by the Church. In fact Pelagius cordially commended chastity, and found the great example of it in Jesus himself. But by excluding the idea of original sin he also a fortiori excluded the possibility that original sin was transmitted by the action which transmits physical life, and that this action is therefore especially sinful. Above all he sharpened by his opposition the doctrines of St. Augustine, the keystone of Western orthodoxy. During the rest of his life, St. Augustine not only worked out and emphasized his anti-Pelagian belief that fucking is especially sinful, but also the anti-Pelagian belief that salvation, like its forerunner grace, lies entirely in God's hand, not in the individual's. He became the forefather of Calvin and Jansen, and thus of the New England Puritans. (Indeed, Jansen read the anti-Pelagian writings of St. Augustine thirty times, but the others only ten.)

Pelagianism was gentle, humanistic, tolerant of man's efforts and severe only on his failures. It denied the rigors of the Augustinian concepts of sin and salvation. It permitted men and women to live as men and women; if they tried to be good, God would help them. But they must always make the first move. God, being man's friend, had not commanded the impossible. Above all, each man was fully capable of virtue and redemption; he had only to be virtuous and redeem himself. Pelagianism was akin to the Hillelist tradition in Jewish teaching: "If not me, who? If not now, when?" To imagine that sin was hereditary and inescapable was to imagine that God was man's enemy. Pelagius was like us.

Not so the Manichees. With the story of Manicheism we enter darker fields indeed and, since we live in a dark, dark age, over which hangs the threat of race suicide, we must accord the Manichees close attention.

The Persian teacher Mani, whose name in Latin is Manes

or Manicheus, and who lived about 215-275, held that Jesus, Plato, Zoroaster and the Buddha were equally great teachers. His cosmogony was extremely complex, and supposed that the creation of the world was only a rather important episode in a long war between the powers of darkness and of light. The upshot was that the world is thoroughly bad, and that men are mainly darkness, but contain each a particle of light imprisoned in him. The best thing that people can do therefore is to get out of this mortal life as soon as is decent, and in the meantime to have as little as possible to do with it. Fucking is bad because it dabbles in matter and even more because it imprisons more particles of light in the babies begotten; it is better to let one's own particle return immediately whence it came.

The powers of light reproduced themselves by *evoking* new powers from one another; the powers of darkness reproduced as we do, and our way is fit only for darkness. At a certain stage in the battle, the powers of darkness had swallowed the powers of light inside them and then, as sometimes happened, the Messenger of God came to them to try to put things right. But God's messenger was beautiful, and the powers of darkness desired the messenger. When they desired, they gave out light mingled with sin. Adam's sin in Eden was fucking Eve, and thus the sin which inheres in all men is physical desire.

The Manichees were persecuted with equal fervor by Christianity, Islam and Zoroastrianism, and the original sect was last heard of in Chinese Turkestan about the year 1000.

In holding explicitly that Adam's sin was carnal, and that mankind's main duty is to die out by continence, and perhaps in the unforgettable image of desire as light mingled with sin, Mani brought to full stature the fear and exclusion of our own origin which has dominated Europe and America ever since. St. Augustine—and here is the point—was nine years a Manichee, and they were the formative years for an intellectual: from nineteen to twenty-eight.

The line of Mani's teaching did not break. The Paulicians perpetuated parts of it in the Eastern Empire from the seventh century. When the Armenian Church caught them, it branded their foreheads with the sign of a fox.

Thereafter were the Bogomils of Bulgaria, the name meaning "beloved of God." More is known of them. They had forgotten Plato, Zoroaster and the Buddha, and were Christians. Their sect arose among an exploited peasantry partly as an expression of nationalism against a foreign nobility.

Thereafter the Patarenes, the name being perhaps from the quarter of Milan, the Pataria, where they first came together. As primitive Manichean preachers begot Paulicianism, so Paulicians begot Bogomilism and Bogomils begot Patarinism. In 1200 there was a Patarene state church in the kingdom of Bosnia, and the sect was finally extirpated not by orthodoxy but by Islam. The Turks put it down when they conquered Bosnia in 1463.

And Patarenes and Bogomils begot Catharism. The Cathars of Provence were the closest to us. Most is known about them because—and the good luck is ours, not theirs —they were burned by Western orthodox fanatics, Dominican friars, who were interested in what their victims did as well as in how they could be downed in doctrinal argument. The Cathars were the victims of the Western or evidence-taking tradition of bigoted savagery, not the Eastern or point-scoring one. Their doctrines and practices and their appalling end still arouse interest and even passions today; it is hard to say how much is interest in and admiration of the doctrine and practice, and how much is sympathy with the victims of the proto-S.S. which was the early Dominican Order. If the State had had gas chambers during the Albigensian Crusade, the Church would have required it to use them.

The name Cathar is probably derived from the Greek word for *pure,* a title they gave to the highest of their three grades of adherent. At the bottom were just people, Christians. A ceremony called Convenenza, the coming together, the appropriateness, could make them Believers. The Believer could be made Perfect by the Consolamentum.[4] This ceremony was a portmanteau of the Catholic sacraments of baptism, extreme unction and ordination; the Perfect was at once ready to live, ready to die, and a priest. Readiness to live and to die were in Manichean doctrine one and the same thing. Over all hung the total asceticism of the Endura, which was nothing less than starving oneself to death. Only one certain instance of it is recorded, but the ideal has a logical place in the doctrinal structure.

Most of the Consolamentum chimed with orthodox doctrine, but among other heterodox lines it contained this: "Have no mercy on the flesh born in corruption, but have mercy on the *spirit held in prison.*" Here are Mani's particles of imprisoned light still on their sin-bound career. The duty of returning all these sad little goods to the one great Good was still not done; mankind had still not committed suicide. Still the greatest sin and the special fallenness of man was his indelible liking for reproducing his kind. The Cathars held to the early Christian custom of the Kiss of Peace at the end of each religious ceremony; each kissed each before they left, but the Perfect of either sex—all Manicheans have always admitted women to as high a degree of initiation as men—might not kiss any one, whether Perfect, Believer, or simple troops, of the other sex. Instead they kissed a New Testament and passed it across the table to be kissed.

It was generation which appalled the Cathars, even more than pleasure. No more pieces of fallen matter must be produced, each with his wrongfully imprisoned spark of light. Hence marriage was worse than what the orthodox called "debauchery." Casual fornication, though wrong, was not as wrong as marriage. Perhaps even buggery, though wrong, was not as wrong as fucking. The very word *bugger* comes from Bulgar, the people who as Bogomils were the Cathars' teachers. The routine charges of the orthodox against the Cathars and their predecessors were perhaps

---

[4] The three grades perpetuate those of the Gnostics, dualists who were around in Christendom even before Mani. Theirs were: hylic (fleshbound), psychic (spiritual) and pneumatic (inspired).

not entirely due to the scandal imagined by people who were themselves much exercised by the rights and wrongs of fucking, but also in part to what really happened. We do not know much about the sexual habits of the Cathars, but their doctrine, in holding that sex without babies was less bad than sex with, permitted people who thought it was only good with babies to imagine what was to them the worst.

The Cathars were defeated in the County of Toulouse during the first half of the thirteenth century by greedy noblemen from the North, most of all by the Anglo-Norman Simon de Montfort. The Church gave these men leave to take the heretic lands for their own. The heretics were then burned at the instance of St. Dominic and his successors. The wars called the Albigensian Crusade were, with the crusades against Islam, the first appearance of the willingness of Western Christians—Christians then, post-Christians now—to exterminate human beings for the sake of power disguised as an idea, proclaiming: "Since our ideas differ and since mine is mine while yours is only yours, I shall kill you." The Dominicans had heretic corpses dug up and burned a generation after their death. They had heretic houses destroyed with the provision that the land should never again be built upon or cultivated. When the castle of Montségur was captured and the Crusade achieved its end, more than two hundred people who would not abjure their faith, most of them women, were herded into a palisade, the palisade was closed, and they were burned alive. The numbers are insignificant to the twentieth century, but we recognize the technique.

Neither Pelagianism nor Manicheism formed us directly; Catholic orthodoxy and the reformed churches which later sprang from it did that. (None of the reformed churches has diverged far from Catholic teaching on the matter of original sin, where, to them, sexual morality lies embedded.) Neither heretical tradition has formed us, and the surviving orthodoxy has; but can we learn anything from their differing careers? Why was it that

Pelagianism, simple, hopeful and God-loving, was not per-secuted and died out as it were of itself, and that Maniche-ism, complex, despairing and world-hating, lasted long and strong and was suppressed only by terrible means?

When we see two wings of a party—and the Catholic Church was simply a long lived and powerful party in European affairs—fall away in such diverse manners, we are forced to ask ourselves the question: what does this teach us about the successful center? If we stand outside the heavy influence of information and exhortation from the center, can we learn anything about the location of that center itself from the fate of its two deviant wings? Was it for instance a true equidistant center, or did it lean more heavily toward the one or the other? And if it did, should we expect it to have been nearer in spirit to the wing which withered peacefully away, or to that which was suppressed in blood and flame after a thousand years of struggle? It is a maxim of common consent that inter-necine warfare is the bloodiest of all.

To see the growth of Western Christianity as the victory of those who were moderate and sensible about life over those who were on the one hand too indulgent to it and on the other too restrictive, may be an error. It may be nearer the truth, or at least nearer to a truth which makes sense to us now, to see it as the victory of the moderate party within the forces of anti-life over the extremists in those forces, while the forces of pro-life withered peace-fully because they could not subsist in a soil so conditioned by the other side. It was not Christ who triumphed in the Albigensian Crusade, it was Mani himself. It seemed he was defeated, but he had won nearly a thousand years be-fore, when St. Augustine left his sect, but carried with him the Manichean, dualist, anti-life, anti-fucking cast of mind.

Chapter 17

Orthodox Christianity

In the last chapter we based ourselves on the things said by the men concerned; we have used their own terms; grace, sin, salvation, and so on. Let us now introduce a word from our day, one they hardly used: orgasm. They hardly used it because they felt fearful and doubtful of it, and we must now examine why.

The teaching which is central to Christianity, even more important than the incarnation and the atonement, and which is unique to the group Christianity, Islam and Judaism, is that God is One *and loves man*. It follows by the nature of human response that as man is loved, so must he love. In the words of St. John the Evangelist: "Herein is love; not that we loved God, but that He loved us." And again: "We love because He first loved us." And, most important of all: "Beloved, if God so loved us, we ought also to love one another."[1] But since God is greater than man, the love man bears to God must be greater than that which man bears to man, and that which man bears to man is only a reflection of that which he bears to God, which

_____
[1] First Epistle, Chapter 4.

is in turn a reflection of that which God bears to him. The greater must be visible through the lesser, it must be felt to be always present, always accessible, always helping and perfecting man.

Now this view of the nature of love, and the causal chain in the genesis of love, is not suitable for men, it is suitable for creatures living before or without the polarity of sex. The love of the Christian God for man—for his creatures —is most like that of a father for his children, and children live before the polarization of sex takes on its function. Men and women, unlike the hermaphrodite sea urchin or the land urchins men and women themselves grow out of and beget, are subject to orgasm. When this is happening, they are incapable of feeling any other love than love for the woman or man they are fucking with, and often they are not even capable of feeling that very clearly. It is the one moment when the greater cannot be visible through the lesser, when men and women, however great their love of God at other times, are wholly absorbed in love for each other, and when any notion of human love being a reflection of anything else is swept aside by the obvious primacy and self-sufficiency of what they are doing. It is the one moment of forgetfulness, of total oblivion for all things, including God.

And this is the more so since, though the faculty of love beomes perforce narrowed and concentrated during orgasm, thus excluding God, the faculty of reason becomes altogether suspended. (Kinsey has described how you can fire a pistol in the room without disturbing lovers at the point.) It was as much the suspension of reason as the narrowing and averting of love from God which made St. Augustine look askance on desire and the pleasure of love. To St. Thomas Aquinas, it was the main objection.

These are the origins of the basic Christian premises that the love of God is better than love between man and woman, that the latter interferes with the former, that chastity is higher than wedlock, and that virgins are holier than wives. Divine love was always an alternative to sexual love, and was free to appropriate its language. Thus Origen in the early third century: "The soul ought to adhere to its spouse and hear his word and embrace him and receive the seed of the word from him."[2] Thus St. Ambrose, echoing St. Paul, wrote in 377 that virginity is better than marriage, but fewer can attain it. Thus St. Cassian wrote in about 420 that chastity is proper to the angels, but man cannot achieve it without grace.[3] Thus St. John Chrysostom in his *Why Women in Orders Ought not to Cohabit with Men* (*ca.* 400) wrote that not only was God a spouse to virgins, but he was also a more ardent lover than men. "We admonish you" he said to virgins, "that you should make as if to sing a certain holy song, both at home and abroad, both day and night, both in the streets and in your bed, both with your voice and with your mind, continually uttering and proposing to your soul: Hear, my soul, and see, and incline your ear; forget evil custom and the King will desire your beauty."[4] "Evil custom" is of course patristic longhand for fucking.

The proposition that virgins are the brides of Christ is common to all those writers who made the first Christian centuries what they were, but, as usual when one wants to find the turns of phrase and habits of feeling which most determined Christianity, it is best to turn once again to St. Augustine. In the following quotations from his *Confessions,* I have italicized certain words. "When my father saw me at the baths, now growing towards manhood, and endued with a restless youthfulness, he, as already hence anticipating his descendants, gladly told it to my mother, rejoicing in that tumult of the senses *wherein the world forgetteth Thee its creator, and becometh enamoured of Thy creature instead of Thyself* . . ." (Bk.

---

[2] M. J. Rouet de Journel and J. Dutilleul, *Enchiridion Asceticum,* Freiburg im Breisgau, 1947, p. 115.

[3] *Ibid.,* p. 782.

[4] *Ibid.,* p. 358.

2). "For there is an attractiveness in beautiful bodies, in gold and silver, and all things and in bodily touch. . . . But yet to obtain all these *we may not depart from Thee, O Lord . . .*"(Bk. 2). "Thus doth the soul commit fornication, *when she turns from Thee . . .*" (Bk. 2). *"By continency* verily are we bound up and brought back into One, whence we were dissipated into many" (Bk. 10).

Obliviousness of God is impiety; to shut out the love of God is blasphemy. How then can a Christian ever feel that the act which is always bound to shut out the knowledge and the love of God is anything but impious or even blasphemous? The Christian concept of God as a single creator who loves us would founder altogether if it were to attempt to take on board the intractable biological fact of orgasm. It therefore isolates it, and the fucking which gives rise to it, in a penumbra of misgiving. It is this quite logical and structurally necessary consequence of the great new theology of Pauline and Augustinian Christianity, so profound, charitable and worthy of all assent in other ways, which has alway prevented it from filling the whole heart and mind of anybody but an ascetic. For the rest of us, because of its insistence that what we perfectly well know in every cell of our body is a right, good and holy thing, is no more than a tolerable shortfalling and a cause of danger, orthodox Christianity can never transcend a certain superficiality and irrelevance.

Among the great religions of the world and of history, Christianity must be squarely qualified as anti-life. It could praise fucking. Some do. It could associate it with sowing or reaping. Some do. It could regard it as an emblem of the fusion of man with God. Some do. It could, and here is the proof of the assertion, it could be quite neutral about it. Some are. But no; the act considered by itself, without question of who or when and why, is felt as a shame and a danger. Only when it is done in marriage and with the desire to have children can it be "excused," or even hallowed.

Now I shall spare the reader all the routine quotations about this from the grudging permission of St. Paul to the snarling hates of St. Jerome, of St. Odo of Cluny, of

Calvin, and inflict on him one only, which sums up all the others. It is a medieval couplet recorded by a Cardinal Hugues de St. Cher and quoted by G. G. Coulton.

> Femina corpus opes animam vim lumina vocem
> Polluit adnihilat necat eripit orbat acerbat.[5]

Jesus himself, in the Gospels, touches only twice and only incidentally on the sexual relations between man and woman. One is the matter of the woman taken in adultery. And the point of this story is neither that he was against adultery nor that was lenient to it, but that he was against hypocrisy. Whether it had been adultery, theft, or pride she was taken in, the moral could have been the same: "Let him among you who is without sin cast the first stone."

The other is the saying that he who desires a woman commits adultery with her in his heart. Again, this is not a saying about adultery; this time it is a saying about the relation between desire and act. "He who hateth his brother," murders him; this makes the same point.

But as soon as the Crucifixion was over, the Manicheism began. The brothers of Jesus, who seem to be there as large as life in the Gospels, began to be erased from the tradition. In the Gospels, they went about with his mother Mary and cared for her, which is exactly what one would expect younger sons to do. But in the tradition they are demoted to being the cousins of Jesus, or at the most sons of Joseph by an earlier, and unmentioned, marriage. One cannot claim that this interpretation is flying in the face of historical fact, but it is certainly flying in the face of human likelihood. Nephews, or elder stepsons, do not so naturally care for a widow as younger sons do. By the end of the fourth century, they had been entirely dropped from the legend, and Helvidius, who had maintained they were just what they seemed to be, had been discredited by the most rancid ascetic of them all: St. Jerome.

The doctrine of the Virgin Birth was central to the whole

---

[5] *Five Centuries of Religion*, Cambridge, 1929, Vol. I, p. 177.
Woman pollutes the body, drains the resources, kills the soul, uproots the strength, blinds the eye and embitters the voice.

story. It chimed with the main philosophical preoccupation of the cultures of the eastern Mediterranean in those days (which was the interaction of general and particular, of idea and thing, of spirit and man) that the savior should have been begotten directly by God, without the interposition of a human father. But as the Manicheism thickened up, so did this emblem of direct interference by spirit, by idea, on the body of mankind through a particular woman pass over into an illustration of a newer attitude, namely that the normal action of flesh on flesh, of particular on particular, was a bad thing. And so there appeared the doctrine of *semper virgo,* of permanent virginity. Not only had Mary never had a man before she bore Jesus, but never afterward either. The Manicheism claimed the central event itself, and then began to seep forward in time, thus excluding the brothers of Jesus from the story.

When the queen of heaven is a virgin, the animal nature of mortal women is bound to give rise to concern. Sometimes, when I have seen the bare-armed tourist girls from the North filing past the notices about "decently clad, covered to the wrist and to the knee" into southern churches, I have understood the alarm of the clergy lest the great event should repeat itself, thereby causing confusion. Each tourist is a sunburned possible Mary.

Many gods and messiahs in legends had miraculous births, were engendered by other than human agency. But I think it is only in Christianity that the process has seeped back up the generations to include the god's mother as well. When the Marian cult grew up within Christianity it became obvious that Mary, like her son, could not have been engendered in the usual way. But she could not have been engendered by the direct intervention of God the Father, as Jesus was, since the uniqueness of that event lay at the heart of the whole religion. The Christian imagination therefore had recourse to a middle way, and the doctrine of the Immaculate Conception began to crystallize, namely that the Virgin Mary had herself been conceived without original sin, which is as much as to say without her parents having enjoyed it. It is interesting that the doctrine first came to the fore about 1200, the heyday of heretical Catharism. It got a strong boost from the Council of Trent, and in the Church of the Santissimi Apostoli in Florence you can see an immaculately conceived Mary, freshly authorized by that Council, stamping on a gentle Satan to whom are chained via the tree of knowledge an Adam and Eve only this instant interrupted in their normal Renaissance love-making. Within a few years the church pictures of the Immaculate Conception changed and changed until the triumphant sexless creature dominated a mere token Satan, and Adam and Eve huddled in opposite corners. However, it did not become obligatory for Roman Catholics to believe in the Immaculate Conception until 1854.

It took time to establish a celibate priesthood, but when once it was established it naturally set the tone and became a dominating force in the Christian sect which, perhaps partly as a result, has shown itself to be not only the most rigid and dogmatic but also incomparably the most alive of them all, the Church of Rome. Monks and nuns living in communities had been celibate from the beginning of Christianity; the institution took up traditions in both Judaism and Greco-Roman polytheism. But it was not until the fourth century that any move was made to limit the marriage of secular priests, that is, ordinary parish priests, in the Western Church. (In the Eastern Church, priests always did marry, and still do.) And it was no less than twelve hundred years before the Church of Rome reached the rigid clerical celibacy which we know now. In the eleventh century, at the time of the full flowering of feudalism, Pope Gregory VII (Hildebrand) sought to impose celibacy on the secular priesthood; his motive was to prevent the growth of a second, parallel cast of feudal lords, passing lands and power from father to son, with consequent loss of spiritual prestige. Later, the appeal of heretical Catharism led the Church to try once more, by enforcing celibacy, to take the wind out of Cathar sails. The issue, as no northern European is likely to forget, was still very much alive during the Reformation, and it was only the Council of Trent itself which, against the advice of the Emperor and the Catholic Kings of France, Poland and Bavaria, finally settled it in favor of general and complete clerical celibacy.

Once it is accepted that celibacy is a meritorious condition, then a tightly organized celibate priesthood will naturally urge everyone else in the same direction, even if only part of the way. By and large those who rise to the top of the Roman Catholic hierarchies are sincere men who practice what they preach, and they are also the men who had the "best" intellectual training, which means in their terms the most rigid, and beginning at the earliest age. It is a solemn thought that most Catholic prelates in responsible jobs have perhaps not made love more than once or twice in their lives, if that. When they want, to find out about it they often turn to doctors. From time to time a theologian writes a book about sex for confessors; he does it by consulting the standard medical dictionaries, and seeing where they can be made to agree with patristic asceticism. Some of these things have to be seen to be believed, but since they are written in Latin they are not often seen by the rest of us. They are the instruments of a carefully perpetuated ignorance, because when knowledge is regarded as sin, ignorance must be transmitted in its stead.

Piscetta and Gennaro, for instance, in *Elementa Theologiae Moralis,* Volume VII, Turin (Nil Obstat 1940), discuss what penitence should be imposed for just about anything you can do in bed except a short quick fuck with the man on top, and (§ 280) argue that if a man with syphilis wants to fuck his healthy wife she has no right to refuse him, because it *may* not be passed on to the child, in which case there would be another soul for the glory of God, and equally (§ 277) if the doctor has told her to abstain at the risk of her life she may still not refuse her huband, because the doctor may be wrong. They also recommend (§ 167) the cauterization or amputation of the clitoris as a cure for the vice of Lesbianism. Not all Catholic writing about sex is like this, indeed the increasing care with which some theologians try to reconcile the cold old dogmas with the warm old facts can be seen as an increasing recognition of the latter. But it is fair to say that the greater part of it is out of touch with the natural release and pleasure which all people could have from their bodies, and which many do. Priests are only physically the sons of their parents; they are spiritually and emotionally the sons of each other. It is a self-perpetuating caste, and the last contact they had with ordinary sensual humanity was about nine hundred years ago, when married priests were still generally tolerated in the Church of Rome.

Of the three vows taken by priests of the Church of Rome, two are not manifestly against human nature. Neither disobedience nor wealth are overwhelmingly necessary to men; many people are very well able to get on without either and not to be torn apart in the effort. Moreover, the vow of poverty has for most Christian priests and monks never been more than a formality. But the vow of chastity is a different matter. It is extremely difficult to live chastely, and generally speaking this vow has not been allowed to become a mere formality. The result is that those who take it are in fact very often torn apart by the difficulty of keeping it, and that most of the temptations which fall to the lot of a Roman priest come under this one heading. It is thus natural that temptation, in this church and in the culture it has determined, should make us think at once of sexual temptation. There is nothing in the life of the layman which necessarily makes sexual temptation any more frequent or more tempting than any other sort of temptation, but there is something which does so in the life of the priest who was for so long his mentor: that vow.

Jesus himself spoke many times more often and more hotly against greed and pride than against luxury. He was no founder of orders, but if he had been, it would surely have been the Sermon on the Mount that would have suggested his rule, and there is nothing about continence there. To suppose that he meant "continence" by "purity" is to suppose him a riddler.

Christianity fails and has always failed us in one of the most intense and fruitful areas of our experience, and the priesthood of its most active sect have deliberately cut themselves off, by their celibacy, from knowledge of this failure. To say, as it has been said, that it is a religion for eunuchs, is going too far; but it is a religion that only ascetics and those inclined to Manicheism will find rings equally true throughout the totality of their need and experience.

There are exceptions. There are places where, because of the survival of pre-Christian religion or close contact with other religions, Christianity has drifted away from Manicheism, and agreed as it were by oversight to preside, in the sense we used earlier, over fucking as well as over everything else. Every visitor to Italy has some tale to tell of a pagan survival; there are villages where the foreskin of Christ is carried on holiday procession just as any other relic would be, a piece of the true cross for instance. And there were until recently churches where you could see plaster casts of sexual organs miraculously cured by the intervention of the name saint among the arms and breasts and feet which you can see everywhere. These things are a good image of what is happening; it is simply that the normal modes of the cult have omitted to withdraw themselves from that area of life, have omitted to qualify it as special and dangerous. And in Brazil, where Christianity, separated by six thousand miles from the seat of orthodoxy, has for four centuries been getting mixed at the edges with Amerindian and African religion, there is a flourishing cult of the pregnant madonna, *A Madona do O,* the madonna of the egg. Brazilian husbands will also slip a small crucifix under their wives just before they come, to insure conception.

The Brazilian cult of the pregnant Madonna is probably

a survival of something which was fairly widespread in Southern Europe in the late middle ages. The Feast of the Expectation came then to be observed a week before Christmas, and there are a good many statues and pictures of the fifteenth and early sixteenth centuries left to attest it. Maria Gravida, Notre Dame de l'Attente, la Madonna del Parto, la Virgen de la Esperanza, Maria von der guten Hoffnung, though not, as far as I know, Our Lady of Expectation, can be found in quite a few churches and museums. Often she had a Christ Child painted in sun's rays on the outside of her robes. She appears also in the form of Opening Virgins; toylike figures which open as a triptych to reveal a little Christ king, or God the Father holding the Crucifixion on his lap, or even half a dozen scenes from the gospels in high relief with a lot of Gothic architecture. She is related to the Black Virgin who can be found in the crypts of many churches; black for the rich earth, honored below ground level, fecundity, fate. The Black Virgin is none other than the old Earth Mother herself; her blackness has always been felt to indicate antiquity as much as fecundity. She is pregnant, with her child, or our fate, or her child which is our fate.

There even exist opening Lady Hamiltons; inside is the Death of Nelson; her womb is his destiny, and through his, ours in the nation he defended.

There are also plenty of madonnas sewing, spinning, weaving, or ornamented with ears of corn, all of which are taken to be symbols of pregnancy. But as usual it was the Italian Renaissance which brought the numen home to roost in the perfection which only normality confers. No mechanical toy, no abstruse symbol, no doubtful and dissident subterranean discoloration, but simply a young woman whose time is on her. In a little chapel at Monterchi in Tuscany all the threads of fate and joy are drawn together in Piero della Francesca's fresco of the Madonna del Parto, Our Lady of Parturition. Her gown is open over her great belly, its seams are already opened at the sides as well, her hand, the hand of work, wanders in

180 / *Eros Denied*

temporary dispossession to greet the muscles where work is called labor, and two of Piero's most lovely and non-committal angels have taken in hand the curtains of her royal tent either to open them in a gesture which answers her gaping clothing or to close them over the mystery which ends her waiting and begins our salvation; one cannot tell.

Piero's majestic picture stands outside the main run of Christian art, as does Bernini's St. Theresa in orgasm. What is remarkable is that we find these things remarkable; here the religion is acting to the full measure of its function, as the protector and sanctifier of all that is good, not simply of most things that are good. But it is going against its own historical nature when it does so.

Chapter 18

Courtly Love and Adultery

The poetry of twelfth-century Provence is certainly one of the hardest of all historical nuts to crack.[1] There it is, masses of it, extremely beautiful, wonderfully rich in form, full of innovations, diverse, charming, dense, much of it readily accessible to us in feeling, and yet in one respect profoundly obscure. It is a commonplace that the troubadours invented love as we think of it; that they invented the passion of love, all the panting and not-daring, the exaltation, the tension, the wildness, the faithfulness through years of refusal, the halo of the lover, the glamor, the overriding claim of passionate personal love on people's lives and thoughts. All this, it has been often pointed out, was unknown in the Greco-Roman culture. There, passionate love was a tragi-comic aberration; something one hoped would never happen in one's own family. There, a passionate lover was moonstruck, a lunatic; laughter and

---

[1] I am indebted in this and the next chapter to *L'Amour et l'Occident* by Denis de Rougemont, which has been translated as *Passion and Society*, London, 1956, and *Love in the Western World*, New York, 1956.

pity were indicated.[2] But in the Provençal culture, he was heard, honored and ennobled, and the more so the more hopeless his love appeared to be. These people invented the idea, still so much alive in common English speech today, of the *hopeless passion*.

The pre-Rougemont view of the troubadours was that they were "respectful aspirants, eager to clothe the caprice of their senses with mystical grace"; I take the phrase from the introduction to one of the standard collections of the troubadours.[3] Rougemont turned this conception on its head, and maintained that they were on the contrary eager to clothe mystical grace with the caprice of their senses. He argues that they were nothing less than full-blown heretical Cathars who wrote in code to evade the persecution of the Church, and that it was no accident this school of poetry died out at the time of the Albigensian Crusade, when undoubted Cathars were suppressed and massacred in the same part of the world. Other scholars hotly contest this interpretation; the whole phenomenon of Occitanian love poetry is fought over by the historians with a ferocity which is only understandable when one remembers that it combines two of the elements which always arouse the highest passions of scholars and recluses: sex and cryptography.

Hermetic it is. I cannot claim to know whether Rougemont is right in saying that the troubadours were actual subscribing Cathars, and that their poems describe the rites and customs. But I do claim that this poetry is not simply the language of love; it is the language of something else disguised as the language of love. So much must be

---

[2] Besides the common examples, see, for instance, *Anthia and Habrocomes* by Xenophon of Ephesus. In this Greek novel of the second or third century A.D., the lovers dare not confess their passion, and their parents cannot recognize the symptoms; it is something shamefully absurd and also quite unfamiliar. In the end the parents are enlightened, and marry the lovers to each other. The wedding night immediately restores their spirits, and Xenophon then comes to his point, which is pirates.

[3] *Florilèges des Troubadours*, André Berry, ed., Paris, 1930, p. x.

clear to anyone who has ever loved, spoken of love, and heard others speak of love.

Let us take some instances. Guillaume de Borneil is forever swearing secrecy not about what he and his lady (the feeling is better conveyed by the *langue d'oc* word *dompna,* Latin *domina*), not about what he and his dompna have done, or said, or sworn to one another, but about what she has told him. This is not a lover's thought, it is a conspirator's. Rigaut de Barbezieux, being continually refused by his dompna, as was usual, finally turned to another who offered him her love at once. After a time he recanted, and sought readmission to the service of his former dompna, but she would have none of him until a hundred knights and a hundred ladies knelt before her and pleaded for her forgiveness on his behalf. In the poem he wrote while he was waiting for this ceremony to be arranged, Rigaut says:

> A tot lo mon soi clamans
> De mi e de trop parlar[4]

Why on too much talking? The story suggests a temporary defection from a secret society or cult, later redeemed by the intercession of former associates, not an amorous infidelity.

Again: Jaufre Rudel passed the whole of his life yearning for a dompna he had never seen, a Princess of Tripoli. He finally managed to get to Tripoli, and immediately died in her arms. The same poet says he will die, not if he does not get a return of his love, but if he does not get a *counsel* of love. This seems to be the language of the neophyte seeking admission or initiation.

Then there is the recurrent personage of the watcher, the *gaita*. He was one who stood on the rooftop, watching for the dawn, so that he could sing out to the lovers, who are assumed to be in bed illegitimately, and they could escape

---

[4] May all the world have mercy
On me and on too much talking.

before the return of the jealous husband. Some of the love-
liest verses in the whole corpus are put into the mouth of
the *gaita,* descriptions of the beautiful but unwelcome
dawn. This is the language of secret nocturnal gatherings
with a lookout posted at the door, not of love. Lovers need
no warning of daylight, and, if they did, the poetic tradition would not have it sung out from the rooftops as by a
muezzin; it would have it whispered through the keyhole.
It is enough to compare this form of expression with the
copious imagery of the beautiful but unwelcome dawn in
undoubted love poetry, where it is seen and resented by the
poet-lover himself; Donne's "Busy old fool, unruly sun,"
for instance, or Romeo and Juliet.

Peire Vidal wrote several poems about the kiss he stole
from his dompna while she was asleep, which seems an odd
thing for a grown man to write about. But if, as De Rougemont maintains, he was using the kiss as a symbol of his
acceptance into a certain grade of initiation in the Cathar
cult, perhaps the Consolamentum, then it does make sense.
The kiss was held against him for some time, but later
allowed him as a gift, and this, which looks like petti-
fogging sentimentality as it stands, would also make sense
if he had somehow rushed his fences over the initiation,
had bluffed or blustered his way in before due time.

Again and again the cloyingness of the troubadours disappears in the solvent of this interpretation, and it is difficult to accept that such excellent poets can have been so
cloying. For instance, Guiraut Riquier's lovely refrain:

> Jorns, ben creyssetz a mon dan,
> El sers
> Aucim e sos loncx espers[5]

which is excessive and conceited if the poet was simply
waiting for his date, as he ostensibly was, is understandable
enough in Cathar terms if he was speaking of his impatience

---

[5] Day, you do grow at my expense
And evening
You do kill me with your long hopes

for initiation into spiritual delights, and even more so if the day was life, and the evening death, or preparation for death. The final grade of initiation in the Cathar hierarchy, the Consolamentum, made life so difficult in the way of abstinence and self-denial that a lot of them did in fact put it off until they were on their deathbeds.

Now there was a certain spiritual conformation to these people, and it does seem fair to assume that if not overtly and, as it were, officially affiliated to heretical Catharism they were at least heavily infiltrated by its feelings and beliefs. But the mind of man, and especially the mind of poets as good as these, is single. You can pick it up and look at it from every side and see a coherent whole; it is not a question of turning over the overt obverse and finding a secret, coded reverse to the medal. The penny-a-peep cast of mind is alien to excellence. It is not in the last resort necessary to decide whether these were spiritual Cathars who clothed their cult and their practices in the images of mortal love, or whether they were mortal lovers who made their flesh-and-blood affairs conform to a Catharistic pattern. Perhaps the best we can say at this distance is that they were both. They gave us verses, to which we are still in fee, expressing once and for all the thought that love and death go together, that to love from afar, without fucking and above all without babies, without more life, is better than to love close in, with all the muddle and day-to-day renewal of love in life.

Jaufre Rudel, the one who loved the Princess he had never seen, put this simply and lyrically, and Arnaud Daniel, the philosopher among the troubadours, put it in full. Jaufre Rudel's formulations were:

> Car nulhs autres joys tan nom play
> Com jauzimens d'amor de lonh.[6]

And:

---

[6] For no other joys please me so much
As the pleasure of love from afar.

> Pus totz jorns m'en falh aizina,
> Nom meravilh s'ieu m'aflam.[7]

To most of mankind it always was and always will be a wonder if the continual refusal of pleasure should set a man aflame. This is a flame that only death can quench, since if life quenched it such a man would quickly conceive another flame more likely to be immune from any but the last quencher. And such a man equips himself for death, not life.

Arnaud Daniel is another matter. It was he whom Petrarch regarded as his master and whom Dante described as *il miglior fabbro,* the best blacksmith (a description which T. S. Eliot has recently revived for a lesser vulcan), and he was indeed a batterer of words and ideas. His language gives scholars pause, and his notions hold up the uninstructed heart over and again by their paradox, their density, their re-entrant quality, their progress back to where we started, which invites the Oriental conclusion that truth is not manifold but one, and therefore *Om,* or, as the Greeks had it, *Ei.* He described himself thus:

> Ieu sui Arnautz qu'amas l'aura
> E chatz la lebre ab lo bou
> E nadi contra suberna.[8]

One can make what one likes of that, either chasing points of doctrine in disguise, or accepting it as expressionism *avant la lettre.*

Here now is his view of love.[9]

The bitter wind clears the branches
That the sweet wind had thickened with leaf,

---

[7] Since every day I lack this,
It is no wonder that I catch fire.

[8] I am Arnold who gathers the wind
And hunts the hare with the ox
And swims against the tide.

[9] Translation concocted with the help of the versions of U. A. Canello, *Arnaldo Daniello*, Halle, 1883; René Lavaud, *Les Poesies D'Arnaut Daniel*, Toulouse, 1910, and André Berry, ed., *Florilège des Troubadours*, Paris, 1930. The original is in Appendix 3.

And the cheerful beaks of woodland birds,
Paired and unpaired, are shut and dumb.
So I stir myself to do and speak pleasant things
To many, for the sake of her who brought me down from the
    heights;
Of which I fear to die, unless she kill my grief.

So clear was the light of my first choosing her
Who convinces the heart by way of the eye,
I needed secret messages as little as dogroses.
My prayers choose nowhere else to go;
All my ease is to hear her will,
And good and graceful words,
For whose service, from crown to foot, I am.

O love, beware—am I truly vanquished?
Even though you turn me away, I fear to make known
Those faults you'd best cut from yourself.
I am straight, brave, and not fickle,
Yet the strength of my heart makes me hide the truth,
That after so much denial I need a kiss
To cool the warmth of my heart; no other balm will do.

If she who enlightens me helps me,
If she who is the citadel of all worth
Accepts my serried inward prayers,
She'll grasp my clear outward thought:
I would be dead: I suffer hope through her,
Which I beseech her shorten; hope which holds
Me high and happy. All other pleasures fade.

The last two verses contain only procedural details.

It seems possible to approach such an extremely oblique
poem only by the oblique method of elimination. It is possible to say that among the things which are not absent
from it is the idea of love. Conspicuously absent, however,
is anything like the frame of mind of a man who has seen a
woman, who loves her, and who wants to live with her and
beget children with her. Arnaud's is a kind of love which
defines itself by its difference from philoprogenitive love;
Dante put him among the sodomites in Hell. (This was a
generic condemnation of infertility, not a specific assertion.)
One senses that if his dompna had borne Arnaud a child,

she would have deprived him of something far dearer than the child could ever be to him, namely the possibility of feeling and writing like this. To him, consummation would have been cancellation, fertility famine, and fidelity treachery. If, as Rougemont would maintain, he was addressing a concept of God in the form of a dompna, (*Meilhs de Dompna,* he called her; Better-than-Lady) we may pity the necessity to do so and admire the product of adversity. If he was addressing a real dompna in terms which suggest that he was disguising something else in her person, we can only stand aghast at the imperialism of the something else, which he allowed to appropriate his human faculty of love. In either case, it is not a love poem; it is an anti-love poem. It stands to love poetry, and Catharistic romantic yearning stands to love, as a cancer stands to the healthy tissue from which it diverts the blood supply and which it pushes aside and supplants. And who knows if we today in the West are not still part of a body politic whose cancer was first so beautifully and mysteriously expressed by the troubadours? As so often, Thomas Mann has drawn the map; in his novel *The Black Swan.*

Rougemont's hypothesis that courtly love as expressed by the troubadours was coded Catharism is difficult and at best uncertain; an integral part of his presentation of it is that the documents which could prove or disprove it have been destroyed by the Church. He makes an analogy with the difficulty a future historian would have in understanding the formation of men's minds today if the works of Freud and Jung had been burned and all he had to go on was our novels and plays and films.

But one certain thing about the troubadours, which it did not need a Rougemont to discover, was that their dompnas were not their wives, nor even the women they wished to marry. They were other men's wives. If the kiss, the welcome, the acceptance they so sighed for, to take it in its literal sense, had ever come to pass (which of course it did not), this would have been adultery. Since it was the whole point of the procedure that nothing human or physical was to come of it, they buttressed this negativity by choosing women who would be kept from them by the agency of other men, those women's husbands. They transshipped their reluctance to come to grips onto a class of strangers whom, in accordance with a normal law of behavior and feeling, they then despised for unwittingly shouldering the burden. The whole stucture of romantic adulterous love rests on that unwitting scapegoat, the husband, just as the structure of so many religions and cults rests on a scapegoat more or less conscious of his destiny.

Now the equation of passionate love with an adulterous situation is still very much with us, and is of course immensely fertile for literature and for general human understanding. In the time of the troubadours, it was still linked with the reluctance to consummate and bear children which, whether formally and overtly or subjectively and obscurely, is Catharistic. But the equation is not one which grows only in the soil of Catharistic attitudes and perceptions; it can and does also grow in what, without meaning any value judgment, one might call the soil of a normal temperament. In Montaigne, by no means a Cathar, it is strongly present. To him—and here he followed Aristotle —marriage was a friendly and solid thing, something chummy, and more akin to other relationships within a family than to the fires of love, which are to be kept outside marriage. The relationship between husband and wife should be more like the relaxed familiarity and solicitous care found between cousins, or at most between brother and sister. The fires of love within marriage, he thought, were something akin to incest, and in this context he remembered how St. Thomas Aquinas held that the main argument against incest was that if sexual love were to be added to the already strong affection between brother and sister, there would be no room left for God at all; which brings us back to our initial interpretation of the doubt and distaste in which Christianity must always hold fucking. In one of his most vivid, if not most exact, aphorisms, Montaigne said that marrying your mistress was like "shitting in your hat before you put it on your head." To him the jovial uproar of sensual fulfillment, which he valued very highly, was not to be had with the easiest and most obvious woman, namely, one's wife.

To take one other example, slightly earlier than Montaigne: *Della Bella Creanza delle Donne* or *Good Form for Women,* written about 1540 by Alessandro Piccolomini, coadjutor bishop of Patras, is in the main a treatise on clothes, cleanliness and manners, very much from a man's eye view. The Italian Renaissance bishop has this to say about the regulation of the love life. The young wife, as soon as she has settled down with her husband, should, after considering the field for a month, two months, eight months, a year, choose a lover, and thenceforth love him totally. She should also totally conceal her love, dissembling every moment of the day, since "secrecy is the nerve of love." There is advice on this in detail, right down to the necessity of avoiding *never* speaking of him, which would arouse suspicion; she must speak of him sometimes, in a natural way, and without emphasis or bashfulness.

The book, like so many on this topic at this time, is cast in the form of a dialogue between a young woman and an older one who advises her.

MARGARITA: You told me a moment ago, monna Rafaella, that her husband and her house should be the things a woman loves above all others in the world, and now it seems you would have the contrary; that her love for her lover must exceed everything else.

RAFAELLA: Yes I said that, so I did; I said she ought to conduct herself in such a way that everybody believes and gives it out that things are like that, but in her inmost heart her soul should go somewhere it is far better off, and what I tell you now is that as for husbands, it is enough to pretend to love them, and that's good enough for them.

And again:

MARGARITA: Do you mean to tell me that a gentlewoman should cheat on her own husband?

RAFAELLA: Cheat, indeed? Straight as a die! The cheating's what you do *with* your husband.

Rafaella goes on to explain that adultery is no shame if no one knows about it, and no wrong either; we find here an early version of the "worldly" morality which informs most of the novels and plays of adulterous intrigue from that day to this, whether or not an unfavorable judgment is later passed on it by the novelist or playwright.

This particular book, like most of the later ones, takes its rise from a society in which the arranged marriage was normal, and justifies the deceit by the prevailing unfreedom in the choice of a spouse. But what interests us here is the strong sense in those quotations that beyond and below the outward and socially perceived marriage there should be a secret and inner marriage with another partner, a marriage of passionate love, which depends for its merit and excitement on secrecy, on tortuous moral justifications, in a word, on difficulty. Only where there are obstacles can passionate love grow, because passion is the awareness and enjoyment of undergoing, and what is undergone is precisely the obstacles; what is suffered is the difficulty.

In an obscure form, and linked with a more or less conscious doctrine that continence is good in itself, passionate, suffering love first appeared and began to batter its head against the walls of obstruction and put its thumb in the thumbscrew in twelfth-century Europe. By the sixteenth century it was free of the alliance with Catharism, and took on the form it still has today. Montaigne complained that we hide in dark corners to do the thing that makes us, but he also took good care that we should do so when he insisted that love should not exist in marriage or, to put it another way, that what exists in marriage is not love, and is lower than what may exist outside.

The course of true love never did run smooth. Love is a hurdler. Love laughs at locksmiths (but it needs locks).

Love will find out a way (but it must be a rough and hilly one). Above all; secrecy is the nerve of love.

Everyone who subscribes to these sayings and whose life conforms to their pattern has somewhere in him chosen to do so. The obstacles are not given; we raise them. The lock is not there, our jimmy calls it up. It is not a fierce and unsympathetic father who forbids the match and forces an elopement, it is one who remembers the difficulties and the inevitable triumph of his own youth, who remembers how his passion flowered as it underwent the obstacles, and benignly wishes to reproduce the circumstances for his future son-in-law. Not a prince compelled to slay the dragon, or choose the right casket, or bring back the apple, or go through fire and flood, but chose and wished to do so; the elders who administered the bureaucracy of ordeal were stage-managed by the prince.

All this, from the troubadours through Piccolomini's treatise and *Romeo and Juliet* right down to Maupassant and this week's film at the local fleapit, is a form of diversionary activity. The one thing that love and fucking cannot be allowed to be is easy, simple and satisfying. We must divert it once again into a specially demarcated area of danger and difficulty, as did the religion which formed us, by seeking obstacles and, where we cannot find them, by erecting them. In preferring the dangerous and complicated adultery to the safe and simple marriage, in seeking ordeal, obstruction and secrecy, we re-enact in social terms the doubts and distaste which assailed the God-loving monotheist when first he conceived that only in fucking was he forced to betray God. A good way to get less of something is to go the long way round to get it.

Chapter 19

Scandal, Accident, Absence and Suicide

I will not reproduce here the argument in the first half of Rougemont's book,[1] that romantic passionate love is death-seeking; I could not do it with his rigor or his insight. In any case, what has been done has been done. The purpose of this chapter is more to discourse round and about the argument, and to adduce more examples of the diversionary activities called scandal, accident, absence, and finally suicide, for which the first three are only substitutes.

Let us start off with two very simple and almost vernacular confrontations of the romantic temper of love with what I would like to contrast as the eirenic temper: eirenic is a patristic word meaning "tending to peace" (O.E.D.). The romantic temper regards love between the sexes as the occasion for suffering, yearning, danger, intense passions and overwhelming but transitory gratifications which can only be spoken of in secret and with bated breath. Its ancestors are Mani, Augustine and Petrarch. The eirenic

---

[1] See note on p. 181.

temper regards it as a normal and steady delight, easy, fruitful, broad, pleasant and accessible. Its ancestors are nameless; contentment remains unsung. Perhaps Boccaccio. . . .

The first of the two confrontations is the full version of the ballad "Dabbling in the Dew," of which the first verse is so familiar.[2]

Where are you going, my fair pretty maid
With your red rosy cheeks and your nut-brown hair?

I'm going amilking, kind sir, she said;
A-rolling in the dew makes the milkmaids fair.

Shall I go with you, my fair pretty maid?
You're kindly welcome kind sir, she said.

Supposing I should lay you down, my pretty fair maid?
Oh then you must help me up again, kind sir, she said.

Supposing you should prove with child, my fair pretty maid?
Oh then I must find a father for it, kind sir, she said.

Supposing I should run away, my fair pretty maid?
Oh then I must run after you, kind sir, she said.

Supposing I should run too fast, my fair pretty maid?
Then the devil shall run after you, kind sir, she said.

What will you do for clothes then, my fair pretty maid?
Oh I can also weave and spin, kind sir, she said.

What will you do for a cradle then, my fair pretty maid?
My brother is a carpenter, kind sir, she said.

The poet is a romantic, the milkmaid an eirenic.

The other confrontation is from an Italian Renaissance comedy called *Florio*. The author was Antonio Vignale, a rather remarkable writer to whom we shall return later when we come to consider the Golden Age myth. It is a

---

[2] Conflating two versions given in *The Everlasting Circle*, James Reeves, ed., London and New York, 1960.

dialogue between a gentleman in love and his wise servant, who belongs to the Figaro tradition.

SERVANT: She is indeed beautiful; loving, gentle and gallant. But even if the whole world agreed she was one of the Thrones of the Seventh Circle of Paradise, and she didn't like me, I'd tell her what she could do with it.
MASTER: Oh, she likes me all right.
SERVANT: She shows it very little.
MASTER: What do you want her to do?
SERVANT: To make you happy, for God's sake.
MASTER: She can't.

That "she can't," or the equivalent "I can't" is the theme song of romanticism. It is a close relative—perhaps a derivative—of the "I mustn't" of Manicheism and orthodox Christianity.

It is unnecessary to present examples of romantic love from European literature; the literature is one big example, and the thing is our culture itself. You find it in the Greco-Roman culture, but in a skeletal form compared with the developments which came later, and only as one thread among many. Take Dido and Aeneas, the noble story in Virgil and the opera of Purcell; Purcell's last aria, the big chaconne "When I am gone," is not only the noblest piece of music ever to come out of England, it is an unsurpassed expression of the lament for unnecessarily lost love. Now why do we find the story noble, and why is Purcell's chaconne, in its setting, so moving? On the surface, the story is ridiculous. There was nothing in heaven or earth to stop Aeneas taking Dido with him when he went on to follow his destiny and found Rome. Neither was married, both were young, royal and eligible; a dynastic alliance with the old state of Carthage would have been an advantage to the new state in its formation. But no; off he goes for no reason, Dido for no reason climbs singing on to her suicidal pyre, and we are all left in tears. Why? Why not giggles?

Simply because there is no reason. There never is.

In the Dido and Aeneas legend, there isn't even a pretense at one, and that is why it moves us; because of its integrity, its refusal to compromise with likelihood. It moves us in the same way that it moves us to see a skeleton. Stripped of the lively and interesting flesh, the bare bones make us gasp and say: "So that's what makes us stand up." Stripped of all invention and incident and especially of all excuse, the story of Dido makes us gasp and say: "So that's what makes our feelings stand up." And mixed with our amazement there is, as there is with skeletons, pity and a touch of ridicule. St. Augustine liked Dido; Pelagius did not.

The flesh with which Manichean Christianity clothed these classical bones is not too complicated. The obstacles fall under only four headings: scandal, accident, absence and suicide. The reader will be able to recall plenty of instances of each kind; think of a love story and see which heading it comes under. *Anna Karenina* uses scandal as the obstacle. The "real-life romance" of Sir William Temple and Dorothy Osborne used first absence and then the accident of smallpox; but since this was real life, the accident turned out not to be an obstacle at all in the end. *Romeo* and *Juliet* combines scandal (the Montagus and Capulets) and accident (the sleeping draught). *Lolita* uses scandal too. (See Lionel Trilling's brilliant article, "The Last Lover," in *Encounter,* October, 1958.) *Werther* and a whole heap of romantic novels down to and beyond D'Annunzio's *Trionfo della Morte* use suicide. The use of suicide as an obstacle, which was the mainstay of the literature of love in the romantic age, is almost as simple as the Dido and Aeneas story; in fact it is the same. Dido committed suicide. If your characters are not going to marry and live (happily) ever after, there is a lot to be gained in simplicity of line and direct impact by cutting the cackle and having them shoot themselves as soon as they meet: death at first sight. Since passion flowers under adversity, let us give it the greatest adversity of all, and at least no one will be able to deny that it is flowering away with the greatest intensity of all in the hereafter, or perhaps in the minds of readers and theatergoers whose curiosity to know what happened next has not been so much disappointed as their belief that passion is ineffable has been flattered.

Scandal, absence and accident only stand in for the one true obstacle of the tradition. Dido and Werther are the heroes of romantic literature; the run of the mill characters are only half-hearted followers. All the romantic plots, all the sighs and the messages and the family obstruction and the declines and the horsewhips and the sales into slavery are there only to postpone death, to keep the story going. Take the blurb on the back of the nearest paperback: "Sweeping across three continents—a story of passionate love and. . . ." Of passionate love and what? We can finish the sentence in our sleep. ". . . a story of passionate love, revolution, plague and war—the novel you'll never forget."[3] Passion is scarlet; love means bloodshed. The commercial film industry is largely dedicated to the dissemination of the idea that kissing and biffing go together. If you can't biff the brother (it can't always be arranged by the scriptwriters) or the husband (that one's out, because it would be adultery, see) then you'd better biff the girl herself. All this is simply a stand-in for the basic equation: love equals death.

A recent article in an English weekly magazine for young girls will serve as an example of the same values didactically put.[4] It is called "To neck or not to neck."

"Can it be wrong when it seems so right?" ponders the girl. Her difficulty, of course, lies in sorting out what's "right" from what's "natural." The two words are not synonymous. [Mark how medieval theology appears in the first paragraph.] Yet, the ability to distinguish is not guaranted to still the pounding of a romantic pulse. [Pre-Rougemont sense.] The walk home after a first date can be like playing patty-cake

---

[3] Jacket from Bernard Dryer, *The Image Makers*, New York, 1958. As if it mattered.

[4] *Honey*, July, 1960.

with an octopus. Decisions, decisions, decisions! . . . I'm dying
to kiss him, but I don't want him to think I let *anybody* kiss
me on the first date. [Scandal.] Stop fretting! A nice girl does
not hand out a kiss—or kisses—on the first date, no matter
how much she likes the boy. If he's worth liking, he'll respect
you for it. [Give him an obstacle; he'll love it.] . . . Old-time
screen star Greta Garbo built a fabulous reputation because
she "wanted to be ah-lone." No-one knew too much about her.
She was mysterious . . . intriguing . . . special. [Like death.]
. . . Whoever heard of a good story without a little suspense?

Quicker than a penguin sliding down an icicle, that's how
quick a necking session can turn into a jam session. And
you're the one in the jam! [There is no mention of contraceptives in the article.]

The only real popularity earned by going too far or all the
way is the dubious distinction of being the top topic of a
male gossip session. Word will get around to your girl friends,
too. Nice, eh? [Scandal with knobs on. Boys don't read this
mag, anyhow.]

More likely he was just testing you. . . . If a boy really
likes you, a slap won't anger him. He will respect you for it.
. . . Familiarity breeds attempt. [Mark the assumption that a
boy's really liking you won't stop him doing something that
is going to make you slap his face.]

Remember, even steel can be melted if consistently exposed to
high temperatures. Keep in the shade where it's cool! END.

That END is a happy comment.

We construct obstacles for our pleasure when we see the
possibility of love, and I have been arguing that we do this
because of a late echo in ourselves of the Manichean doctrine, which is also strongly present in mainstream Christianity, that fucking is a bad thing. But may there not also
be another reason? Is it only God that we may betray
when we love? Is there any other pattern where the impulse to love is measured against the betrayal inherent in it?
There obviously is, and it is a pattern of far more universal
validity than the Manichean one. We may also betray our

wives or our husbands by seeking to repeat what we already have. Fewer people now believe that God himself as an independent being outside of ourselves will suffer for, or punish, our love for a fellow mortal, than that this is exactly what a flesh and blood spouse will do. It is the normal substance of our daily lives to do the sum: do I want her (or him) more than I mind hurting my wife (or husband)? For the heartwhole and unmarried, obstacle-racing is Manichean and that alone. But for the married, their own past is also an obstacle, and a concrete one.

It is possible to feel that one never makes love without betraying someone. Even the very first time, there is perhaps an obscure rupture of subterranean bonds with the parents. Few mothers can regard their daughters-in-law and few fathers their sons-in-law without a low swell of jealousy, at least unrecognized, at least at first. And the children know this. The secrecy of the first affair before marriage, the tears at the wedding service, are evidence. "My mother wouldn't understand" and "I could never tell my father" are as much forbearance as they are a statement of general lack of contact between the generations.

So much the more so later on. No marriage or liaison was ever broken up by unfeigned, equal and simultaneous consent of both people. Someone is always betrayed. As well as a jealous God we usually have a ditched mate or at least a mildly wounded parent breathing down our necks when first we make love with a new person, whether in circumstances of divorce, or in the far more common circumstances of before or outside marriage.

What is the actual form in which youngish people in our society put to themselves the reason for not going to bed with a new person when they want to? It comes in two parts: "Firstly it would be wrong, and secondly, Mary (or John) would be hurt by it." But these two parts are not of the same kind. The first is constant, is indelibly ingrained in us, and will remain true in our minds the next morning. The second is subject to our own feelings and decisions. We know that if we go forward with a new person and grow to love him (her), we shall care less and less whether John (or Mary) is hurt or not. We also know that in time John (or Mary) will stop being hurt in any case, and will find someone else. If we have children, we will balance in our minds the harm that would come to them from a broken home with the harm that would come from a patched-up or unreal continuing marriage. Then we decide what to do. Or alternatively, if we are "swept away by passion" we shall already have decided not to decide, in other words, to go ahead.

Equally, we shall also look at it the other way round and say "although it would be wrong to go ahead, it would hurt Jane (or Henry)—our potential lover—if we did *not*. It would also hurt us ourselves." The dilemma is presumably familiar to everyone over eighteen except priests. But it is manageable, it is within our own capability and decision, and we know that it will all be the same not a hundred years hence but probably two. Few people's lives are wrecked by changing husbands or wives or lovers; those whose lives are wrecked are romantics, Manichees; they are neo-Didos and wee Werthers. They have decided their lives are going to be wrecked, whether for vengeance on the mortal cheat or because they are in thrall to the Cathar pattern.

It is a manageable dilemma, but it leaves its mark on us; it over-scores the same traces as those left by Manichee-Christianity. There are two weights engraving that pattern; the general and permanent one of our culture and its origins in religious insight, and the personal and transient one of the human betrayals we act through in our individual lives.

So strong is this double-scored pattern that it will often glow with its own light without any outside reference at all; we shall see some examples of this in Chapter 21. But often it will glow with reference to a concrete cause which is manifestly, when you come to look at it, not there; to a flesh and blood cause which is erected into an obstacle as unreal, as capricious and voluntary, as the suicide of Dido or the horsewhips, accidents, and declines of the romantic tradition. To conceal adultery because of the hurt it would do to the spouse is a fairly common pattern of life, and when it becomes a dominant or repeating pattern, the flesh and blood spouse is being erected into a romantic obstacle. A good example of this pattern is in the novel *The Philanderer* by Stanley Kauffmann (1954). This book achieved notoriety as the object of an unsuccessful prosecution in the wave of Grundyism which overcame the British Director of Public Prosecutions in 1954, but it deserves fame for the light it throws on the process, the reverse of those we have been considering, where the *wife* is made into an obstacle to fruition in love, where marriage is inverted into the unreal and romantic obstacle to happy adultery.

The novel tells the story of an advertising executive in New York who likes to lay a good many girls, and lives in perpetual terror of his wife finding out. From apartment to apartment he goes, collecting the plaudits of different women for his prowess, and looking over his shoulder all the time for the gossip, the awkward chance meeting, the discovery. He fears this, he believes, because his marriage is the most important thing in his life. He is compelled to sleep around by some inner bug, arising perhaps from a childhood experience, and his compulsion makes him repeatedly risk all that is dearest to him. But it becomes increasingly clear as one reads on that "all that is dearest to him" is no more than a phrase. We never see his wife actually being dear to him, or his marriage actually being important. He merely assumes and insists that it is, thereby capriciously making it into an obstacle to happy promiscuity, almost using it as a condiment. The wife has no idea she is being used in this way, and since she is an unconscious, insentient element in her husband's life (as far as this pattern goes), she might just as well not be a person at all; she might just as well be a wedding ring, a morbid condition, or a moral absolute. In fact one inclines to the conclusion by the end of the book that she is precisely that —an embodiment of a moral injunction; she is no more than a justification for the statement "I know I shouldn't." We may justify this statement by reference to a jealous god, or to the traces he has left in us although we no longer accept his real existence, or again we may justify it by reference to a marriage which is important to us. But there is a temperament which will assess the importance of a marriage not so much by the pleasure and meaning to be found in it as by the convenience with which it may be adduced in support of a pattern of doubt and guilt which is none other than the Manichean refusal itself.

When Blake saw " 'Thou shalt not' writ over the door," he felt it had been put there by priests who were "binding with briars his hopes and desires." Many people in this century feel that it has been put there by their wives or husbands. *The Philanderer* is an instructive study of the masochistic temperament which must have a jailer. If the hero of the novel had told his wife he lived in perpetual terror of her discovering his infidelities, his marriage might have broken up, in which case he would have been free to philander without hindrance. Or it might have survived, in which case he would have been free to build a relationship based on knowledge and understanding, one in which he regarded his wife as a person, and not as an absolute or a wedding ring. But in either case he would have been free, and freedom was the one thing he could not accept.

There are countless other patterns in the great game of obstaculation, and countless ways of looking at each; you do not walk far into this field without bumping up against the perimeter wall of understanding. Where there's a man, there's a lover, and where there's a lover there's an obstacle. At least in the West. Dante, a Christian poet if ever there was one, folded the search for understanding back on its own starting point with the terrible line *Amor, ch'a nullo amato amar perdona.* "Love, who forgives no beloved for loving." The line is melodious, profound, unforgettable, and quite, quite untrue.

Chapter 20

Love's Loss Was Empire's Gain

Semen, being as we now know concentrated half-children, and having always been felt to be concentrated children or at least the concentrated catalyst necessary to the conception of children, is and always has been a powerful symbol. The more physical a culture is in its picture of the world, the more importance it accords to the body itself in its feeling of how things work, the more powerful will be the feelings attached to semen, and the more will rules and taboos about it come to the fore. Yogism, being physical through and through, a picture of the world seen from the body outward, has for centuries enjoined attention to the control of the physical substance which makes bodies; being a Manichee-like matter-hating system, it has also enjoined retention and caution. Yogis learn to copulate without orgasm; they have to be able to control the body so well that it will do the opposite of what it wants. The retention of semen in intercourse is parallel to the use of the urethra and the rectum to suck in water by reversing the normal peristaltic motion, and to the ability to vomit water from the stomach. The reversal of the natural direction of peristaltic movements is held to be a way of cleansing impurities from the body; the retention of semen is held to be a way of conserving vital strength.

The Manichean refusal of pleasure and love which lies near the heart of the Christian picture of the world, has clothed itself from time to time in different forms. The nineteenth century, being an age of physical preconceptions, the age when for the first time the concepts of energy and especially of stored or kinetic energy became familiar, clothed the Augustinian asceticism, the theological doubts and inhibitions of an earlier time, in a physical form. It was then that the possibility of regarding man as a machine became a normal part of people's minds, and in certain respects the new mechanical blueprint of man fitted very neatly over the former theological one. It was also a mercantile age, and this caused man to be felt to be something like a bank or a firm.

It is easy to see the analogy. The more energy you draw from a machine, the less there is left; you must not overload it. The more money you draw from a bank or a firm, the less there is left; it must not overspend. Therefore the more a man fucks, the weaker he gets.

In this chapter we come to some material which may surprise us in that such extraordinary things can have been believed so recently. When one says "the Victorian attitude to sex," what picture does it call up? Probably for most of us a picture of stern disapproval, expressed by the persecution of "deviants," ornamented by one or two piquant facts: they put frilly knickers on piano legs and separated books written by men and women on their shelves. But there is a great mass of published material, not yet subjected to historical reassessment, which contains fully developed scientific rationalizations of these attitudes. Of this, the work of William Acton is the clearest and the most vivid example that I have come across.

Action was a specialist in diseases of the urinary and genital systems who worked first in Paris and later in London. His book, *The Function and Disorders of the*

Reproductive Organs, went through six editions between 1857 and 1875. It was thus presumably an influential book; one learns from the book itself that Acton's opinion was much sought by educators and parsons, by general practitioners, and above all by ordinary people of the upper middle class in London whose sex lives were giving them trouble. As he reads the following quotations, the reader should bear in mind that this is what was believed by the best informed people in London less than a hundred years ago. It is probably what his own grandfather believed.[1]

In his opening pages, Acton sets the tone by pleading that working-class young men should be lectured in institutes on the merits of fatigue as a means of reducing desire, and that cultivated parents should not permit their children to read the classics. For desire and an inflamed imagination lead to one thing and one thing only, loss of semen whether in intercourse or not, and loss of semen is loss of vigor, health and ultimately sanity.

My own opinion is that taking hard-worked intellectual married men residing in London as the type, sexual congress had better not take place more frequently than once in seven or ten days; and when my opinion is asked by patients whose natural desires are strong, I advise those wishing to control their passions to indulge in intercourse twice on the same night. I have noticed that in many persons a single intercourse does not effectually empty the *vasa deferentia* and that within the next twenty-four hours strong sexual feelings again arise; whereas, if sexual intercourse is repeated on the same night, the patient is able to restrain his feelings so that ten days or a fortnight elapse without the recurrence of desire.

A few pages later he has misgivings about having recommended this gambit for getting rid of the horrible

---

[1] The quotations are taken some from the 1857 edition, some from the 1875 edition. In successive editions, Acton was forced to modify his claim that intellectual and artistic excellence was dependent on sexual abstinence, but with this one exception he is increasingly delighted to notice that his views are gaining ever wider acceptance.

thing once and for all, and qualifies it by writing: "This, however, is only a guide for strong, healthy men."

I maintain that in highly civilised communities the continuance of a high degree of bodily and mental vigour is inconsistent with more than a *very moderate* indulgence in sexual intercourse.

[Describing orgasm in men:] The nervous excitement is very intense while it lasts, and, were it less momentary than it is, more mischief would probably result from repeated acts than ordinarily happens.

A medical man called on me, saying he found himself suffering from spermatorrhoea. [Loss of semen between orgasms and without erection.] There was general debility, inaptitude for work, and disinclination for sexual intercourse; in fact, he thought he was losing his senses and the sight of one eye was affected. . . . I asked him at once if he had committed excesses. As a boy, he acknowledged having abused himself, but he married seven years previously to his visit to me, being then a hearty, healthy man, and it was only lately that he had been complaining. In answer to my further enquiry, he stated that since his marriage he has had connexion two or three times a week, and often more than once a night. This one fact, I was obliged to tell him, accounted for all his troubles. . . .

The ill-effects of marital excesses are not confined to the offending parties. No doubt can exist that many of the obscure cases of sickly children born of apparently healthy parents arise from this cause.

The whole book is based on the assumption that any loss of semen whatever is dangerous, but that the worst dangers can be avoided by indulging in intercourse very rarely. If you slip, you may find the thing has got out of control, and the system leaks, exactly like a worn-out machine or a carelessly run commercial enterprise. As a long-stop visitation behind all the other horrors, there lurks the threat of spermatorrhoea.

The first thing to do, then, is to see that children are brought up in such a way that they will not fall prone to this dread runaway reaction.

I tell them [parents] the best preventive step to be taken is to watch their children—if not actually to warn them against what it is hoped they are ignorant of: to develop all the muscular powers of their charges by strong gymnastic exercises; for, as anyone may observe, it is not the strong, athletic boy, fond of healthy exercise, who thus early shows marks of sexual desires—it is your puny exotic, whose intellectual education has been cared for at the expense of his physical development.

[And again:] Slight signs are sufficient to indicate when a boy, otherwise apparently healthy and fond of playing with other boys, has this unfortunate tendency. He shows undoubted preferences. He will single out some one particular girl, and evidently derive a more than boyish pleasure from her society. His *penchant* does not take the ordinary form of a boy's good nature. . . . His play with the girl is different from his play with his brothers. His kindness to her is too ardent. He follows her he knows not why. He fondles her with a tenderness painfully suggestive of a vague dawning of passion. No-one can find fault with him. He does nothing wrong. Parents and friends are delighted at his gentleness and politeness, and not a little amused by the signs of early flirtation. If they were wise they would rather feel profound anxiety; and he would be an unfaithful or incompetent medical adviser who did not . . . warn them that such a boy ought to be carefully watched, and removed from every influence calculated to foster his abnormal propensities.

But of course if loss of semen in intercourse is a danger, loss of semen any other way is even worse. The self-sufficient machine or reservoir of energy which is a man may be permitted to part with his vital substance now and then for the procreation of more men, but if he loses any for no return, then he is in the position of an idling machine or an investor so misguided as to spend his capital.

Wet dreams can be avoided by will power, and by eschewing soft mattresses and drinking after eight. The greatest watchfulness must be exercised over the thoughts and actions during the day. Broken sleep is good, and so is an enema of cold water or opium before retiring. Acton himself had tried passing an instrument up the rectum to press on the vesiculae, and thus mechanically inhibit the emissions, but he found that too much local irritation resulted. More successful was the cauterization of the urethra with silver nitrate, or the passing of a bougie[2] once or twice a week. Association with females should of course be shunned.

I need hardly add the obvious advice that he should above all things leave off any acquaintance he may have formed with immodest women. His reading should be of a nature calculated not to tax the strength, and strict injunctions should be given to abstain from the perusal of any work containing allusion to the subject of his complaint, or any work which would be likely to produce erotic ideas.

A page or two later, Acton warns against quacks who exaggerate the effects of nocturnal emissions, and prescribe over-energetic remedies.

If wet dreams are bad, masturbation is worse. He quotes with approval the following passage from *Les Pertes Séminales Involontaires* by Claude-François Lallemand (three volumes, 1836-42), which is perhaps the prime example of the great literature of masturbation-phobia:

However young the children may be, they become thin, pale and irritable, and their features assume a haggard appearance. We notice the sunken eye, the long, cadaverous-looking countenance, the downcast look which seems to arise from a consciousness in the boy that his habits are suspected, and, at a later period, from the ascertained fact that his virility is lost. [Mark the assimilation of virility to virginity, as something which can be lost once and for all.] . . . Habitual masturbators have a dank, moist, cold hand, very characteristic of vital exhaustion; their sleep is short, and most complete marasmus comes on; [wasting of the body: S.O.E.D.] they may gradually waste away if the evil passion is not got the better of, nervous exhaustion sets in, such as spasmodic contraction, or partial or entire convulsive movements, together with epilepsy, eclampsy, and a species of paralysis accompanied with contraction of the limbs.

---

[2] From the French for candle. A sort of rod instrument for opening it up.

A jerk, after all, is simply a habitual masturbator.

Acton himself is quite methodical about this; he divides the effects of masturbation into three chapters headed: "Insanity arising from Masturbation," "Phthisis arising from Masturbation," and "Affectations of the heart arising from Masturbation." The first chapter contains actual observations, obtained in lunatic asylums, of the course of the generally recognized clinical entity of masturbation insanity. The treatment in all three categories of complaint consists primarily of stopping the habit.

The ordinary remedies for phthisis are of no avail unless we at once check the cause of the complaint, namely, *sexual excesses.*

The remedies are as mechanical as the conception of man and his functions which underlies the whole book.

If the practice of masturbation be ascertained to exist, steps must be taken to check it. In young infants the habit may be corrected by the ordinary mode of muffling the hands, or applying a sort of strait-waistcoat.

Among what may be called the prophylactic remedies for self-abuse, the *sponge-bath* stands pre-eminent. . . . the bather should sit down in the centre of the bath, with his feet on the floor, and then, having drawn back the foreskin, for one or two minutes briskly squeeze the [cold] water over his back, chest and abdomen and thighs, taking care to lead as much as possible towards the genitals.

Nor is the "ordinary" practice of sleeping with the hands tied behind the back to be disdained by grown men.

The book is informed by a gruff solicitude for the troubles of men, and has nothing whatever to say about the corresponding troubles of women. Even in the sections on anatomy and pathology women only get a cursory glance after the interesting business is over. The contrast between the careful directions for the examination and treatment of the sexual organs of men, full of hints how to avoid pain and useful turns of phrase for jollying them along when you can't avoid it, and the impatient distaste which appears in the corresponding passages on the examination of women, is quite striking. About men, Acton writes like a bluffly affectionate elder brother, warning, exhorting, even from time to time forgiving. About women he writes like a vet. There is a fairly full description of orgasm in men, but none of orgasm in women: because he didn't believe it happened. He does not even argue that those who believe such a thing does happen are wrong, he never even mentions the possibility. He is concerned from time to time about the lesser question whether women are capable of sexual feeling at all, and concludes that on the whole this is only "a vile aspersion."

In a state of nature, wild female animals will not allow the approach of the male except when in a state of rut, and this occurs at long intervals, and only at certain seasons of the year. The human female probably would not differ much in this respect from the wild animal, had she not been civilised, for as I shall have occasion again and again to remark, she would not for her own gratification allow sexual congress except at certain periods. . . . Love for her husband and a wish to gratify his passion, and in some women the knowledge that they would be deserted for courtezans if they did not waive their own inclinations, may induce the indifferent, the passionless to admit the embrace of their husbands.

I should say that the majority of women (happily for society) are not very much troubled with sexual feeling of any kind.

I am ready to maintain that there are many females who never feel any sexual excitement whatever. Others, again, immediately after each period, do become, to a limited degree, capable of experiencing it; but this capacity is often temporary, and may entirely cease till the next menstrual period.

As a general rule, a modest woman seldom requires any sexual gratification for herself. She submits to her husband's embraces, but principally to gratify him: and were it not for the desire of maternity, would far rather be relieved from his attentions. No nervous or feeble young man need, therefore, be deterred from marriage by any exaggerated notion of the arduous duties required from him. Let him be well assured on my authority, backed by the judgment of many, that the married woman has no desire to be placed on the footing of a mistress.

She assured me that she felt no sexual passions whatever. . . . Her passion for her husband was of a Platonic kind, and far from wishing to stimulate his frigid feelings, she doubted whether it would be right or not. She loved him as he was, and would not desire him to be otherwise except for the hope of having a family. I believe this lady is the perfect ideal of an English wife and mother.

[Moreover:] Women give many more gonorrhoeas than they receive. In fact they originate the disease.

However grotesque they may seem to us now, Acton's beliefs are important for an understanding of Victorian England, and thus for an understanding of the motives of empire and of mercantile values. Acton wrote during the revolution in the English educational system with which we connect the name of Thomas Arnold. His book is full of quotations from the advice he gave to public school masters. The Arnoldian public school was only partly an institution for the instruction of Christians and gentlemen, it was also an institution for the formation of mechanistic Manichees. In an atmosphere of spying, flogging, repression and fear, which seems to us probably crazier than anything since the witch-hunts of the sixteenth and seventeenth centuries, generations of men were educated in a carefully maintained ignorance of the fact that fucking is pleasure, and pleasure for both parties, is the nodal point of the family (an institution which was praised in all other respects), and is free from disastrous consequences.

If every value and every force surrounding an adolescent tells him that his bodily affections must at all costs be transformed and sublimated into physical effort, intellectual prowess, competitive zeal, and manly friendship, how can he not found empires? If virility is held to be something which is lost, not acquired, in concourse with women, what is left for him to do but organize the whole world? The

medieval Manichees and the troubadours had no steamships
and no telegraphs; they stayed put. The retentive machine-
men of the nineteenth-century English bourgeoisie had
these things, and therefore turned up in Rangoon and
Nairobi, bombarding surprised Buddhists and animists with
distorted energy. One of the nostalgic phrases about the
British Empire is: "Never has the world had so boyish a
master." It is true. The nineteenth-century British Empire
was not acquired in a fit of absence of mind, it was acquired
in a fit of absence of women. When Mem Sahib turned up,
she destroyed it.

Acton's quotation from Lallemand is not really a description of the results of masturbation; it is a description of hell.
It bears comparison with a passage in the prototype of all
British public school stories, Dean Farrar's *Eric, or Little
by Little*, the epic of an inferior public school in the Isle
of Man at which Farrar was a pupil in the 1840's.[3]

"Oh young boys, if your eyes ever read these pages, pause
and beware. The knowledge of evil is ruin, and the continuance in it is hell. That little matter—that beginning of evil,—
it will be like the snowflake detached by the breath of air
from the mountain-top, which, as it rushes down, gains size,
and strength and impetus, till it has swollen to the mighty and
irresistible avalanche that overwhelms garden, and field, and
village, in a chaos of undistinguishable death.

Kibroth-Hattaavah! Many and many a young Englishman
has perished there! Many and many a happy English boy, the
jewel of his mother's heart,—brave, and beautiful, and strong,
—lies buried there. Very pale their shadows rise before us—
the shadows of our young brothers who have sinned and suffered. From the sea and the sod, from foreign graves and
English churchyards, they start up and throng around us in
the paleness of their fall. May every schoolboy who reads this
page be warned by the waving of their wasted hands, from
that burning marle of passion, where they found nothing but
shame and ruin, polluted affections, and an early grave.

---

[3] First edition, 1858, p. 101. There were thirty-six editions in
Farrar's lifetime.

In the superb tub-thumping of this passage Farrar was really describing the effects of what Acton would have called "sexual excess" and in particular of masturbation, the big bugbear. But the convention of the time would not allow mention of such things, so he makes the passage follow on a description of how Eric failed to stop his ears while lewd stories were being told in the dormitory, stories in which, as Farrar put it, "the vile element" had a place.

The masturbation phobia of the Victorians and of certain earlier religious writers is interpreted by Freudians as a form of castration phobia, and it seems to me that this particular *reductio ad castrationem* is not absurd. One may think of the theme song of Victorian nannies: "If you play with it, it'll fall off." I have even seen an Italian book called *Il Problema Tonsillare è Problema Nazionale e di Razza* [The Tonsillary Problem is a National and Racial Problem] (Milan, 1940), which solemnly argues for some hundreds of pages that people who have had their tonsils out sweat easily, are enfeebled in reason and emotion, cannot work properly, etc. It all seems perfectly crazy until you equate tonsillectomy with castration throughout, and thus with the old beliefs about masturbation.

It would be a mistake to think that Acton's and Farrar's values have disappeared from the educational scene, at least in England. For example, I went to an English public school from 1937 to 1941. We laughed at Farrar (we did not know Acton) but we had nothing to put in his place. I left that school at the age of seventeen without having encountered a single sentence, a single image, a single breath of a notion in all that swift and efficient educational machine which could have informed me that girls like fucking too, or that any form of sexual activity whatever was anything but a stupid and regrettable loss of some precious capital of physical energy and moral integrity with which I was brought into the world by presumably insensible parents.

The temper of Britain today is largely explicable only in terms of the quest for something else to do with the derailed sexual instinct which our best educated men of a certain age can no longer apply to the self-imposed tasks of empire. That is on the civilian side. The military and imperial strands of British life are still breathing the air of William Acton. It was recently reported in the press that a soldier who had fainted while the Queen Mother was inspecting his unit had been *held upright* until she had passed. Why was a man's fainting such a disgrace? In June, 1958 the *Daily Express* carried this news item: "The Coldstream Guards are taking strict precautions to stop men fainting at the Trooping of the Colour. . . . Men below the rank of sergeant are to be confined to barracks, and married men condemned to bachelor barrack beds on the night before big parades."

Chapter 21

The Cheshire Scowl

In Alice Through the Looking Glass there is that smiling Cheshire Cat on the branch of a tree which keeps disappearing from the tail forward till at last there is nothing left but the smile. In most of us today, systematic beliefs about sin and damnation have long since disappeared, and all that is left is a negative feeling of doubt and guilt. Manichean Christianity was a scowling Cheshire cat, and all that is left is the scowl.

A startlingly clear example of the Cheshire Scowl, the very essence of the phenomenon as it were under laboratory conditions, is to be found at the end of a novel called *Das Schiff,* translated as *The Crossing,*[1] by the German poet Hans Egon Holthusen. The characters have had an affair on an Atlantic crossing and are talking about it.

"Women aren't prudish, you know, they don't want to be treated like injured innocents, they like being guilty . . ."

"How do you know that?" I turn my head towards her in astonishment. "You can't actually know that yet!"

---

[1] London, 1959.

Her face jerks up. "But I do know it!" she retorts in a child-ish fit of temper, pounding the arm of her chair with her open hand. It is this refractory loveableness of hers which snatches at me and completely overwhelms me. "And I know too," she continues, "that I was to blame for everything that happened—as well as for everything that hasn't." She turns away, leaving me sitting there with a racking emotional pain somewhere in the region of the heart.

"My God, Mercy!" I exclaim involuntarily. "You're too sweet for words! If I only could do what I want to in these next few minutes!"

She doesn't answer, and I make one last attempt to fortify my tottering sense of guilt. "So we're both to blame then. But the question remains, what for, and in the sight of whom? Not in our own, if I understood you rightly, but . . . condemned by some court of love which exists on a different plane. By the whole, I should say, the meaning and law of the whole. We've fallen short, somehow, of the totality of love. The word love must after all have a general meaning, and wherever a pair of lovers comes into being it places itself under a certain law and must abide by it. Or don't you agree?"

She jumps to her feet. Her eyes are turned westwards out to sea, in the direction of the sinking sun. I can't see her face now. There is such an air of remoteness about her that the words stick in my throat. She coughs twice and without turning round, says, "Darling, could you fetch me another cup of tea?"

The hero does not really believe in the idealistic court of love stored up in heaven; he is only casting about in his mind for something to put behind the Cheshire scowl, and seizes without much hope on the irrelevant outlines of the German idealist tradition. The one thing he cannot do is admit that perhaps their affair has been entirely guiltless. "So we're both to blame, then. But the question remains, what for, and in the sight of whom?"

There are many other halfhearted cat-bodies with which we still try to bolster up that scowl, barely rationalized notions sketched in to conceal from ourselves the fact that if there is no cat, there cannot be a scowl.

One such notion is a naive faith in science, which is also a way of demarcating the area of sexual love as special and dangerous. The first books on sexual behavior to appear publicly after the Victorian interregnum were heavily scientific in form. Krafft-Ebing's *Psychopathia Sexualis,* Havelock Ellis' large series *Studies in the Psychology of Sex,* even Freud himself, right down to and including the much more accessible works of Kinsey; all these assume that in a lessening degree Latin and Greek terminology, and in an increasing degree statistical tables, are necessary to contain a subject matter which might otherwise jump out and destroy us. Through no fault of its own, this tradition has encouraged the feeling that though it would be rash for untrained people to observe the cat on the branch, a biologist or zoologist, skilled in saving his life if necessary, may do so, with due caution. The scientist is right to feel that his special skills can be useful in this field, but the rest of us are wrong if we feel that they uniquely qualify him to enter it.

Then there is the school of thought which placatingly describes the scowl as "mysterious and beautiful." Many of the booklets written at present to teach children how they were made, and much of the teaching in schools too, rely heavily on this approach. The reproductive organs and their function are said to be far more mysterious and beautiful than, for instance, the respiratory or digestive organs and their functions. They are *said* to be, but one may doubt if many of the writers of these booklets really believe it. If we were to challenge them to enumerate the mysteries in orgasm, fertilization, pregnancy and birth, they would probably not find them any deeper or more numerous than those of digestion, circulation, the chemistry of cell nutrition, or the physics of cell reproduction. If we were to ask them why they felt pricks and cunts were more beautiful than mouths and eyes, they would probably be quite startled. The phrase is there to set children on their guard against something dangerous and special, to let them know that they are being taught something quite extraordinary. They must approach it with the very greatest care, holding out a lump of sugar, a ritual formula of protection.

Another talisman to get safely past the scowl (and often into the domain of pornography) is the word "art." This is more transparently ridiculous, and is not favored by the better educated. Here are two examples. From a booksellers' advertisement of 1888:

The beautiful frontispiece, a facsimile of that charming statuette, the "Venus Callipyge," with the unabridged descriptive letterpress from the inimitable "Secret Museum of Naples," must prove a source of admiration to all "Art" students; indeed no effort seems to have been spared . . . *etc., etc.*

And here is the photographer's foreword to an English periodical of today containing photographs of naked girls.

It has always been my contention that the many thousands of readers who take a keen interest in figure photography, would sooner or later, grow weary of some of the "trash" served up to them under the guise of "art studies" (French pronunciation of course). Under flowery titles, numerous booklets have found their way to the bookstalls, and regretfully have done much to discredit the high professional standard of figure photography established by such photographers as Roye and John Everard in the 1940's. Happily, those craftsmen are still producing quality work, and in recent years a small handful of other specialists, and I hope I may include myself amongst them, have entered the field. We few together with such photographers as Andre de Dienes of America, and Serge de Sazo of France have done much to lift the art of figure photography back to its rightful place, and although we all work individually, I feel that we, in reality, work as a group in the fact that we take pride in our particular metier, which is a most exact and difficult branch of the photographic profession.

There are countless other tricks of varying degrees of absurdity. There is for instance the custom, enforced I believe by the police, of erasing the maidenhair from photographs of women in nudist publications. Nudism is an ascetic cult; the pleasure is Manicheism with knobs on. Let

s all get together naked and enjoy the frustration; it is like
he early Christian custom of testing one's chastity by going
o bed naked with a naked person of the opposite sex and
doing nothing, the custom which Gibbon described so
sardonically. Even in a crowded country like England
here is no difficulty in finding secluded beaches and woods
where one can take all one's clothes off, if that is the sole
purpose.

But the photographs of this harmless and to many people
pleasant cult must be "touched up" in order to get past
the Cheshire scowl. The practice says to the scowl: "This
seems to be a photograph of a naked woman, I agree. But
it does not fall within your competence because, as you
see, I have depilated her. Therefore she can arouse no
passions which would be offensive to you; she is not, as you
can see for yourself, *really* a woman at all." If the scowl
still had a cat-body behind it, such a quibble would not
hold water.

Then there are the irrational phobias of those who
accept the scowl at its face value, as something which must
be complied with, something which strikes terror into the
heart of and by itself. Schoolboys tell a story about the
young lovers who got locked together and had to be taken
to the hospital, he clamped within her on a stretcher, and
separated by medical intervention. You can hear timid
young men, the product of scowl-education, telling each
other in terrified voices how it is quite likely that the exer-
tion of fucking will prove fatal on the spot. Some Anglo-
Saxon men are kept continent by the fear of blackmail, the
fear that the girl may faint with pleasure and then what
will they do, by the fear that the ceiling may fall in on them
as it did on Attis, by almost anything.

Much of the fear with which the possible real results of
fucking are regarded, the fear of venereal disease and un-
wanted pregnancy for instance, is no more than the effect
of the Cheshire scowl. Indeed the most unpleasant thing
about it is the way it lumps together pregnancy and disease
as two similar things which may happen if you go against

it. Those who are well and truly in thrall to the scowl are equally appalled to find that new human life has resulted, and that disease and pain have resulted; both seem a retribution.

We are at the terminal moraine of Manicheism. The glacier itself has melted in the country and class out of which I am writing this. We are a hundred times more likely to look with admiration toward France and Italy and Sweden, where we think they make love easily and without fuss, and toward Africa, the Caribbean and Japan, where we think they make a positive glory of it, than toward our own past and its fears and inhibitions, its fear of God and its even more potent fear of closing the reason to God's access. And yet the scowl is still there on the branch above us, and the moraine is still steep to our feet.

Here is a poem by Kingsley Amis which is one of the best expressions yet to come out of our time of the scowl without cat-body, the moraine without glacier, the prohibition without a cause. (There is also a pretty electrifying description of the same thing, death while waiting for girl, in his novel *Take a Girl Like You*.)[2]

Nothing to Fear

All fixed: early arrival at the flat
Lent by a friend, whose note says *Lucky sod*:
Drinks on the tray; the cover-story pat
And quite uncheckable; her husband off

Somewhere with all the kids till six o'clock
(Which ought to be quite long enough):
And all worth while: face really beautiful,
Good legs and hips, and as for breasts—my God.
What about guilt, compunction and such stuff?
I've had my fill of all that cock;
It'll wear off, as usual.

Yes, all fixed. Then why this slight trembling,
Dry mouth, quick pulse-rate, sweaty hands,

---

[2] London and New York, 1960, p. 273.

As though she were the first? No, not impatience,
Nor fear of failure, thank you, Jack.
Beauty, they tell me, is a dangerous thing,
Whose touch will burn, but I'm asbestos, see?
All worth while—it's a dead coincidence

That sitting here, a bag of glands
Tuned up to concert pitch, I seem to sense
A different style of caller at my back,
As cold as ice, but just as set on me.

This poem is a true statement of where we stand. But it is an Oedipean self-blinding operation in the sight of history. It is not a "dead coincidence": ask William Acton, ask Arnaud Daniel, ask St. Augustine, and behind them all, ask St. John the Evangelist: "We love because He first loved us."

Chapter 22

Libertinism: The Religious Phase

I described above the close debt of orthodox Augustinian Christianity to the Manicheism it so horribly suppressed, and its distant indifference to the gentle Pelagianism which died out without a shot fired. We come now to another strain in the history of feeling about sex in Christendom, one which it is even harder to interpret than heretical Manicheism or Pelagianism, and this is the strain which one may conveniently call libertinism. It is harder to interpret because the records have been burned with, if possible, even greater thoroughness than those of the other heresies; because the tradition lacked a teacher of anything like the stature of Pelagius or Mani; and because there is thus little continuity between one "outbreak" and the next.

In this and the next two chapters I shall consider three related structures of feeling which belong to this tradition: libertinism, sadism, and what I call sexual stakhanovism. By libertinism I mean the way of life which valued promiscuous sexuality as a form of self-expression and as a revolt against orthodox Christianity. I distinguish two periods in the history of libertinism in Europe. The first ran from the early Christian era to its fullest development in the seventeenth century; it was not a revolt against Christianity itself, but against the asceticism in Christianity. It was in general based on a rival conception of the Christian God to that held by the Churches, and so qualified as a heresy. The second ran from about 1700 to the French Revolution; it was in revolt against Chirstianity itself, and had affinities with the systematic atheism of the Illumination. It was not a heresy, but an outright rejection of Christianity and Christian ethics. The earlier phase of libertinism had a theological background of some interest; the later was the fruit of a period of class tension, and had rules and regulations of the utmost complexity, like a highbrow game. True libertinism has been extinct now for a century and a half.

By sadism I mean the doctrine of the Marquis de Sade, which was formulated as an extreme variant of libertinism toward the end of its second period. As a revolutionary antithesis, it was in total and nihilistic revolt agaitn religion, religious ethics, and the whole structure of society at that time and, implicitly, at any other time. As a primary phenomenon it is a type of temperament which existed unsystematized before Sade, and exists today, and presumably will exist as long as society permits the free play of those elements in the formation of children which give rise to it in the individual temperament, and that will probably be always.

By sexual stakhanovism I mean promiscuity for its own sake. Stakhanovism, which is a common pattern now in Europe and America and for all I know elsewhere, is not in revolt against anything much. The dynamic forces of theological and class struggle, which moved its predecessor libertinism, are defunct, and stakhanovism is the freewheeling effect. Stakhanovism corresponds to those patterns on the other side of the fence which I labeled the Cheshire Scowl: it is the Cheshire Leer.

One might sum up the feeling structures which we discussed in the preceding chapters as "anti-fucking." Libertinism, sadism and stakhanovism are not therefore "pro-fucking" so much as "anti-anti-fucking."

Probably the first teacher of Christian libertinism whom we shall ever hear of was a second-century Alexandrian called Carpocrates. Theologians describe his followers and certain similar sects of that time and later as Licentious Gnostics. The phrase brings us straight to the heart of the riddle. Carpocrates and presumably his son Epiphanes, who wrote a book advocating outright sexual communism, and their sect, were not in recation against the dualism and Manicheism which was all around them in the early Christian communities. They did not say: "Fie upon you for being against matter; we say that matter is especially good, and we will therefore have lots of it and glory in our senses." On the contrary, they were themselves dualists. They held matter was not only bad but *so* bad that the best thing to do was to raise oneself miles above it by perfection and initiation, and then one could do what one liked with it. One should even demonstrate one's superiority to matter and thus one's closeness to God by what in a more material man would have been sin. We shall never know, but it seems likely that the first doctrinally licensed promiscuity to appear in Christendom was by no means under the stars of fertility, community and joy in matter, but under those of sterility, pride, and contempt for matter.

The wheel of temperament runs full circle. Though the rites of the Carpocratians might have been indistinguishable from those of the pagans before them, yet their motives would have been closer to those of the Manicheans with their cult of chastity. And yet again, what does this mean? To have an orgy because matter is especially good and needs helping on is perhaps not so different from having an orgy because matter is especially bad and needs to be reminded of it. The articulation of paganism and Christianity is an obscure page in history.

Orgies in a religious context, cannibalism, black mass, blood-drinking, scatophagy; the medieval and later inquisitors handed out the charges with only moderate discrimination between one group of heretics and the next. It is hopeless to try to sort it all out, but reading the attempts which have been made[1] one does seem to catch sight of four related motives for religious libertinism. They are (1) the hatred of matter which belongs to the dualist tradition, (2) the opposite feeling: a positive good residing in the act of fucking at certain times, which is a survival of pagan religions, (3) a wish to do that which will annoy a priesthood found oppressive and sanctimonious, and (4) a dedication to a God opposite to that of the priests, namely Satan, who is partly the anti-God of Christianity and partly the sole survivor of Olympus and Valhalla. But what the relations are between Satanism, witchcraft, Mediterranean and Nordic polytheism, Manichean dualism, and Carpocratian religious libertinism—this remains to be worked out.

At the time of the Reformation, among, for instance, the Anabaptists of Münster and among Low German and Flemish sectaries who were called Pifles (corruption of Publican, in turn corrupted from Paulician—see Chapter 17 above) the dominating motive of religious libertinism seems to have been the third; it was an expression of defiance by the individual conscience, and as such it was related to the impulses which gave rise to the Reformation itself and, in the Anglo-Saxon world, to the reformation within a reformation which was Dissent. But nothing is less promiscuous than a Congregationalist, and it would be a good study to inquire why these, who went farthest in throwing the priesthood overboard, went no distance at all in throwing chastity over and adopting promiscuity or libertinism. Many times between the fourteenth and the eighteenth centuries Christians got together to throw out the

[1] E.g., Norman Cohn, *The Pursuit of the Millennium,* London and New York, 1957.

priests and establish direct contact between the individual soul and God. When the contact was established, some heard God say: "Now you may lay whom you please." Others heard him continue to say what he said through the mouths of the priests: "Fucking is always a danger and usually an abomination." It is the latter sects which have survived: though libertinism may be human, it cannot be Christian in the long run.

The "spiritual libertines" in medieval and Renaissance Europe held that salvation was general and impersonal and did not depend on the correct ordering of action or thought, still less on confession and penitence. Grace abounded in all circumstances, and was too strong to be impeded by sin. Heaven and hell were in this world, and the after-life was often rejected. Heaven was knowledge of one's own divinity, hell ignorance of it. Among the recurrent formulations of the tradition were: "Every rational creature is in its nature blessed," "We have no longer any need of God," and "We ride the Holy Trinity like a saddle." There is much here in common with the European pantheist tradition, and even more, perhaps, with Buddhism. "We have no longer any need of God" makes exactly the same point as one of the principal funny stories of Zen Buddhism. A young master went to visit an old master at his hideout in the hills. As they were sitting on the older master's favorite seat, a lion roared in the distance. The younger master jumped, and the older one said: "I see it is still with you," meaning: "I see the passions are still with you, and in particular the passion of fear." After lunch the older man went to rest and while he was away the younger wrote the character for Buddha on the seat. When the elder returned he was about to sit down, but noticed the holy name, and hesitated. "I see it is still with you," said the younger. To this temperament the fear of god and the love of god, in a word the awe of God, is a mortal passion which must be sloughed off before understanding can be reached.

It is not fertile or interesting to say that the "spiritual

ibertines" were Buddhists without knowing it. But it may be fertile and interesting to think that some of them were of a temperament which was crushed in Europe as a deviant minority but which was in the ascendant in Eastern Asia, and devised the religious system which has made the people of Eastern Asia what they are.

Since the spiritual libertines believed in a grace far more abounding than did the orthodox, they were free to give rein to such thoughts and actions as their individual natures suggested, without the fear of thereby impeding its action. Whatever was, was holy. Thus some stole, some brawled, many swore—a thing which it is harder for us to realize may have been a great release—and, which is what interests us here, many fucked regardless. The *Homines Intelligentiae,* a Low Country sect of the early sixteenth century, called fucking "the acclivity," or the upward slope, which was a technical term of the mystical tradition meaning the ascent to God. The Blood Friends, a German sect of about 1550, elevated it into a sacrament, the sacrament of *Christerie.* They reverted to the practice, condemned by St. Paul, of taking the love feast of the holy communion one farther; if love between mortals is an emblem of divine love, they felt, why stop short at eating and drinking together?

One of the last of the sects of spiritual libertines, and the one which it will be most convenient for us to dwell on, since it arose in England and its adherents wrote in English, was the sect of Ranters, who flourished and were suppressed during the Commonwealth. They were in many respects like the Quakers and the Diggers; pristine communists, total egalitarians, revolutionaries to the point of nihilism. The Diggers went too far in the economic sphere, the Ranters went too far in the sexual sphere; only the Quakers trimmed their sails to remain in existence as the lightship of peace they now are, the one good and durable fruit of that time of collapse.

The Ranters belonged to the tradition of unlimited grace. One of them dated a letter: "From Heaven and Hell, or from Deptford in the first year of my reconciliation to myself." Men and women called each other "fellow-creature." All were equal, and all saved and blessed. It was necessary only to be reconciled to oneself to be reconciled with God, whose creatures we all are without distinction between saved and damned, between good and bad. They themselves used the word *libertinism* as synonymous with revolution or general overturning; what they overturned were the two pillars of St. Augustine's thought: election and chastity.

The Ranters are usually represented in the history books, when at all, by the pamphleteer Abiezer Coppe. But he was a confused and cacophonous prophet compared with another writer, Laurence Clarkson. The following are quotations from Clarkson's pamphlet, *The Single Eye* (1650), of which a few copies have survived contemporary burners. I make no apology for the length of these extracts; stakhanovites of today should know their origin.

As I have said, so I say again, that those acts, or what act soever, so far as by thee is esteemed or imagined to be sinful, is not in God, not from God; yet still, as I said, all acts that be are from God, yea, as pure as God.

I pleaded the words of Paul, "That I know, and am persuaded by the Lord Jesus, that there was nothing unclean, but as man esteemed it," unfolding that was intended all acts, as well as meat and drinks, and therefore till you can lie with all women as one woman, and not judge it sin, you can do nothing but sin.

Sin admitting of no form in itself is created a form in the estimation of the Creature.

Consider what act soever, yea though it be the act of Swearing, Drunkenness, Adultery and Theft; yet these acts simply, yea nakedly, as acts are nothing distinct from the act of Prayer and Praises. Why dost thou wonder? Why art thou angry? They are all one in themselves; no more holiness, no more purity in the one than the other.

But once the Creature esteemeth one act Adultery, the other honesty, the one pure, the other impure; yet to that man that esteemeth one act unclean, to him it is unclean. . . . Yea again and again it is recorded that to the pure all things, yea all things, are pure, but to the defiled, all things are defiled. . . .

This is, in fact, indistinguishable from the ethical tradition, or rather anethical tradition, of Buddhism. The clearest and most subtle expression of it is in the first of the above quotations. It forces the essence of sin back where Clarkson holds it belongs, in the estimation of the sinner and nowhere else.

But he goes over now to a new tack:

My privilege doth not in the least approbate thee, yea thee that apprehendest the title to swear, whore or steal etc., because to thee it is unclean, therefore not lawful for thee; neither canst thou upon the bare report hereof say, well, if it be but as a man esteems it, then I will esteem it so too. Alas, friend, let me tell thee, whatever thy tongue saith, yet thy imagination in thee declares said things against thee; in that thou esteemest them acts of sin, thy imagination will torment thee for this sin; in that thou condemnest thyself, thou art tormented in thy condemnation, with endless misery; so that I say, happy is the man that condemns not himself in those things he alloweth of.

The pamphlet now proceeds with increasing density and eloquence toward a peroration where the insights become mystical.

No matter what Scripture, Saints or Churches say, if that within thee do not condemn thee, thou shalt not be condemned; for saith the History, "Out of thine own mouth" not another's "will I judge thee." Therefore remember that if thou judge not thyself, let thy life be what it will, yea act what thou canst, yet if thou judge not thyself, thou shall not be judged. For; "I came not into the World to condemn, but to save the World." But if the reproach and slander of Saints and Churches do cause thee to question thyself, then art thou ready to say within what they report without, I am guilty of what they accuse me. . . .

The Lord declared that those filthy abominable works of darkness (by thee so apprehended) shall be destroyed and damned. But how or where shall they be damned? That is in the sayings of this text; "I will make darkness light." Oh that thou wert[2] purely minded, then thou wouldst see that sin must not be thrown out, but cast within, there being in the Vat, it is dyed the same colour of the liquor. As Saffron converts milk into its own colour, so doth the fountain of light convert sin, hell and devil into its own nature and light as itself: "I will make rough ways smooth." Now is it damm'd and ramm'd[3] into its only Center, there to dwell eternal in the bosom of its only Father. This and only this is the damnation so much terrifying the Creature in its dark apprehension.

Therefore my beloved ones, that supposeth your service is perfect freedom, by having only light into another's life, know this, that if light without life, thy service will be perfect bondage, and therefore it is when a creature is drawn forth to act in another's life, instead of triumphing over sin, he will be conquered in sin; so that I say, till flesh be made spirit, and spirit flesh, so not two but one, thou art in perfect bondage; for without vail, I declare that whosoever doth attempt to act from flesh in flesh, to flesh, hath, is and will commit Adultery; but to bring this to a period, for my part, till I acted that so called sin, I could not predominate over sin; so that now, whatsoever I act, is not in relation to the Title, to the Flesh, but to that Eternity in my Form, the Representation of the whole Creation; so that see what I can, act what I will, all is but one most sweet and lovely . . .

In conclusion here is one more of Clarkson's tenebrous insights; a perfect expression of the revolutionary, antithetical aspect of libertinism:

No man could be free from sin till he had acted that so called sin as no sin.

It is the paradox Dostoevski worked on. Some actions and attitudes come to us from the Christian fathers wrapped

---

[2] I amend "this were" in the text, assuming it to be a misprint, to "thou wert."

[3] "Rammed" is hermetic Ranter language for "Godded."

in a cocoon called Sin. But this is an opaque wrapping, as long as it is there we cannot understand or know what is inside. It is only by unwrapping the cocoon that we can learn the true nature of the action or thought; what it can do and not do, what its real effects on others may be, whether we want it for our own or not. As long as it is wrapped, we are condemned both to ignorance and to curiosity.

Not to unwrap it is to remain in a world of mysterious, unexplained desires and prohibitions, great lumps of autarchic injunction which move menacingly around, bumping each other with sinister, soft thuds, and squashing puny individuals under their irrevocable weight. To unwrap it is to enter into a lighter realm where things are themselves because that is what they are, and where we can pick our way unsquashed among the manageable entities of human nature, which is what we have, and not what we think we ought to have.

In museums, we replace the solid castings which cover machines by transparent covers, because we want the children to see how things work. But no greenpainted steel casing around a crank case or a gearbox, no cover or shield or lid was ever so opaque as the wrapping with which we conceal the workings of desire and pleasure from our children and ourselves.

One of the mechanisms by which libertinism went from heresy within Christianity to outright rejection of it was rakery. Rakery was libertinism freed of its aspect of "acclivity," no longer used as a means to a higher or truer conception of God, and no longer claiming for fornication the sanction of general salvation on this earth, but existing as a simple reaction against the Manicheism in Christianity. The rake did not deny that he was damned; on the contrary, he meant to enjoy the progress to hell as much as he could. It was a defiance, not a wiping of slates; the word itself is an abbreviation of "rakehell." But it was an even less tenable spiritual position than that of the early religious libertines, and naturally went over in time into fully fledged atheistic libertinism, where the libertine was equally skeptical of both salvation and damnation.

Where there is an English example available, it does not seem worth going abroad, so let us turn to the best known English rake, Rochester, who shows these transitional characteristics very well. He admitted the standards and the framework of ideas of his own day, and deliberately went against them. This he did not out of any philosophical compulsion or personal vision of life, but out of idle impatience and fretful sloth.

Rochester was an inverted Puritan. He pursued whoring with the same hot vigor that the Puritan divine abominated it. Fucking in love eludes his grasp; it is always in squalor, drunkennness, shame and loud laughter. Again and again he returns to the theme of impotence in love, contrasted with potency in whoring; after the folly of the King and his Ministers, it was his main concern, and gave him some of his best lines. This, from one of the two poems called *The Imperfect Enjoyment,* is a good expression of that particular predicament, brothel-courage. "Naked she lay," be begins, "clasped in my longing arms, I filled with love, and she all over charms." But his prick

> Now languid lies, in this unhappy hour,
> Shrunk up and sapless, like a withered flower.
> Thou treacherous, base deserter of my flame,
> False to my passion, fatal to my fame.
> By what mistaken magic dost thou prove
> So true to lewdness, so untrue to love?
> What oyster, cinder, beggar, common whore
> Didst thou e'er fail in all thy life before?
> When vice, disease, and scandal led the way
> With what officious haste didst thou obey?
> Like a rude-roaring Hector in the streets
> That scuffles, cuffs and ruffles all he meets;
> But if his king or country claim his aid
> The rascal villain shrinks and hides his head.
> E'en so is thy brutal valour displayed,
> Breaks every stews, and does each small crack invade.

But if great Love the onset does command,
Base recreant to thy Prince, thou dost not stand.
Worst part of me, and henceforth hated most,
Through all the town the common rubbing post
On whom each wretch relieves her tingling cunt,
As hogs on gates do rub themselves and grunt;
Mayst thou to ravenous shankers be a prey,
Or in continuous weepings waste away;
May stranguries and stone thy days attend;
May'st thou not piss, who didst refuse to spend,
When all my joys did on false thee depend.
And may ten thousand abler men agree
To do the wronged Corinna right for thee.

This is a fair picture of the mental set of the rake, of the anti-Augustinian who reacts into damnation and accepts it. He distinguishes quite confidently between two reasons for fucking; lewdness and love. He is caught in the fear of love which leads him to lewdness and this conditions him in turn so thoroughly that when he does seek to make something of love, the original fear is reinforced by an uncontrollable physical response, or rather lack of response. Upshot: he curses his prick with the diseases you get from whoring, and degrades the girl he loves to the function of a whore in his imagination. It's the damnation that does it. The vision of hell to come reaches out and surrounds the feelings and deeds of this life with wisps of sulphur smoke. Already, for him, hell and wrong work, and heaven and right don't. He can whore, he can't love.

Rochester writes in a convention of knowing blame and satire on the mighty. A wise man, so goes the convention, would have no part in such doings, but there are many foolish men, and some of them are in high places, not excepting King Charles II himself. Rochester is foolish too, and since this particular folly leads to damnation, why then the best thing is to guffaw and snigger our way through life, occasionally sparing a thought for the repentance that might or might not be got round to at the end. Rochester himself did at least appear to repent on his deathbed, though his biographers differ about whether he meant it. If my interpretation of him and of rakery is right, he probably did mean it.

Most of Rochester's verse expresses defiance of accepted custom in general and of Christian morality in particular. At his best, his very wit stands in the way. He was pouring experience into little polished vessels, and you admire the craft more than the content; indeed so much so that it takes time to identify the content for what it was: trivial reaction. At his worst, he assumes a hectoring and scathing tone, belaboring women as unfortunately attractive but fundamentally vicious, and marriage as "the clog of all pleasure, the luggage of life." He was too much blinded by the very intensity of his reaction, the shallow compulsion of his drinking and whoring, to notice its philosophical overtones.

There is sometimes a kind of careless violence, the fruit of his whole-hogging reaction, which makes you sit up. For instance, this about Nell Gwynn:

> She was so exquisite a whore
> That in the belly of her mother
> She placed her cunt so right before
> Her father fucked them both together.

Or this:

> Oh that I now could, by some chymic art,
> To sperm convert my vitals and my heart,
> That at one thrust I might my soul translate
> And in the womb myself regenerate.
> There, steeped in lust, nine months I would remain;
> Then boldly fuck my passage out again.

But only rarely does the ranting and roaring and sniggering stop, only rarely does he give himself time to see a true thing and set it down well. I can't leave him without quoting one of these pauses:

> Have you not in a chimney seen
> A sullen faggot, wet and green,

How coyly it receives the heat
And at both ends does fume and sweat?

So fares it with the harmless maid
When first upon her back she's laid;
But the kind, experienced dame
Cracks, and rejoices in the flame.

Chapter 23

Libertinism: The Irreligious Phase

The second stage of libertinism, that which reached its clearest definition in France just before and during the Revolution of 1789, is something closer to us than the spiritual libertinism which wenched its way to God, or the rakery which whored its way to hell.

The aristocratic French libertine of the later eighteenth century carried the reaction farther than any of his predecessors; he reacted through heaven and through hell right out into a God-free country where fucking became its own reward. He was promiscuous for fun, and because he could be. He was rich, and unburdened by too much social function; in one sense he was no more than a particular flower on the stem of that age-old model and ambition, the cultured nobility. He differed in that he put his grace, his learning, his chivalry and his wit to use, not in war, politics or conversation, but in bed. He regarded fucking as a continuation of conversation by other means. He also embodied in the sphere of sexual relations the aimless and irresponsible elegance which in the economic and political spheres is still usually Lesson One of Modern History in our schools.

And this movement—not a movement in the political sense: the way their spirit moved away from the majority around them—their movement was still only a reaction. Their predecesors had rejected chastity, but not God. They rejected both chastity and the god which enjoined it; they therefore found themselves in trackless territory; a moral wilderness. But they were men, and like other men in wildernesses, they began to make tracks and rules. When a system of rules grows up, it must stand comparison with the other rules all round it, and must run the risk of offending. This is what happened to the libertines; they allowed a code of conduct to grow up, and their code offended. To an extent not always apparent from the history books of later ages which did not like to dwell on such things, the French Revolution protested against and swept away not only privilege, prepotent wealth and autocratic institutions, but libertinism as well.

The literature of eighteenth-century French libertinism is enormous, and ranges from works of great beauty and insight to the boring trivia of *lectures galantes*. Here I discuss three men only, one painter and two writers: François Boucher, Andréa de Nerciat, and Choderlos de Laclos. In these three, one can perhaps adequately trace the movement from irresponsible, trackless gaiety and grace to the objection from the society round them which finally put a term to the experiment. The objection, as we shall see, was not religious; it grew from roots in political ethics.

Boucher painted the look of libertinism, and Nerciat described the feel of it. Laclos wrote down its rules in vitriol and thereby destroyed it. Boucher, the court painter of Louis XV, lived with and for women. He painted his wife (she is the fair girl with the small head in his earlier pictures) and he painted three of the five O'Murphy sisters, one of them over and over again. If you walk into the Wallace Collection in London, you are in his world. It takes a moment or two to realize that these are not "images" of this or that, of scenes from classical mythology, or of "court

life" in eighteenth-century Paris, seen from outside or re-
layed for the benefit of provincials or posterity. They are
Boucher's life, they are what he wanted to see, and did see,
every day. He is as much present in his pictures as the
swains and shepherdesses, and he is thinking and feeling as
they are. Toying and fucking are the ordinary forms of communication between human beings, not extraordinary or
loaded with emotion. Where we talk, the libertines touched;
where we interest, they excited. If there were young women
around, they would naturally be naked or nearly. Young
men would be too, but one can sense the veil that came
over Boucher's perception of his men subjects; painting a
man and a woman together could only cause a postpone-
ment of what they wanted to do. Therefore he hurried, and
retired. Very few of his men are as good as most of his
women. These are calm pictures; the people in them look
calm, and the compositions though intensely voluptuous
are without tension. The figures look open-eyed at each
other, aware of each other's feelings and of their own. There
is no grab or snatch in this view of love, no swooning or
hectic pressure; it's as cool as conversation.

And the same is true of his overtly erotic works.[1] There

---

[1] Strictly speaking, one is not entitled to call these pictures
"Bouchers." I know them only from reproductions in three German works from which much of one's information in this field
unfortunately has to come: *Geschichte der Erotischen Kunst,* and
Grosse Meister der Erotik, by Eduard Fuchs, and *Die Erotik in der
Kunst,* by Kary von Karwarth. Unfortunately, because Fuchs and
Karwarth, who both wrote in the first quarter of this century,
were so unscholarly and had such a tin ear for history that their
assiduity is almost wasted.

The often repeated story is that Boucher did a series of four or
six erotic oil paintings for the Pompadour's bedroom, that when
Louis XVI acceded to the throne he ordered *"ces cochonneries"* to
be removed, and that, according to one version, they fetched up in
the Wallace Collection; according to another, they were burned by
the British Customs about 1865. They certainly did not land up in
the Wallace Collection; this seems to be a confusion with the other
ones, perfectly presentable, which did. I have been unable to check
the story about the Customs, or to find any trace where the pictures might be if they have survived.

is no possibility of reproducing these pictures now in a book for general sale, so I must ask the reader to get his eye in by thinking of a famous Boucher, say the Diana, or the O'Murphy lying on her front, and then imagine these others. There is a picture of a dark young man, partly clothed, fucking a naked girl from behind as she leans over a bed. She is, or is very like, the familiar O'Murphy: he has a stylish twist, almost wrench, to his stance. Amorini sport on remotish clouds. You can see that they have only just begun, and that she has not yet got her heart in it, though he has; there is a trace of lumpishness about her, but a fiery thrust and impetus about him. He wears an expression of lyrical objectivity. The picture makes two clear and separate statements; these people are fucking, but over and above that, they are feeling such and such. By no means is there any feeling of guilt, or of ecstasy, or of blind abandon; these people feel this, it says. Others would feel otherwise.

There is one of a young woman washing in a *bidet* while another sits by her and watches her face. This is the beginning of a Lesbian encounter, and again the fact that they are soon going to make love is not the main point; the main point is what precisely they feel. The larger woman, the butch figure, is watching for the green light. The younger one is putting off the moment when she has to show any light, green or red. It is a static, latent sort of picture; like the other, it fills in part of the map in the territory which the libertines occupied, but which the main stream of the arts in Christendom has left cloudy, saying: "Here be nameless ecstasies."

These are two cool and explicit images of the beyond-land which is usually excluded as too intense, too dangerous to be depicted. But Boucher also attempted an image of a part of the beyond-land which is usually considered too comic and too pathetic to be attempted, unless perhaps in a spirit of gross satire. This is a picture of two girls buying dildoes from a young man who has a basket of them for sale. It is a grave, sweet, kindly picture; the girls want the dildoes, the man wants the money, that's all.

The look of libertinism is a surprise to us now, because we are conditioned by the century of romanticism which came after. Try this one on your friends. Ask them which of the professions love most resembles: medicine, religion, the law, politics, or war. Very few will say politics; but those who do will be best equipped to understand Boucher and libertinism.

What Boucher depicted, Nerciat described. Because Nerciat wrote little that was not overtly erotic, and that little is rather poor, he is less known than Boucher. His family was by origin Neapolitan, spelled Nercia, but his father was already French; he was an official of the *Parlement* of Burgundy. Andréa de Nerciat was born in 1739 and passed most of his life as a soldier. His company was axed in 1775, and he went to be court musician and theater manager in two or three little German principalities. He returned to Paris during the Revolution, and in 1797 was Madame Bonaparte's personal guard. He ended his days in the service of the King of Naples, after having been imprisoned in Castel Sant' Angelo by the French on a charge of spying. Although by trade a military officer, his life was peaceful; he was an organizer who oscillated between the arts and semi-clandestine diplomatic service, without patriotism or enthusiasm. He was twice married, and had two sons by his first marriage. Besides his erotic novels, he wrote some military and some printably amorous poems, both very weak, and a play called *Dorimon,* of which I have not been able to find a copy.

His erotic novels are considerable for two reasons, which are connected. By virtue of their craftsmanship, they seem to me the highest achievement of the European erotic or "pornographic" novel; and they give an unsurpassed window on the values of the laughing, exploiting phase of libertinism in France. This is not to say they are realistic novels; but you can learn a good deal about a society by the best light reading which remains from it. What they found funny and what they found charming are the next most important questions about people after what they thought good and what they held true.

The limits of this praise should be obvious. The general level of achievement in the European erotic novel is not high, and to excel in it is therefore not remarkable by general literary standards. And the way of life of the French libertines, as Laclos knew but Nerciat did not, was without possibility of development or issue. To be its best chronicler was thus only to be the best chronicler of something rather small.

The most famous of Nerciat's novels is *Félicia, ou mes Fredaines.* This is not so overtly or continuously erotic, and is easy to come by on open sale, but it does not show him at his best. His two best works are *Les Aphrodites,* published in 1793, and *Le Diable au Corps,* published posthumously in 1803. They have not often been reissued, and are now very difficult to find. They are real novels, in the sense that the characters have family and financial backgrounds in which you get interested; in this they differ from all-out mercenary pornography, which thinks it is letting the reader down if ever the characters get out of bed for a page or two. They are also quite funny; they are the true froth on the thinnish beer of libertinism; and they are always pleasant and kindly in tone. There is no trace of sadism in them; guilt, degradation and squalor were as foreign to Nerciat as romantic swooning and yearning. He describes with admirable control the physical and conversational graces of fucking, the carrying over of normal modes of being into the area considered abnormal by Manichees and romantics. His characters make mistakes, laugh, and start again; they talk with their bodies, are sad, are gay, express meanings in touch. There is a scene in *Les Aphrodites* where he has a complicated orgy all prepared over several pages, everybody set in exactly the manner he wants to be, tension running very high, when somebody bursts in with bad news about a friend. "What?" they say; "No! Really? How dreadful. Why, last time I saw her she seemed all right. But tell us more. . . ." Meanwhile erections go down, thighs close, and characters and reader become engrossed in a story of financial and family misfortune. Several pages later they carry on with the orgy.

Nerciat's tone is one of unruffled delight interrupted by equally unruffled absurdities. The motto of *Les Aphrodites* is "*Priape, soutiens mon haleine!*" There are unforgettable lines; the English are "boring philosophers and sad fuckers." There is a passage where a girl is describing a man's prick to another girl that throws new (or perhaps old, but forgotten) light on humanist architecture: "I supposed that after elevation and diameter you were going to call the glans *capital* and count inches *moduli*." There is the description of promiscuity itself: "A few excursions here and there are only swordcuts in water." Sometimes cool flippancy degenerates into silliness; there is an orgy of seven men and seven women where he gives a table of who did who in two hours (7 times 7 equals 49).

The background of action to the stories is often that of libertines visiting and dining with each other, but sometimes it takes place in a sort of tremendously superior brothel, subscription payable once a year, like a club. The brothel is democratically run; committee meetings discuss whether to admit homosexuals. Often there is a feeling of shutting oneself away from the world, recluses of pleasure, while catastrophic changes are in preparation outside.

As indeed they were. The libertine is often socially superior to his prey. In *Les Aphrodites*, for instance, there is an educated servant called Nicole, and one of the set pieces of erotic description depends on her not knowing who was with her in her darkened bedroom. A certain nobleman had marked her down and presented himself to her as—what?—as a good lover. No more. She was passive to his choice, so passive that she did not even know she had been chosen; and when he came to foreclose, she did not know who it was that had chosen her. The incident carries us to Laclos and the *Liaisons Dangereuses*.

Like Nerciat, Laclos had something farther south than France in his ancestry; the history is obscure, but *Choderlos* is thought to be the remnant of a Spanish family name. Like Nerciat he was a soldier, but from there on the bourgeois artillery officer was as different as could be from the court fribble. Nerciat was unmoved by the great events of the time; Laclos served the Revolution. Nerciat was all elegance and lightness; Laclos was an intellectual, an organizer of anything he could lay hands on, a strategist of fortification and siege, the destroyer of the Vauban myth in an exemplary piece of deblimping, who drew up not only the death warrant of libertinism and the birth certificate of modern bourgeois morality, but also a system of street numbering which underlies the one still in use in Paris.

Laclos himself set down the genesis of his view of love, and that of many other intellectuals too, in a poem he wrote when he was young. It is called "The Right Choice," and I give here an English prose version, in spite of its length, because it illuminates the question: what kind of man can change the moral patterns of an age, and what kind of experience makes him that kind of man?

The first twenty lines decry intellectuals (*beaux esprits*) at the expense of men of action. Then he tells his story:

You must know, then, that two young men once lived together as good friends in the same lodging. The one, who was called Pamphilius, was famous in all the town for his wit; he made up epigrams, tales, and verses and every month he was praised in the newspapers. The other had a different destiny; he was easygoing and cared for nothing; he slept late, ate and drank well, and ended the day in digestion. In fact, since lives like his go unobserved, his name has not come down to us. Some may think I shall be embarrassed by this, but I don't find anything surprising about it; if one name is lost, there is always another. I know plenty in like circumstances whose very line has been continued under a borrowed name. As for my hero, if he must have a name, I hereby name him Cleon, by my own authority. Now that he is named, all I need say is that he was the friend of Pamphilius; in any case, both were young and fresh, good company, and passably well-made.

There came to live under the same roof the charming Isidora, dark and startling, lively and light of mien, whose eyes awoke desire, and with it the hope of forgiveness. Youth is tempted by less; soon, our friends were admitted to their neighbor's friendship. At first it was no more than civility, and thus far their success was equal; but desire, in the guise of chivalry, soon made two rivals of two friends. But how, some austere critic may ask, if they are rivals, can they be friends? Nothing is simpler, and here is the mystery; as a literary hero, Pamphilius had a sovereign disdain for his rival. Such a competitor was nothing; he could well be allowed to dispute the prize. Cleon, as modest as he was worldly, had the greatest respect for all good intellectuals; and respect stifles anger. So each, for opposite reasons, was a rival, not an enemy.

Success goes first to Pamphilius; his sweet language, his easy tongue, charm the ear and captivate the heart; when she listens to him, the most docile beauty secretly blames her unjust severity. At first it is enchanting praises, and eloquent looks go with them. Later, he treats of the happiness of Lovers in his discourse, but with delicacy. Then he fires up, and his ardent speech paints the happy ecstasies of sweet pleasure. And what does his rival say to all this? Nothing; or rather two words, badly arranged.

And thus the swift days passed between Isidora and Cleon and Pamphilius, when love, or the occasion, changed the fate of all three.

It was summer; more, it was evening. Seeking to escape the heat, our Beauty, at peace and alone, was dreaming in her boudoir, and taking the air. Her self-forgetfulness and her thin clothes, both artless, enhanced her charms. Thus Venus, to enchant the world, let herself be seen without adornment. Our two friends, led by the same hope, both arrived and were both received. Once more, Pamphilius was master of the situation, and spoke best when he spoke most. To what he said, Love lent again a sweeter charm, a more flattering air, and as she listened, the delightful Isidora felt her heart glow with a new fire which, no sooner born, consumed her. Everything betrayed her, even the care she took to hide her secret thoughts. Her eyelids lowered over her lovely eyes made her look yet more touching; she said nothing, but a burning sigh came to those just open lips; the lilies of her skin were now all roses; her breast heaved with excitement; the expressive softness of her whole manner declared a moment of happy weakness. Thus would Albano have painted pleasure.

"The enchanting power of intellect!" she said at last; "What flattering magic makes your voice able to cause such happiness? Delightful talent! Doubtless your works also offer these charming images? I wish to see them. You will read them to me, and as you read them, you will make them yet more beautiful." One can see that by this the Beauty was offering her lover an opportunity of seeing her again, and being alone with her, without the inconvenient Cleon. But the praise went to Pamphilius' head. Drunk with glory, even more than love, he cried: "My verses? Nothing could be simpler; you shall see them; you shall see them this very day." And went.

His calmer rival let him go, and sought better. Silently he went to Isidora; he saw her beautiful, he saw her defenseless. And in that moment an audacious gesture stood him in stead of eloquence. The Beauty cried out and complained of the offense; all unsurprised the silent lover let her have her say, and still advanced. He did so well that, in spite of her resistance, he found the way to her heart, took it, and installed himself there as victor. In that situation, time seems short, and both easily forgot their friend Pamphilius. But he saw everything, because he unfortunately came back suddenly. You think Isidora was confused? You are wrong; she sought no excuse, and freedom reigned in her manner. Only Pamphilius was out of countenance; he knew everything but what to say.

The Beauty at last, with a sweet smile, said to him: "My dear, be frank; you love your works better than me. And be happy; I promise to read them; I am already admiring them in advance from here. But you should learn that a generous woman wants to reign alone in her lover's heart. If you want to laugh at my expense, you can. You have my secret, but I warn you that I have little fear of a couplet or a satire; because, between ourselves, nothing you say can outweigh what Cleon did."

It would be too easy to say that Pamphilius spent the rest of his life avenging himself on Cleon. But Cleon is the first appearance in Laclos' works of the libertine against whom he turned all the icy artillery of his intelligence and the scorching fervor of his morality and his compassion. Moreover, Laclos' own attitude never changed. In this poem, Pamphilius does not rail against his conquerer, he implies he's done an excellent job and anyone with more sense than a poor soppy egghead would do just the same.

So *Les Liaisons Dangereuses* (1782) was taken at the time, and often since, to be a sort of celebration, or at least a neutral statement, of libertinism. It was held to be a pernicious and damnable book, to open which was at once to do likewise. Almost everyone who has written about it has noted how perfunctory are the wages of sin; the he-libertine, Valmont, is killed in a most off-hand sort of duel, and the she-libertine, Merteuil, is disfigured by smallpox, all in a hurried chapter or two. Merteuil's punishment is not even related to her crimes.

But the mere analysis of libertinism, since it was carried out by a novelist with such a prodigious command of his medium and such a patient knowledge of the modes of love, was enough to condemn it and to play a large part in its destruction.[2] One must assume that Laclos knew what he was about.

The Comte de Valmont and the Marquise de Merteuil, hating love and life, and loving not each other but themselves, part, and dedicate themselves to humiliating people in bed and writing each other long letters about it. Their first operation is the "corruption" of a young girl who is engaged to a man they have reason to dislike. Merteuil advises Valmont by letter. This done, they knock off two or three minor characters in a formal procedure which they, and by inference all libertines, know well; it is analyzed in four stages by Roger Vaillant in his *Laclos par Lui-Même*;[3] the stages are, the Choice, the Seduction, the Fall, and the Rupture. Much of what Vaillant says is extremely acute, but I would prefer to see the stages laid out as the Choice, the Declaration, the Foreclosure, and the Rupture. The Declaration, in libertinism, is not something the man makes; it is something he extracts, and when it is

---

[2] That Nerciat, Sade, and others were still celebrating libertinism ten or even twenty years after the appearance of *Les Liaisons Dangereuses* does not show the latter had no effect on society; only not on those writers. Nobody was celebrating libertinism thirty years later.

[3] Paris, Editions du Seuil, "Ecrivains de Toujours," 1953.

extracted, it gives him the right to proceed to the Fore-closure, or the fucking. In the right three of these stages, Valmont operates like all libertines of the time. But in the fourth stage he and his adviser Merteuil differ from the kindlier, sillier libertines you find in Nerciat and the other literature. The kindly libertine sees the rupture as some-thing to be done with as little bloodshed as possible. There were several gambits; the best, if you could pull it off, being to pass the girl on to another man, usually of course a younger and less experienced one, without either party noticing. The absence of any feeling for a stylish rupture is what most sharply differentiates the stakhanovism of to-day from true libertinism; but more of that later.

The purpose of Valmont and Merteuil in the rupture was to humiliate the girl and to glorify Valmont. The more pious and virtuous the girl, the more inaccessible in general belief, the greater the glory to Valmont; all he had to do was to arrange for the fact that he had had her—the word "had" is the correct one here—to become known in such a way that no one suspected him of noising it abroad.

The bulk of the story is taken up by Valmont's en-counter with the Présidente de Tourvel, who is the em-bodiment of the new bourgeois morality; happily married, faithful to her absent husband, and devout. Valmont, for the first time in his life, falls in love, partly because he can-not easily get her and partly, Laclos suggests, because her better values infect him. He does get her in the end, though it takes a lot of pushing from the Merteuil, and he does in-flict his horrible style of rupture on her, though again pushed by the Merteuil; he actually copies out the letter of rupture she suggests to him. The scene in which the Présidente yields ("Picture a woman sitting unmoving and stiff, her face unchanging, seeming neither to think nor to listen nor to hear, from whose eyes fall rather continuous tears, but falling without strain. . . .") and then describes the way she hopes to redeem the situation by transferring her love to Valmont, is one of the greatest pieces of pathos in the history of the novel; it does not seem at all extrava-

gant to suppose that it can have played a part in bringing
about the Revolution which cut down the libertine aristocrats and installed the bourgeoisie. And anyone who can
read today the Merteuil's draft letter of rupture and not feel
the sword of revolution jump centuries to his hand can
hardly be human. The letter is built round the reception of
the phrase "*ce n'était pas ma faute*," "it was not my fault,"
and has a cadence to it, a lyrical crescendo of shallow
cruelty, that puts it among the masterpieces of moral poetry.
Laclos here condemns evil in the same hypnotic litany that
the old Jews used to praise God.

But there is a conundrum; what was Laclos in favor of,
after all? It is easy to see that he was in favor of the Présidente and her values, and against Valmont and Merteuil
and theirs. But where are these good values, except in the
bare references to the devoutness and fidelity of the Présidente and, rather more strongly, in the gentleness and op-
timism of her character? People should not be libertines;
that is clear, not so much from the perfunctory visitations
which fall on Valmont and Merteuil as from the horrible
cruelty of Valmont and the terrible pathos of the Présidente. But what should they be? What do this devoutness
and this happy and faithful marriage actually feel like?

We never see the Présidente being devout. It is a puzzle
why Laclos put that in; he was far from an orthodox Christian himself, so of course was the revolutionary current
of opinion which he went with, and which he so much
strengthened with this novel. It is conceivable that he saw
farther ahead than any of his contemporaries and intuited
that the new ruling class of France and Europe after the
Revolution would be devout, but it is more likely that he
was using every possible stick to beat his dog.

We are not told, either, what the faithful marriage was
like. The Présidente's husband, the Présidente de Tourvel,
is away from Paris doing a job in Burgundy; he is a
working man, and this establishes a contrast with the prepotent wealth and idleness of the libertine aristocrats. But
why wasn't his wife with him? Why, when she found that

a sort of love for Valmont was growing up in her and threatening her love for her husband, did she not run to him? Or tell him? And here we come to the one big flaw of this almost perfect work; she did tell him. She wrote to him, saying something about what was happening, and Valmont intercepted and read the letter. Valmont was always intercepting letters, and all the others Laclos gives us in the book. But not this one.

The episode is presumably there to increase the pathos of the Présidente's lot; she writes to her husband, perhaps asking his help and advice, or at the least letting him know something is wrong so that he can come back if he wants to, and then the libertine intercepts the letter and she is left believing that her husband doesn't care; even this solace is denied her in the general siege and humbling. So why did Laclos not write that letter for us, showing what the Présidente's marriage meant to her? It would not have cost him much in terms of his plot; the husband was not going to get it, and Laclos would not have had to bring him into the story. But it would have been an opportunity of setting out the positive side of the bourgeois morality he so passionately defended by inference. Was it that he did not want to blur the continuous impact of denunciation which informs his analysis of the *mores*? That he wanted nothing positive to stand comparison with the—one is tempted to say incomparable—blast of negative judgment he blows? Or was it that he shirked the difficulty of standing *for* something, he who stood against something with a skill and fervor as prodigious as any of the great writers who made us what we are?

We don't know. But we can tell that the impetus behind his denunciation was not simply a respect for religion and fidelity. In 1783, when he had finished *Les Liaisons Dangereuses,* he wrote two essays on the education of women, both unfinished, and never published until 1903. These are Rousseauist works; they accept the social contract, and one of the chapters even begins: "Nature creates only free beings; society creates only tyrants and slaves." Laclos

imagines that women were first subjected to men because
they were weaker, and were forced to do all the dirty
work. From this slavery they partially escaped by inventing *coquetterie,* but the men caught up with them by
inventing jealousy, and in eighteenth-century France they
were just as much slaves as they had ever been. Woman, he
implies, could only regain her freedom and dignity by becoming once again what she had been in the state of nature,
man's companion and equal, as well as his wife and mistress. I give some extracts from these essays in Appendix
4, partly to back up this part of the argument and partly because they are so agreeably written. Laclos never published
them, presumably because he couldn't think how to finish
them; yet again he shied from the positive aspect. But they
do show, even if it was not obvious from the book itself,
that the steam power behind *Les Liaisons Dangereuses* was
not religious, still less puritanical, but political. The prési-
dentes of France were an oppressed class; they were in a
form of slavery to the Valmonts, from which only a revolution could save them. Laclos thought of it as a revolution
in education, but there were other revolutions on the way
too.

His negative blast brought them closer. Libertinism, born
of anarchism, contempt for matter, and the doctrine of the
primacy of feeling and self-expression in reaching God, had
dropped God, and had formed rules in the wilderness. The
rules incurred the censure of one of the greatest moralists
who ever wrote, and coalesced with the rules of feudalism,
of irresponsible wealth and functionless power to form a
target. The target came under fire in 1789, and within fifty
years the revolution was complete in Western Europe.

Chapter 24

Sadism

Everybody knows that in countries where homosexuality is illegal, which means mainly England and the United States, the great majority of homosexuals are just like the great majority of the rest of the population, and that most of us don't even know who they are. The ones who annoy us or make us laugh or excite our pity are the dissatisfied ones, the ones who can't get what they need in private, and are so thwarted, or stupid, or filled with exhibitionism, which are not specifically homosexual things, that they go around making passes at heterosexual men and boys. These are the ones who "get homosexuality a bad name." Take the broader instance of "normal" heterosexuals. Most of us get what we want in private, but a few of us are so thwarted or stupid or exhibitionistic that we go around making passes at women and girls or men and boys who don't want us. This does not "get heterosexuality a bad name," because the collective knowledge and wisdom of everyone about heterosexuality (since so many of us are that), tells us that these people are a minority.

Is sadism like this? It is possible to suppose, and will remain possible until studies of sadism as good as recent studies of homosexuality confirm or disprove it, that the sadists who make themselves and other people miserable or ill or dead, are simply the thwarted, stupid or exhibitionist minority of that particular craft, and that for every one of these there are ten or a hundred well adjusted people, filling what they call responsible jobs and never raising an eyebrow, who are perfectly happy beating each other up in private. It is a way of life and, like homosexuality, goes on a sliding scale: there's some of it in many people who don't swear by it.

Insofar as some people find that the greatest sexual pleasure comes from administering and receiving what Sade called "a severe general shock to the nervous system," and that the more severe it is the greater is the pleasure, sadism is presumably as old as mankind, or older. But it was the Marquis de Sade (1740-1814), starting from the tradition of French libertinism, the later, irreligious phase which we discussed above, who first raised this idea to the level of a general view of man and society. He was certainly a considerable writer, with a good style and plenty of impetuous fire which, when what he is saying is not quite crazy, which is only sometimes, is rather engaging. Most writing about him is as crazy as what he wrote himself; a notable exception is Simone de Beauvoir's *Faut-il brûler Sade?*

He spent most of his life in prison, and wrote copiously there. His two best novels, from the narrative point of view, are *Justine* and *Juliette*. The best from the point of view of doctrinal exposition is *La Philosophie dans le Boudoir*. All these have been reissued many times. He also wrote an enormous catalogue of the various ways people could chew each other and slit each other up called *Les Cent Vingt Jours de Sodome*. It is often said to be the most horrible book ever written, but only some degree of ignorance of one's own nature could allow anyone to be really upset by it; it would certainly worry someone who had not come to terms with his own sadistic impulses.

Sade was a mirror man. He took the piety and conformism of his time and turned it on its head, declaring that the only pleasure was to fly in its face, and that the correct ordering of society would be a point by point inversion of the system around him. It is useless to look in Sade for anything which is not already there the other—or usual—way up in the writings of *bien-pensant* moralists of his time.

Take for instance the introduction to *La Philosophie dans le Boudoir*.

Lubricious women, let the voluptuous Saint-Ange be your model. Follow her in despising all that contravenes the divine law of pleasure, by which she was bound all her life.

Young girls, too long constrained by the absurd and dangerous bonds of a fantastic virtue and a disgusting religion, imitate the ardent Eugénie; destroy and trample underfoot, as swiftly as she did, all the ridiculous precepts which have been inculcated in you by your idiot parents. And you, amiable debauchees, you who since your youth have had no restraint but the capacity of your desires, and no law but caprice, let the cynical Dolmancé be your example. Go as far as he does if you, like he, wish to tread the flowery paths which lubricity prepares for you; be convinced at his school that it is only by extending the domain of taste and fancy, in sacrificing everything to pleasure, that the unhappy thing known as man, thrown against his will into this sad universe, can succeed in snatching a few roses from the thorns of life.

Throughout his writing there is a passionate, personal and reactive hatred of God and virtue, things of which he had a much clearer idea than most of his contemporaries, or than any of ours. He was a case for conversion if ever there was one; nothing to build, only invert what there was, and he would have been a good stodgy bishop.

"It is most certain that I shall spare nothing to pervert her, to degrade her, to overturn in her all the false principles of morality by which she may already have been bemused; in two lessons I mean to make her as depraved, as impious, and as debauched as I am."

"The depravation of custom is necessary in a state."

"Do you really think, Eugénie, that the piety which would bind man to so idiotic, inadequate, ferocious and despicable a Creator is an entirely necessary virtue?"

"O Thou of whom I have not the least idea . . ."

"He doesn't believe in God, I hope?"

". . . this divine infamy . . ."

Guillaume Apollinaire[1] quotes from a pamphlet by a certain Ange Pitou, who was in prison with Sade during the Revolution, the following dialogue, which puts it all in a nutshell.

SADE: What are you reading there?
PITOU: The Bible.
SADE: Well, Tobias is all right, but that Job is just a story-teller.
PITOU: Stories, sir, which will turn out to be realities, both for you and for me.
SADE: Realities? You believe in those fables, and yet you are laughing?
PITOU: We are both mad, Monsieur le Marquis; you for being afraid of your fables, and I for laughing at my realities.

Sade spent twenty-seven years in eleven different prisons; most of his work was written in the Bastille itself. He was more than once imprisoned for beating up girls, but the greater part of his imprisonments were for fraud, riot and for political reasons. One can sum up one aspect of his career and his significance by imagining the sort of temperament which can *think of nothing better* to do with a naked girl than beat her up. It is an extreme example of a diversionary activity.

Sade was transferred away from the Bastille to another prison on July 4, 1789, ten days before the sack which started the Revolution. But Apollinaire holds it possible that the sack itself was partly caused by Sade's habit of

[1] In his *L'Oeuvre du Marquis de Sade,* Paris, 1909.

writing descriptions of how the prisoners were tortured and throwing them out of the window, and by declaiming the same down a drainpipe to some inflammable humanitarians who were gathered round the bottom. This is in keeping; it would have been his private pleasure to do so, and again his private pleasure to gloat over the massacre and destruction which resulted.

He had also said to Pitou: "Why am I so frightful, and why is crime so charming? It immortalizes me. It must hold sway in all the world." Conversely, he gave instructions in his will that he was to be buried in his own woods, and acorns were to be sown over his grave "so that . . . the signs of my tomb should vanish from the face of the earth, as I flatter myself my memory will be effaced from the spirits of men."

Self; unique renown, or unique oblivion. It leaps to the eye when you read Sade's novels that his pleasure was buggery. When the pious virgin Eugénie arrives at the party in *La Philosophie,* the first thing that happens to her is she gets buggered, and the bugger remarks: "Now you are a woman." Sade also takes it for granted that buggery is more fun for women than fucking, and one may speculate how much the early habituation of a man to a form of sexual contact where the woman does not normally answer his pleasure with her own, may propel him down channels of solipsistic gratification, of not caring or noticing what is happening to anyone else. In several senses, Sade buggered the world, and it did not answer. Real philosophers and artists and statesmen fuck it; it answers in joy, and gives birth to things that work.[2]

---

[2] We must recognize that Sade was the forerunner of just one thing which has, even if doubtfully and provisionally, been found to work in our age; psychodrama, or the group therapy technique of setting the mentally ill to act out their conflicts in extemporization on a stage. Sade was sometimes in lunatic asylums as well as prisons, and in one of these he organized the first psychodramas.

At the asylum of Charenton there was both a Director and a Medical Superintendent. The former was a certain M. de Coulmiers, a former Premonstratensian monk who, under the Empire, had become Minister of Constituent and Legislative Assemblies. He was

But the frantic excitement of all Sade's writing prevents him being able to give a cool map even of the sado-masochistic lock. This has been achieved in our day in a French novel called *Histoire d'O*,[3] which achieved a *succès de scandale* when it was published because everyone thought they knew who was concealed behind the pseudonym of "Pauline Réage." It has an introduction by the conservative writer Jean Paulhan, of which more in a moment.

The following passage gives the clearest picture I know of that particular landscape. The heroine is taken blindfolded by her lover to a mysterious place where she is fucked and buggered by four men in succession, without knowing which is her lover. She is then enrolled in the confraternity as follows.[4]

You are here at the service of your masters. In the daytime you will carry out such duties as may be assigned to you for the upkeep of the house, such as sweeping, or arranging the books and the flowers, or waiting on table. There are no

---

a believer in the sovereign virtues of dancing and acting as a remedy for alienation; he had a box in the asylum theatre, to which he invited his friends. The audience was the quieter lunatics and invited guests. The Medical Superintendent was a Doctor Royer-Collard, one of the old school, and against de Coulmiers he wrote as follows to Monseigneur the Senator the Minister of the General Police of the Empire, on August 2, 1808:

". . . And that is not all. There has most imprudently been established a theatre in this house, under the pretext of getting the lunatics to act plays, and without any reflection on the disastrous effects which such a tumultuous concern must necessarily produce on their imaginations. Monsieur de Sade is the director of this theatre. It is he who chooses the plays, apportions the parts, and takes the rehearsals . . . It is not necessary, I think, to remind your Excellency of the scandal of such a departure, or to represent to you the dangers of all kinds which are attributable to it. If these details were known to the public, what idea would they form of an establishment where such strange abuses are tolerated? Moreover, how can they be reconciled with the moral sector of the treatment of alienation? The patients, who are in daily communication with this abominable man, . . ." etc., etc.

[3] Sceaux, 1954.
[4] Pp. 17-20.

harder ones. But you will always leave what you are doing at the first word or the first sign which may require you to turn to your only real function, which is to offer yourself. Your hands are not yours, nor your breasts, nor in particular are any of the openings of your body which we can explore and into which we can enter in turn at our pleasure. As a sign to keep it constantly in your mind, or as constantly as possible, that you have lost the right to withdraw, when you are in our presence you will never entirely close your lips, or cross your legs, or press your knees together (as you will remember you were forbidden to do when you arrived). This will make it clear to you and to us that your mouth, your belly and your buttocks are always open to us. In our presence you will never touch your breasts; they are excluded from your corset to show that they belong to us. In the daytime, when you will be fully dressed, you will raise your skirt if you are ordered to do so, and you will satisfy any of us who requires it, with your face uncovered, in whatever manner he requires, always excepting the whip. The whip will only be used on you between sunset and sunrise. But, over and above that which may be given to you by any of us who desires, you will be punished by whipping in the evening for ignoring the rules in the daytime; that is to say, for having been less than pleasant, or raised your eyes toward whoever is speaking to you or taking you; you must never look any of us in the face. When we are in the costume we wear at night, that which I have on now, and our sex is uncovered, this is not for convenience sake; this could be otherwise assured. It is for insolence sake, so that your eyes should be fixed there, and should not be fixed elsewhere; so that you should learn that this is your master, to which above all your lips are destined. In the daytime, when we are ordinarily dressed, and when you are dressed as you are now, you will observe the same manners, and your only duty will be to open our clothing, if that is required of you, and to close it again when we have finished with you. At night, moreover, you will only have your lips with which to honor us, and the opening of your thighs, because your hands will be tied behind your back. You will be naked as you were brought in just now. You will only be blindfolded when you are to be maltreated and, now that you have seen how you are whipped here, when you are to be whipped. On this subject; if it seems convenient to us that you should get used to the whip, this is not so much for our pleasure as for your own instruction. Indeed, on the nights when no one wants you, you will wait for the servant whose duty it is to come to you alone in your cell and give you what you ought to have, since we shall not wish to give it to you. So in effect, what with this and the chain which will be fixed to your collar and will keep you more or less flat on your bed for several hours of the day, it is not so much a matter of making you feel pain, or cry aloud, or shed tears, as by means of this pain to make you feel you are compelled, and to teach you that you are entirely devoted to something outside yourself. When you leave this place, you will wear an iron ring on your ring finger, by which you will be recognized; by then you will have learned to obey those who wear the same sign—and they will know when they see it that you are always naked under your skirt, however ordinary and dull your clothes may be, and that this is for them.

Later she is whipped at some length, and branded down her belly and thighs to show that she is their property; she takes pride in the palpability of the brand marks under her skirt.

In his introduction, Paulhan has offered this story as a substitute for a document the loss of which to historians has always tormented him; it is an account of the reasons why some slaves in the Barbados revolted *against* manu-mission. They demanded the restoration of slavery, and Paulhan suggests that they were in love with their master in the manner of the heroine of the novel. In the course of his introduction he writes of the intense surprise he feels when contemplating the nature of women: "They speak to those half-crazed things, children, whom we admit to our company . . ." and, of women themselves: "I am often surprised that there are any." His political moral is: "The excessive kindness of the father, the schoolteacher, and the lover, is paid for in the crepitation of bombs, in napalm, and in the explosion of atoms."

The limitations of sadism as a practical way of life are severely factual. I am not thinking here of the law; if there is a law which says people should not murder each other in bed, or even use branding irons, the sadist may make a logical claim for a society in which such laws would not exist, and he would be allowed to do those things. No; I am thinking of the pattern of gratification itself. If pleasure consists in this severe general shock to the nerves through the infliction and the undergoing of pain, then more pleasure can always be procured by more pain. It is very different from the normal drill where you proceed through fucking to coming, and that is that; the pleasure is there, and is over and done with until the next time, which may be in a week or in ten seconds. The degree of pleasure depends on a host of things, but mainly the together-goingness of the lovers. Of that there can be more or less, but a desire to have more of it will not lead to planning. Of pain there can also be more or less, and the desire to have more of it is bound to lead to planning. "Next time I will hurt her (him) more. Last time I only . . . and that was pretty good. Next time I will . . . and that will be even better." But the end of pain is unconsciousness and death, and then you aren't inflicting pain any more and the whole thing falls to the ground. Under the dispensation of sadism, the imaginable extreme of pleasure is self-canceling. Under the ordinary dispensation, the imaginable extreme of pleasure is available whenever you want it, given good health, good will, and good luck. Sadism capriciously removes the aim of pleasure from the realm of the possible, thus erecting an obstacle to happy fucking as unreal and unnecessary as those of romantic and puritanical manicheism. Nobody compels the sadist to seek the impossible; like all the others before, he can't bear the heat of the possible.

It is the very same dilemma of self-destruction as that which bedeviled Christian asceticism. If God is pleased by virginity, the more virginity there is the better pleased He will be. But the more virginity, the less people are born to be virgins, and the less pleased is God. The pleasure of God in virginity, like the pleasure of the sadist in pain, is subject to diminishing returns and in the logical extremity cancels itself out.

Lastly, Sade—how could he not; he wasn't a fool—

foresaw and desired thermonuclear weapons. "To attack the sun, to expunge it from the universe, or to use it to set the world ablaze—these would be crimes indeed!" We await a study by the heirs of Kinsey on the correlation between sexual habit and desire on the one hand, and political and military attitude and policy on the other.

Chapter 25

Stakhanovism

> These natural freedoms are but just;
> There's something generous in mere lust.
>
> —From A Ramble in St. James' Park, sometimes
> (wrongly) attributed to Rochester.

Twentieth-century Stakhanovism is the offspring not immediately of eighteenth-century libertinism, but of nineteenth-century "debauchery," and it is there that we should start our account of it, as best we can. Because of the puritan restraints of the time in writing and even more in publishing, it is quite hard to find documents which give the true feel of Victorian debauchery. In the novels on which we rely for our general picture of the age, there may be an occasional mention of a young man penitently redeemed in the nick of time by his uncle—to have his father redeem him would have been going too far—or on the other hand an uncle, not redeemed in the nick of time, who now lives in Nicaragua, or Paris, and is terribly sunken-eyed and unmentionable. But we would no more expect an account of what they had been rescued from or not rescued from than we would expect the Air Force to press for disarmament. We are left with the impression that it could have been late nights with friends at the club. Even the St. John's Wood side of life, the respectable and mellow adulteries of the leafy suburb, were not chronicled at the time; that was left to a student of Victoriana, Sir Michael Sadleir, whose novel, *Fanny by Gaslight,* was published in 1944.

The patterns of adultery and marital strain were of course recorded in nineteenth-century France, but in Flaubert and Balzac and Zola you will find no picture of debauchery. Maupassant is perhaps the only writer of the time to give an inkling, though even that is faint. The Russian novelists were as reticent as the English.

No, it is best to go to the pornography of the time for a true picture, to put on one side all that is "romantic," that is wishfully linking fucking with ecstasy-to-death, which is most of it, and look for a book which has the marks of realism. The most considerable is an anonymous memoir called *My Secret Life,* published about 1888.

It is eleven volumes long, four thousand pages—as a matter of fact they are quite small pages, but still—and a copy is alleged to have been sold in 1926 for $17,000.

The author appears to have been a rich Englishman, and the unflagging length of his book reflects the unflagging length of his active life. It gives an artless picture of the sex addict, the one who can't stop, doesn't want to stop, can't think of anything else to do, is bored by having the same girl more than a week, hasn't had enough, will never have enough, can't have enough. He had a kink; he liked to get into girls who were still full of another man's seed. It's clear that, like the sadists, such a man is only worrying about the effect on himself; this particular kink is an emblem of positively desiring no response. His obliviousness to the tears, disasters and muddles he caused with his stupid money—he did not even take a sadistic pleasure in them—makes the book painful to read. It is a compulsively long and factual account of what it is like to be a compulsive collector of physical contacts. Although he paid for most of his experiences in money, he was a thief of touch; it is full of near rapes and surreptitious fumbles, and whenever a woman liked it, he was astonished.

The author of *My Secret Life* is like William Acton seen in a mirror. Acton's values were all based on a compelling physical fear of orgasm, the anonymous author's are all based on a compelling physical itch for it. God, society, morality and love are not real to either; both are engineers, the one of Manicheism, the other of promiscuity, and both are technicians of exclusion. To exclude fucking from what may be done, and to exclude it from what may, even for twenty-four hours, be left undone, are the same thing.

So much for the extremes of a mechanistic age. But what about the stakhanovites of today? Here we do not need documents, the people are all around us. Let us first narrow the field a little, and exclude very young people who have not yet developed a pattern of life but are casting about in the first impetuosity and free joy of sex, finding out what sort of thing suits them and what does not; let us talk of men of, say, twenty-two and up and women of twenty and up.

In the last fifty years, there have been sharp technological changes which, probably far more than social or economic ones, have made the map of sexual morality look different: indeed they have probably partly caused the social ones. First: contraception. None of the present techniques of contraception is very new except the pill; in the eighteenth century they had condoms and Dutch caps. What is new now is that they work. Until rubber technology reached its present condition, the apparatus was either so robust that you threw it away in despair of pleasure, or so unreliable that you might just as well never have used it. The rhythm method was known at different times and places, but since the doctors have still not got it quite buttoned up, it is not surprising that it affected things little. The only sure way was what the doctors call *coitus interruptus,* when the man gets out just before coming. To be any good at all, this depends on tremendous presence of mind; the woman has to come first then, before she has cooled off, the man has to get to the point where he's sure he's just going to come, and then get out. Both people feel like stranded whales.

But in recent decades, for the first time, with those two homely, simple, cheap and not too offputting devices, the rubber and the diaphragm, coition in itself is no longer a sufficient cause of pregnancy. (Nor even a necessary one; but artificial insemination does not concern us here.) To be sufficient, it must be one kind of coition, namely coition without contraceptives. There is a choice.

Likewise, the fear of disease has been removed, or very largely so. And here it is convenient to digress.

Gonorrhea has to all intents always been around in Mediterranean and European cultures. (The word is Greek for *flow of seed.* The white discharge was held to be an escape of semen out of season.) Egyptian mummies have been found to have had it. The strains of gonococcus no doubt went up and down in virulence, as they still do, so that at some times and places it was a terrible disease, the fear of which overflowed into people's everyday thoughts, and in others it was nothing worse than a cold.

The presence of gonorrhea in ancient and medieval Europe is not disputed, I think. But there is dispute about syphilis. In December of 1494 there was an outbreak of what seemed to be a new and worse sort of venereal disease among the French occupation troops in Naples, and it was immediately given one of its most permanent names, *il morbo gallico,* the French Evil. The new disease spread —or was recognized—throughout Italy and Europe, and in course of time the whole world, down to the tragic depopulations of certain South Sea islands in the eighteenth century. Some said it came back from America with Columbus' men, some said that it was a visitation on the

French soldiers for their imperialistic adventures, and there were other theories. Most scholars now think that the disease was endemic among the American Indians, and was in fact brought back by Columbus' men, but some still hold that it was present in medieval Europe and merely flared up in 1494.

The name *syphilis* comes from a Latin poem published in 1530 by the Veronese humanist Girolamo Fracastoro; it was called *"Syphilides, sive morbi gallici libri tres,"* "The Syphilid, or three books on the French Evil." *Syphilis* was Fracastoro's corruption of the classical *Sypilus* or *Sypilis,* who appears in Ovid as one of the sons of Niobe, a hardly mentioned shepherd boy. In the allegorical narrative which ends Fracastoro's poem, Syphilis is a shepherd boy in Hispaniola, who defies the sun-god in his demand for observances. The sun-god punishes him by sending a new plague on earth, of which the boy Syphilis is the first victim. Most of Fracastoro's poem is taken up with an account of the disease and of various treatments for it, and routine mythological conceits. He was not a very good writer and would probably not be remembered if he had not hit on an acceptable name for an intractable trouble.

In the Renaissance, and for different lengths of time afterward in different parts of the world, gonorrhea and syphilis were taken to be the same thing; gonorrhea was the early symptoms, syphilis the late. This mistake had a tragic and stupid result; the perfectly good cures which medieval Arab physicians had found for gonorrhea were discarded and forgotten because they didn't cure syphilis. Nineteenth-century microscopy separated the gonococcus from the treponeme, as it is called now, or the spirochete as it was called then, and made possible the succession of treatments which, ending with the antibiotics, have at last —not brought the diseases under control—but made it unnecessary that anyone should die of syphilis or be maimed by either.

Throughout European history, fucking has been something which could make you ill if you had bad luck, and since 1494 it has also been something which could kill you, with the hellish, using the word in the strict sense, refinement that it would often kill you only after twenty or thirty years of apparent moderate health. The slow and ineluctable progress of the pox—*majestic* was Baudelaire's word—was an emblem and reflection of the eternity of hell itself. If God did not punish you for the sins of your youth, the disease would. Or, with equal force, the punishment of God was executed by the *sbirri* of ailment: buboes, chancres, shambling, idiocy, an early and stinking death. When the spirochetes were first seen corkscrewing and wiggling under the microscope, they themselves took over the role of God's *sbirri*. (See Thomas Mann's *Doctor Faustus, passim*.) It is not always realized that, among other things, penicillin has abolished an enactment of hell in our midst which was a part of the very structure of our conscience and our personal freedom.

All that is past. Though they have not been abolished, probably never will be, and may recrudesce in resistant strains, the venereal are now cut down to the scale of other diseases.

Mid-twentieth century people then, for the first time in the history of Christendom, form the pattern of their sex lives with pregnancy a matter of choice, and with little fear of disease. They also, by and large, approach it without fear of hell, or at least without a recognized fear of hell.

The withdrawal of the big penalties of hell and bastardy has allowed a sort of neo-libertinism to appear in people of various inclinations; a patternless, unstructured, socially and spiritually functionless "sleeping around."

Among stakhanovites are many subdivisions. There are the knee-jerkers, who cannot refuse an invitation or a challenge. One lascivious glance, one idle caress, and all is up with them. They wake up in bed with a stranger. Many people are a bit like this when drunk, some people are like it all the time.

There are the novelty addicts; so many wonderful men

left to receive, so many wonderful gifts left to explore. Men novelty addicts are depressed by a crowd of girls; it shows the scale of the problem. This may be why lecturers at American women's colleges are often rather sad and quiet.

There are the virility provers, and their female counterpart the seductiveness provers. Look, I can still do it. No need to worry yet. Many people have a burst of this in early middle age, but some get that way even in their twenties. Some of these succeed in convincing themselves that they can in fact do what everybody has always been able to do, and find a better use for their faculties. Others can never quite convince themselves and go on and on until it is beyond their power to convince anybody.

There are certain non-mercenary kinkies, who need to do something that they feel they can't explain until they are actually in bed, and keep on trying partner after partner until they find one who likes it. But this is not pure stakhanovism; it is stakhanovism for a purpose.

There are the hypotenuse-hunters; men (rarely women) who have a sado-masochistic lock with a wife or a regular girl friend which works by the man having other women in order to be dominating and free, and the wife or girl friend taking pleasure in a devotion abject enough to encourage him.

There are the wife-punishers; they are trying to achieve a hypotenuse situation, but made a mistake about their wives. This is not a durable situation.

There are the actual triangulators whose own desire to have two women at once fits in with a Lesbian complaisance in their wives.[1]

There are the scalpers; got to hold our own among the boys.

And, overriding and permeating all these, there are the free, warm reactors. The cult of freedom, warmth and

[1] There was a recent novel about this: Tereska Torres, *Dangerous Games,* tr. from the French, New York, 1957, London, 1958.

gregariousness is a reaction, sometimes against the supposedly cold and constricted people all round, or, more often perhaps, against the past. As the libertines reacted against the Augustinianism in Christianity and finally against Christianity itself, as Victorian debauchees reacted against the mechanistic prohibitions of that age, so do contemporary stakhanovites react against the Cheshire scowl which is all that is left of Catharism.

There are large sectors of society in our cities and towns and commuter belts now where stakhanovism is the convention, and not only in the youngest of the three generations, but in the middle one too. In these sectors the pale ideals and pale sanctions of the stakhanovite way of life reign as prim and awful as the disapproving morality of the "suburbs" which Bloomsbury and D. H. Lawrence attacked in England from different angles forty years ago. There are two moral traditions facing each other now, as there always were, but the terrain has changed. They are exhausted and irrelevant traditions.

It is easy to see that a pendulum has been swinging in sexual morality in the West for the last four hundred years, taking about a century each way. We can count ourselves lucky to live in a century with an even number. It might go on swinging, perhaps faster owing to communications, but it is hard to see why it should now that so few people believe in the things that made it swing, the things that I have been outlining so far. It seems more likely to me that there will next be a time of perfect sexual freedom, by which I don't mean everybody laying everybody else regardless, but perfect freedom for everyone to live in the manner he has been conditioned to by chance and society, or has chosen by introspection and will. A time when men can be faithful husbands, unfaithful husbands, stakhanovites, orgiasts, homosexuals, whoremongers, kinkies, or monks, and women can be faithful wives, unfaithful wives, stakhanovites, orgiasts, Lesbians, whores, kinkies or nuns, exactly as they choose, and when this will rate the same sort of interest—which will still, thank God, be considerable—as whether they are parsons, journalists, school teachers, miners, electronic engineers or shorthand typists. But only the same sort. In this condition they will find their own way into the right life for them in accordance with those forces in society and themselves which cause them to seek that way and not another, and the individual causing factors will be stronger than the social ones. Above all, if the ban on knowing about and talking to people with a different sort of sex life from the accepted one is reduced, there will be less reason for people to be unhappy in this or that way of life because of ignorance. If it ever disappears entirely, then there will be no reason.

It's easy to see that some of the ways of life I listed above have got a long way to go before they escape the blanket ideal of chaste teenager, faithful spouse, and reach this millennium. But if they do, will there be more or fewer people in each of them? It is my hunch that there will be fewer, and my rather firm conviction that there will be at most no more. When we persecute one deviation, we probably swell the ranks of another without much reducing those of the one. If all persecution were to cease, I can see no reason why the ranks of any should increase.

PART VII

PROJECTION

Chapter 26

The Golden Age

In the last section we discussed some of the historical elements which have contributed to make us exclude sex from the realm of the normal, and feel bad about it. We have discussed the *why*. We must now turn to the *how*. In what ways do we do this excluding?

In two ways: by hypocrisy and by projection. I do not propose to dwell on hypocrisy; its workings are familiar to all except hypocrites, and even to some of them. It depends on the level where you set up the barrier between yes and no. If you say no with your voice and yes with your mind, you are a hypocritical liar. If you say no with your mind and yes with your heart, you are a hypocritical Anglo-Saxon. If you say no with your heart and yes with your balls, you are a neurotic, which is the deepest-dyed of all hypocrites. (If you say no all through you are a monk; if yes, a man.)

Projection on the other hand is more complicated and less familiar in its workings, and we do a tremendous amount of our excluding by this means. Projection is the system of feeling which says: "We don't do this, but other people do lots of it."

Here is the famous chorus which ends Act I of Tasso's *Aminta* (1573). The trailing rhythm and cumulative rhyme scheme of this poem in the Italian passed into our own pre-conscious notions of how a language should sound with Milton's *Ode on the Nativity* and, for a reason I cannot quite make out—did Bach read Tasso?—into our idea of how music should sound with the slow movement of the First Brandenburg Concerto. Its form lies behind much in our arts that delights us by going on longer than we had any right to expect.

But to the content:

O lovely golden age; yet not because the river ran with milk and the grove dropped honey, not because the earth gave her fruit all untouched by the plough and snakes went without spite or poison; not because the dark cloud then forebore to spread its wings or because the sky laughed with light and calm in an eternal spring from dawn to dusk, nor yet because the pilgrim hull brought not war nor goods to others' shores; but only because that empty name without a thing, that idol of error and idol of deceit, that which the healthless herd came to call Honor (and made it tyrant of our nature) mixed not its dark toils among the happy courtesy of the loving flock; nor was its stern law known to these souls bred in freedom; but the golden law that nature wrote: what you will, you may.

Then among streams and flowers the children of love without bows and without arrows raised sweet carols; shepherds and nymphs sat down, mixing caresses and whispers with their words, and with the whispers kisses closely clinging; the naked virgin then discovered her fresh roses which now she hides in her veil, and the sharp, new apples of her breast, and often, in the spring or in the lake, the lover was seen playing with his beloved.

You it was first, Honor, who veiled the source of delight, denying water to the thirst of love; who taught lovely eyes to hide within themselves and hold their beauties secret; who gathered hair in nets which had floated on the breeze; who made sweet lascivious deeds into deeds of contrariety and reserve; who imposed a check on words, and art on movement; it is your work alone, Honor, that what was once love's gift should be our theft.

And our pains and our complaints are of your capricious making. But you, the lord of love and nature, you, tamer of kingdoms, what are you doing in these cloisters which cannot comprehend your greatness? Away; trouble the sleep of the famous and the powerful, and leave us alone, us the forgotten and lowly multitude, to live after the way of the ancient people. Let us love; for the life of man has no truce with the years, and runs.

Let us love, for the sun dies and is born again. Its brief light hides from us, and sleep brings on eternal night.

The myth of the Golden Age is so potent that few writers or artists in this century bother to write it up. It is in all of us all the time; it informs much of what we feel and say. It is simply the feeling that somewhere, at some time, things must have been better. Whenever we say "nowadays" we are recalling the myth. How often in an ordinary day's talk do we hear that word? Things ain't what they used to be. The decline of standards. Those were the days. The good old days. Man was born free and everywhere is in chains. You have nothing to lose but your chains. In the beginning was the Word. It is so strong it even gives rise to little surfs of repetition when speech breaks over it; English "in this day and age," German "heutzutage," . . . Always these words precede a statement of loss, of impossibility. "Not in this day and age." In that day and age, they could do it, feel it, think it, get away with it, enjoy it, be free from it; whatever it is. Not now. Things have changed. Everything is altered for the worse. Change and decay in all around we see. *O tempora, O mores.*

In Christianity, it is institutionalized in the story of the Fall. Archeologists have claimed to know where the Garden of Eden was. The central image of Christianity is redemption, but we only needed a Redeemer because we had earlier lost out on the Golden Age. "The Second Adam . . ." To follow it in other creeds and peoples would be one way of writing a Summum Anthropologicum. Psychologists who lean toward the ontogenetic would say it is a construct in myth built on the experience of each of us individually. Generally speaking, we were golden when we were young, literally so; and if not, our brightness of spirit, our heedless generosity, and our sexual potency are well rendered by the image of gold. Some would push it farther and say young people themselves have a golden age of content to look back to in their mothers' wombs.

The European tradition finds money to be the root of all evil, and the main plank of its golden age myths is communism. Communism of land, goods, products and, patrists that we are, women; not so often of men. The myth of positive contentment and innocence lived equally long and strong both in the Greco-Roman culture and the Christian; in fact it linked the two. The pagan writer Seneca thought we deserved to lose it, which is a Christian attitude, and the Christian writer St. Clement of Alexandria thought it had included sexual communism, which is a pagan attitude.

It is the sexual communism of the Golden Age which interests us here. We have already quoted Tasso's evocation of it, perhaps the finest of all. Here is Theocritus, XII, 15-16:

"They loved one another with an equal yoke; men were indeed golden in those days when the loved one loved in return."

Eros was the god of love and the word for love between human beings; the god grew out of the word, as we saw before. And once again a little god grew up like grass between the paving-stones; he was called Anteros, and is mostly forgotten now. The sources for him are Pausanias (VI. 23), and some pieces in the Greek Anthology. In Pausanias he is described fighting with his brother Eros in a painting on the wall of a gymnasium. Both were the sons of Venus, and they are fighting over a palm. They are described also by the Italian Renaissance mythologist Cartari, who explains that the palm they are fighting for is the palm of victory in a contest about which loves the more and the better.[1]

Eros existed to say "I love you." Anteros existed to protest: "I love you back, just as much as you can possibly love me." Eros had a bow to shoot love into people's hearts. Anteros had a whip to punish those who did not return their lover's love. Not to return devotion was a most undue thing, a most unusual thing, worthy of censure. The right web of life demanded a return, otherwise you tore the web; nature, or the gods, would punish you. Their agent would be the offended principle, the offended word itself; back-love, Anteros.

Anteros is the Golden Age, the age when all lovers loved reciprocally and calmly, when there was no frustration in desire and no disappointment in love. The Greeks put it back before their time, but at least they had a name for it. Christian Europe has not; we remember Eros, though we deny him; we forget his partner and antithesis, his necessary obverse.

A passage from Diodorus Siculus is often quoted as a version of the Golden Age myth. It seems to be a mixture of mythology and anthropology, that is to say a secondhand account of a distant but real people, suffused with the elements of the myth. Two Greeks are taken prisoner by the Ethiopians, and then pushed out to sea without means of propulsion in an open boat. This is a good mythical beginning. But they are pushed south, a factual detail which makes one think of Madagascar. They come to an archipelago of seven islands, and one thinks of the East Indies. The people of these islands have cleft or double tongues, which they cleave still farther back, and this enables them to talk to two people at once. (Here the mind turns to Yogism, where people slit the tendon connecting their tongues with the floors of their mouths in order to be able to turn it back and block their throats with it, which is considered a useful accomplishment for spiritual purposes.)

---

[1] Vincenzo Cartari, *Le Imagini dei Dei de gli Antichi*, 1556.

The people have hairless bodies. (Hereabouts we oscillate between India and Southeast Asia). Their social organization is based on clans and tribes; the oldest man is the head of each clan of four hundred people. (This could be almost anywhere). There is communism of wives, and the children are brought up communally. (A projection of something nearer home? Or is it one of the more happy-go-lucky phases of Hinduism?) They have oil and wine, but also edible snakes, and things which seem to be rice and cotton are described, as well as how they are used. There are hot springs, and our stars are not visible. (This narrows it down a good deal.) The language is a written one; there are seven characters, each of which can be pronounced in four different ways. (China?) Moreover, the writing goes from top to bottom of the page. All in all, good guessing-ground.

The tone of Diodorus Siculus' account is admiring; he presents this mysterious people as living happily in an excellent and mechanically regular climate, untroubled by property or jealousy. Like much work by anthropologists of our own day, it is a mixture of observation and of homage to the myth of the Lotus Land, which is the same as the Golden Age, being removed only along another dimension.

Let us jump now into Christian Europe and take an example from a time when people reacted after a millennium of Augustinian Christianity with a form of the myth which concentrates quite wholeheartedly on the sexual aspect of primitive communism; the *Cazzaria*, or "Prickery," of the Italian Renaissance writer Antonio Vignale (see Appendix 5). This tragi-comic work narrates the origin of human society in terms of how the various bits and pieces of people, and especially their pricks and cunts, came together to form individuals. In the beginning there was no society, and no people; there were simply *membra disjecta* which did exactly as they pleased, there being as yet no bonds of law or custom. Society arose through the operation of injustice or perhaps original sin itself, which made necessary classes and alliances of classes. The big pricks kept the pretty cunts to themselves, so the little pricks and ugly cunts revolted; it is a familiar strand of European political theory. But what interests us here is that in seeking for an image of primitive anarchy, of the good old days before anything as unpleasant as society was needed, Vignale should have chosen the sexual organs themselves. He made a *reductio ad absurdum* of the feeling that the Golden Age *was* fucking; there were not even people then, just the most important bits of people. In allowing themselves to be formed up into something so violent and unreasonable as people, the very principles of freedom and pleasure were the victims of tragedy, a continuous tragedy which is still enacted in all our lives. Indeed, it is only superficially a comic book; the regret which informs it sometimes seems as passionate as Christian contrition itself.

In the Renaissance there were many visual images of the Golden Age, there was much laboring over the mythology the Greeks used to express perfect human love, and all this implies the statement that it is lost, that it was once and may or may not be again. We will take as an example four paintings by Agostino Carracci now in the Kunsthistorisches Museum at Vienna.

Agostino, the less famous brother of Annibale Carracci, and mainly an engraver, was at home in the erotic. Wittkower (*Art and Architecture in Italy, 1660-1750*) holds that the Carracci family saw the erotic and the "obscene" as part of "low life," as part of the genre paintings which they, as much as any others, invented, and which have continued ever since. But certainly the grand-manner frescoes of Annibale Carracci in the Palazzo Farnese at Rome are erotic, and certainly too the erotic pictures which we are about to describe are grand. I do not think it is possible to maintain that they relegated the erotic as subject matter into a special category of quaint or miniature observation. It seems to have been part of the main stream of life to them.

The four pictures in question are usually called *The*

Golden Age or *The Four Loves.*[2] They are *Reciprocal Love, The Golden Age, Lethean Love* and *The Scourge of Love*. The two children in *Reciprocal Love* are Eros and Anteros. The picture is just what the title says it is; a picture of multiple answeringness, of general fulfillment, of the lost state of affairs when love calls up love and there are no loose ends.

The second picture, *The Golden Age*, is the same.

The third, *Lethean Love*, shows groups of boys and girls bathing separately, while between them Eros douses his torch in a river which has the quality of making you fall out of love.

The fourth, *The Scourge of Love*, shows Anteros again. Here he is being pulled along in a cart drawn by two lovers and is whipping their backs because one of them failed to return the love of the other. There are suicides in the background, and Dr. Kurz has shown that they include two characters called Timagoras and Meletes who killed themselves respectively from chagrin at not having called up an answering passion and remorse for not having answered the initial passion. (The picture follows a plate in that obscure and marvelous hodgepodge of early Renaissance philosophy and mythology and teaching on love, the book *Hypnerotomachia*, or the Dream-Love-Battle, by a Venetian friar called Colonna, who wrote as Poliphilus.)

Agostino Carracci was not a great painter, but he was a very competent and interesting one, and these pictures are his best. But eighty years, and the Council of Trent, had passed since Aretino and Giulio Romano collaborated on their unprecedentedly straightforward view of fucking, and Agostino Carracci put quotation marks round his pictures; he explicitly moved them into the realm of myth. He took them out of the houses and woods of Italy at the turn of the sixteenth and seventeenth century and set them back not only a millennium and a half, as Giulio Romano

<hr>

[2] This account of them is based on Dr. Otto Kurz's article, *"Gli Amori dei Carracci,"* in the *Journal of the Warburg and Courtauld Institutes*, Vol. XIV, pp. 221 et seq.

had set his back, but into the never-never land before the Fall. It couldn't be "us, now" it had to be "them, then."

A number of rather hot and hurried-looking Dutch and Flemish pictures arose out of Agostino's achievement, answering the forms and the general point in mythology. There is even an English drawing which Dr. Kurz holds derived from it. It is a *Nymphs and Satyrs* by Isaac Oliver. Oliver carried the removal one stage farther by making the men not men but satyrs; an alienation gambit which we discuss in the next chapter.

If we leave aside William Blake, whose work is full of the Golden Age of free love, but who is almost a cultural tradition in himself, and so not assimilable in a book of this length, by far the best expression of the myth in English verse is the *Rapture* of Thomas Carew. This is neither a short poem nor an unknown one, but I should like to quote it here because one of my purposes is to give a general idea of the erotic in the European tradition, and it seems to me that the *Rapture* is the high-water mark of erotic writing in English. Never before or since has our chaste old language been bent with such ease and fire to the task of describing our only origin and our greatest pleasure. This poem, and the Song of Songs in the Authorized Version of the Bible a few years before, are about the only things we can read in English and feel that we are not after all left entirely speechless compared with all those well-rounded Latins.

A Rapture

I will enjoy thee now my Celia, come
And flye with me to Loves Elizium:
The Gyant, Honour, that keeps cowards out,
Is but a Masquer, and the servile rout
Of baser subjects onely, bend in vaine
To the vast Idoll, whilst the nobler traine
Of valiant Lovers, daily sayle betweene
The huge Collosses legs, and passe unseene,
Unto the blissful shore; be bold, and wise,

And we shall enter, the grim Swisse denies
Only tame fooles a passage, that not know
He is but forme, and onely frights in show
The duller eyes that looke from farre; draw neere,
And thou shalt scorne, what we were wont to feare.
We shall see how the stalking Pageant goes
With borrowed legs, a heavie load to those
That made, and beare him; not as we once thought
The seed of Gods, but a weake modell wrought
By greedy men, that seeks to enclose the common,
And within private armes empale free woman.
    Come then, and mounted on the wings of love
Wee'le cut the flitting ayre, and sore above
The Monsters head, and in the noblest seates
Of those blest shades, quench, and renew our heates.
There, shall the Queene of Love, and Innocence,
Beautie and Nature, banish all offence
From our close Ivy twines, there I'le behold
Thy bared snow, and thy unbraded gold.
There, my enfranchiz'd hand, on every side
Shall o're thy naked polish'd Ivory slide.
No curtaine there, though of transparant lawne,
Shall be before thy virgin-treasure drawne;
But the rich Mine, to the enquiring eye
Expos'd, shall ready still for mintage lye,
And we will coyne young Cupids. There, a bed
Of Roses, and fresh Myrtles, shall be spread
Under the cooler shade of Cypresse groves:
Our pillowes, of the downe of Venus Doves,
Where on our panting lims wee'le gently lay
In the faint respites of our active play;
That so our slumbers, may in dreams have leisure,
To tell the nimble fancie our past pleasure;
And so our soules that cannot be embrac'd,
Shall the embraces of our bodyes taste.
Meane while the bubbling streame shall court the shore,
Th' enamoured chirping Wood-quire shall adore
In Varied tunes the Deitie of Love;
The gentle blasts of westerne winds, shall move
The trembling leaves, & through their close bows breath
Still Musick, whilst we rest our selves beneath
Their dancing shade; till a soft murmure, sent

From soules entranc'd in amorous languishment
Rowze us, and shoot into our veines fresh fire,
Till we, in their sweet extasie expire.
    Then, as the empty Bee, that lately bore,
Into the common treasure, all her store,
Flyes 'bout the painted field with nimble wing,
Deflowring the fresh virgins of the Spring;
So will I rifle all the sweets, that dwell
In my delicious Paradise, and swell
My bagge with honey, drawne forth by the power
Of fervent kisses, from each spicie flower.
I'le sieze the Rose-buds in their perfum'd bed,
The Violet knots, like curious Mazes spread
O're all the Garden, taste the ripened Cherry,
The Warme, firme Apple, tipt with corall berry;
Then will I visit, with a wandering kisse,
The Vale of Lillies, and the Bower of blisse;
And where the beauteous Region doth divide
Into two milkie wayes, my lips shall slide
Downe those smooth Allies, wearing as I goe
A tract for lovers on the printed snow;
Thence climbing o'er the swelling Appenine,
Retire into thy grove of Eglantine;
Where I will all those ravisht sweets distill
Through Loves Alimbique, and with Chimmique skill
From the mixst masse, one soveraigne Balme derive,
Then bring that great Elixar to thy hive.
    Now in more subtile wreaths I will entwine
My sinowie thighes, my legs and armes with thine;
Thou like a sea of milke shalt lye display'd,
Whilst I the smooth, calme Ocean, invade
With such a tempest, as when Jove of old
Fell downe on Danae in a storme of gold:
Yet my tall Pine, shall in the Cyprian straight
Ride safe at Anchor, and unlade her fraight:
My Rudder, with thy bold hand, like a tryde,
And skilfull Pilot, thou shalt steere, and guide
My Bark into Loves channell, where it shall
Dance, as the bounding waves doe rise or fall:
Then shall thy circling armes, embrace and clip
My willing bodie, and thy balmie lip
Bathe me in juyce of kisses, whose perfume

Like a religious incense shall consume,
And send up holy vapours, to those powres
That blesse our loves and crowne our sportful houres,
That with such Halcion calmenesse, fix our soules
In steadfast peace, as no affright controules.
There, no rude sounds shake us with sudden starts,
No jealous eares, when we unrip our hearts
Sucke our discourse in, no observing spies
This blush, that glance traduce; no envious eyes
Watch our close meetings, nor are we betrayed
To Rivals, by the bribed chamber-maid.
No wedlock bonds unwreathe our twisted loves;
We seeke no midnight Arbor, no darke groves
To hide our kisses, there, the hated name
Of husband, wife, lust, modest, chaste, or shame,
Are vaine and empty words, whose very sound
Was never heard in the Elizian ground.
All things are lawfull there, that may delight
Nature, or unrestrained Appetite;
Like, and enjoy, to will, and act, is one,
We only sinne when Loves rites are not done.
    The Roman Lucrece there, reades the divine
Lectures of Loves great master, Aretine,
And knows as well as Lais, how to move
Her plyant body in the act of love.
To quench the burning Ravisher, she hurles
Her limbs into a thousand winding curles,
And studies artfull postures, such as be
Carv'd on the barke of every neighbouring tree
By learned hands, that so adorn'd the rinde
Of those faire Plants, which as they lay entwinde,
Have fann'd their glowing fires. The Grecian Dame,
That in her endless webb, toyl'd for a name
As fruitless as her worke, doth there display
Her selfe before the Youth of Ithaca,
And th' amorous sport of gamesome nights prefer,
Before dull dreames of the lost Traveller.
Daphne hath broke her barke, and that swift foot,
Which th' angry Gods had fastned with a root
To the fixt earth, doth now unfetter'd run,
To meet th' embraces of the youthfull Sun;
She hangs upon him, like his Delphique Lyre,
Her kisses blow the old, and breath new fire;

Full of her God, she sings inspired Layes,
Sweet odes of love, such as deserve the Bayes,
Which she her selfe was. Next her, Laura lyes
In Petrarchs learned armes, drying those eyes
That did in such sweet smooth-pac'd numbers flow,
As made the world enamour'd of his woe.
These, and ten thousand Beauties more, that dy'de
Slave to the Tyrant, now enlarg'd, deride
His cancell'd lawes, and for their time mispent,
Pay into Loves Exchequer double rent.
　　Come then my Celia, wee'le no more forebeare
To taste our joys, struck with a Pannique feare,
But will depose from his imperious sway
This proud Usurper and walke free, as they
With necks unyoak'd; nor is it just that Hee
Should fetter your soft sex with Chastitie,
Which Nature made unapt for abstinence;
When yet this false Impostor can dispence
With humane Justice, and with sacred right,
And maugre both their lawes command me fight
With Rivals, or with emulous Loves, that dare
Equall with thine, their Mistresse eyes, or haire:
If thou complaine of wrong, and call my sword
To carve out thy revenge, upon that word
He bids me fight and kill, or else he brands
With markes of infamie my coward hands,
And yet religion bids from blood-shed flye,
And damns me for that Act. Then tell me why
This Goblin Honour which the world adores,
Should make men Atheists, and not women Whores.

Carew has more here than splendid sensual poetry and
an appeal to the Golden Age; he has a program. We must
learn to treat Honor, which was Tasso's bugbear too, as
a masker who only denies tame fools a passage, and later
on we must arise in open rebellion against him, and deride
his canceled laws. What was honor, to Carew and to Tasso,
and to Donne in his Elegies? I think it was a concept of
economic and political power, not a religious one. Honor
required Carew to draw his sword and fight (like an in-
fidel) if anyone spoke ill of his mistress, and a fortiori if
anyone threatened to take her from him. It is an attack on

marriage and fidelity as political institutions, not as religious ones. Indeed, the neat map he draws of the situation in his last couplet tests the concept against the assumedly higher values of Christianity. Here is honor, he says, which forces me to go against my religion in drawing blood; would not an opposite concept which forced Celia to go against her religion by being a whore be equally justifiable, or unjustifiable?

Donne, too, in the love poems of his youth rails at fidelity and chastity as the constructs of lay, political honor, not as the constructs of religion. He did not retrace his steps and contradict himself when he became a Dean and wrote the religious poems; he made a knight's move.

Carew was the friend and, in some respects, admirer of Lord Herbert of Cherbury, the first English metaphysician, whose *Autobiography* contains what is to us a very silly and surprising account of the man of honor. When Herbert was ambassador in Paris, he used to challenge and be challenged to duels about whose glove a girl of twelve had picked up or thrown down. There is no suggestion that he cared in the least for the little girl, either in an avuncular way or in a Humbert Humbert way; he cared only for an autophagous system of values and penalties, perhaps more akin to gambling than to love. The code of honor in the seventeenth century was a poor leftover rag of the "Arthurian" code, which was itself a splendid example of diversionary activity. If you spent all your time charging around looking for damsels in distress and giving and taking mighty knocks with the nearest knight who might have caused the distress, you never got round to fucking the damsel. Herbert's game in the embassy nursery is the *reductio ad absurdum* of the tradition, and Carew's *Rapture* expostulates.

Lord Herbert of Cherbury's brother, George Herbert the poet, took a view opposite to that of Carew:

If God had laid all common, certainly
  Man would have been th' encloser: but since now

God hath impaled us, on the contrary
  Man breaks the fence and every ground will plough.

Carew and the golden agers, according to George Herbert, were not seeking to go back beyond the bad human custom of honor, which is against religion, to the Golden Age of freedom before the Fall; they were seeking to overthrow religion itself. There never had been a time when women and goods were "laid all common"; God had impaled and fenced us from the start, and communism, whether of goods or of people, was against the divine will. To this view, the Golden Age myth must appear as an act of human imperialism toward God, seeking to carry him along as the flag of what is no more than rebellion and contumacy. One may inquire which of these two seventeenth-century poets was the better man, but there can be no doubt which was the better Christian.

The other view got a new lease of life in the work of the nineteenth-century sociologists Bachofen and Morgan, and of Marx himself. To them, the Golden Age was a perfectly real thing which had happened in the primitive past, even more real than it had been to Rousseau and Laclos. They interpreted their sketchy knowledge of contemporary tribal life as confirmation that the Golden Age still existed here and there, and consequently had probably also existed in our own past. Marx tended to see the institution of marriage as having grown in the same way as the accumulations of power and capital which it was his principal concern to overthrow. The clever and strong got not only the field, the cows, and the money, but also the women, more than their share of them, and at last the average man revolted and insisted on the institution of monogamy. (Just as they insisted later, according to this scheme, on the institution of the bourgeoisie.) Vignale's allegory of the big pricks keeping all the pretty cunts to themselves and being overthrown by the little pricks was applicable to most Christian thinking on the origin of marriage in non-Christian societies, until twentieth-century anthropology traced patterns of kinship and taboo.

Whatever else he may or may not have at a certain moment, man always has discontents. As soon as he notices a discontent, he has already imagined a state of affairs where it would be absent. He may then contemplate the animals or the angels, but this will lead him to a glum immobility which is both useless and unattractive to his fellows; such a cast of mind will breed itself out by counter-selection. He is far more likely to conceive that things either were or are going to be better, or both. A belief that things were better, a belief in the Golden Age, is quite useful; it gives rise to historical scholarship and criticism at one end of the scale, and a decent respect for the traditions of the land at the other. A belief that things are going to be, and even more can be made to be, better is very useful indeed, and especially attractive to young people of the opposite sex; it is therefore selectively perpetuated. It gives rise to revolution and reform at one end of the scale, and to ardent activity of one sort or another all the way along it. A belief that things both were better and can be made to be better again is the most approved of all, and thus the most selectively favored by breeding. It gives rise to the temperament, calm yet active, careful of the past yet solicitous for the future, which is preferred by most moralists of our species, and celebrated in all the myths of fall and redemption.

Yet all three beliefs are false. Things were never better, and never will be. They were only different, and they will only be different. Discontents have been removed, and will be removed. But the removal of one brings in another of equal size, or two more of half the size; this is the law of the conservation of discontent. Man is a half-happy, half-miserable creature, and to believe objectively that discontent, any more than energy, can disappear is to suppose that man might have been or might become other than human.

The Golden Age and the millennium are the names we give to these beliefs. We attribute to these ages freedom from the particular discontents that irk us in the time and culture we inhabit. We in the West attribute to them now, and have attributed to them for a couple of thousand years, material and sexual communism. It is our choice; we need not have attributed these things to them. We could without contradicting our nature as human beings have attributed to them autocracy, or monasticism, or bellicosity, or unrelieved physical immobility, or even, come to that, a prevalence of graceful green rabbits three feet high. Our choice identifies our discontents; they are property and chastity. By their Golden Age shall ye know them.

Now it would not be interesting to say that our culture has *too much* property and chastity; too much for what, or compared with what? The stock comparison would be with the Golden Age itself, which is a myth. But it does seem meaningful to say that it has *so much* of these things that they, and not other things, elbow their way into the contrary mirror of our collective dream. Our desire is to have less of them, and we project our desire in myth.

We have this, but we dream of that. If we had that, it is easy to see that we should dream of this; there is the usual tension between reality and dream. One is tempted once again to say: "we have too much of this; otherwise we should not dream of that. It is *wrong* that we should have so much of this. Let us put our dreams into effect and have more of that." But to say or feel this is to postulate that there is a part of us which sees the reality of our daily lives, judges it lacking, and makes up the lack by selecting the dream which will best balance it. In this postulated map the daily reality lies to one side of that central part of us, and the dream lies to the other.

Some hold that this central dreambuilding and myth-building part of us is indeed real, and is our essence. But among those who do hold this, there is no agreement what it is like. This disagreement is one aspect of the history of thought. That is so even within one culture. But if we were to take the tension between reality and myth-dream in different cultures, believing that their essential humanity was halfway between the two in each case, we should by no means get entities which would resemble each other so closely as to enable us to say: "Here is man; I have found him." We should on the contrary get a spread of essential humanities even wider than that which we get between the reality and the myth-dream within each culture.

On the one hand we build the daily reality of society, on the other we dream dreams and build myths. But it is not one part of us which builds the society and the other which builds the myth; it is we, we ourselves as whole individuals, who do both, just as one and the same pair of hands can both chop wood and make a gesture. There is no transcendent adjuster sitting in our minds.

The fact that we dream and mythicize about material and sexual communism does not mean our society is *wrong* to have so much property and chastity, it merely means it is the sort of society which has a certain amount of property and chastity and which dreams about their opposites. If ever the dream and the myth become the daily reality, then we shall be able to say that, according to the values which at that point began to prevail in our society, we had hitherto been wrong.

Chapter 27

Animals, Foreigners and Women

> *Even the dolphins burn*
> *with human love.*
>
> —*Alessandro Adimari*[1]

Better, freer and, above all, *more* sex is one of the things
we project into our Golden Age myths. *They* used to do
a lot of it, we say, until things went wrong. Or alternatively, they (Adam and Eve) didn't do any of it at all
until things went wrong. But one way or the other, it is
certainly part, and a big part, of all our *they* feelings. If
ever things were better, it was certainly because they
ordered these things, meaning sex, differently in Eden, and
we project tremendous sexual activity onto them, whoever
they may be, far more often than tremendous abstinence.

And the Golden Age is by no means the only direction
in which we project it. Even the dolphins, according to
the Renaissance allegorist, burn with human love. Without going as far as that, it is certain that from the Greek

---

[1] Emblem 53 from *Emblemi Amorosi,* a Renaissance bestiary in
which the animals are used as emblems of different kinds of love.

satyr on we have tended to import animals onto the human scene when we wanted to symbolize or call to mind physical love. The first female nudes in Christian iconography are the mermaids on churches of the "dark ages"; there are examples at Pavia and Verona. These little creatures, with their twin tails spread wide and curling up to be held in their own hands, are a sort of lightning conductor for Augustinian and Manichean Christianity. Nakedness? Yes, of course there's such a thing as nakedness. Look, these creatures do it, funny little things, but people don't. Never make that mistake; nakedness and copulation are all right for satyrs and mermaids and things like that, but not for people.

Consider too all the animals to which we still attribute tremendous sexual prowess. Ferrets (mistakenly, as the ferret-fanciers organization in England never tires of pointing out: they want ferrets to be like people, therefore chaste), rabbits in a hundred stories (whambam, thankyou mam, etc.), stags (rutting: evocative word), pedigree bulls (the morals of a . . .), rams, goats, and so on.

Consider the reputed existence of enormous collections of pornography here and there in the world. I mentioned earlier the belief that the Vatican has the biggest of these. It is also believed that the custom of segregating erotic books originated in the Vatican Library. Other details of the story are that the collection was built up, particularly by certain named popes, from books and pictures sent in by parish priests who had received them at the deathbeds of penitent parishioners. The fact is that there is no such collection at all. It is also said in Rome that there are locked rooms containing erotic frescoes in the Farnesina and the Villa Madama. There are none; the rumor probably arose because Raphael worked at both places, and Giulio Romano was Raphael's assistant, and therefore. . . .

But when we come to people, the habit of attributing tremendous sexual activity to them, to the others, to anybody but ourselves, is very well established. In England, it is said that Wales is the place. How many stories depend on the surprise of finding a virgin in Wales? I have heard educated and traveled men argue seriously that the quality of sensuality is higher in Wales than elsewhere in the British Isles. The girls of Nottingham are supposed to be especially attractive and accessible. In Italy, it is Sicily. Any discussion among *hommes moyens sensuels* in Italy about sexual customs comes to a resigned halt at the mention of Sicily. Down there, the feeling is, they never do anything else. It's not worth discussing, because it's impossible to make out any pattern or value in the general welter of lechery. Every country, every group, has its symbolic shrine of Venus to which is attributed "above-average sexual activity."

The foreigner, of course, is even more likely to be sexmad than this or that group in our own country. European literature is full of lecherous Turks and Moors—Monostatos in *The Magic Flute* and a thousand others. Jews were alleged to be given to buggery. There are Chinese scrolls showing Mongols riding their women on horseback, and the Japanese call menstruation the Manchu sickness. In England, almost everything to do with sex has always had a foreign name. We call rubbers French letters, cunt-licking Frenching, simultaneous cunt-licking and cock-sucking *soixante-neuf*, kissing with the tongue in the other's mouth French kissing. We call a diaphragm a Dutch cap, a masturbation machine a Dutch husband or wife, and buggery the Italian manner. A hundred years ago it was considered morally dangerous for young ladies in low-church upper middle-class families to learn French; they might read French novels. In 1960 there was a film on at a Soho clip-joint called "The Frenchman's Dream."

The French, of course, call a French letter an English overcoat, and say "the English have landed" for menstruation, just as they call taking French leave "taking English leave." They also call flagellation the English vice, and all of western Europe combines to pin buggery on the Bulgars.

We hold that the Chinese go on fucking for hours at a time, and there is a legend that the women's cunts run sideways instead of fore and aft. (Some sort of assimilation to the *cheongsam*?)

But above all it is on the Negro that we project our sexuality. White erotic literature is full of images of the buck nigger who alone can assuage the inordinate desires etc., etc., and of the doe-eyed, compliant yet fiery native woman or mulatto or *métisse* or *négrillonne* whose embraces once tasted can never, etc., etc. And what rich overtones there are of sadistic superiority for the white man and masochistic inferiority for the white woman. Colored people are earth, they are low, animal, pure impurity, "mud" as Mellors has it in *Lady Chatterley's Lover*. They are black, and so belong to the delightful devil and his forces of ruttish wrong. On a slightly more sophisticated level, they are simple and primitive and friendly, without the inhibitions that come with the machine society; with them we can roll back into the true warmth and understanding of the Golden Age.

Above all, of course, *They* have enormous pricks. This is something we simply can't get over. It provided the central episode of Terence Rattigan's play about T. E. Lawrence, *Ross*. It provides the point of countless "funny" stories and underlies most race riots and racial persecution. It lies as image of the extreme sensual experience, half agony, half bliss, behind the world picture of some white women, and behind the world picture which more white men believe their women to have. In some circles, where Negroes are unfamiliar, it may be the first thing we mention to them. I remember the gasp of incredulity with which an American Negro in Rome said about some society women at a party: "They ask you . . . the length of . . . your prick."

The, as it were, official ethnological view about this is that it is probably not so. Myrdal says it is a common belief "which has not yet been checked by scientific research," and quotes an anatomist who said he had "never had any occasion to remark any appreciable difference. . . ."[2] This view is so far accepted that in educated and liberal circles in New York and London and Paris it is a kind of unmentioned joke that anybody can ever have believed the story.

So it is amusing to turn to a black sociologist on the matter. A. da Silva Mello, in his *Nordeste Brasileiro* writes that sexual attraction is important as a factor in natural selection, and nowhere more important than in northeastern Brazil.[3] Ethnologists should not, therefore, limit their studies to the dimensions of heads and hands, but should study the sexual organs too. As far as he can judge, the *caboclos* and *mulatos* of the northeast, whether they are short or tall, have penises superior to those of other peoples both in size and in serviceability. Probably their psychology accords with their physical equipment. He has noticed that in white men with a dash of black in them the skin of the penis and scrotum is often quite black, as though there were a natural affinity between blackness and sexuality. "Another superiority in the sexual, which is to say racial, equipment of its bearer?"

"After all this," he asks, "where are we to place that tall, strong, bulky man, with his blue eyes and his golden hair, his large hands and feet, and his small, sometimes ridiculously small, sexual apparatus?" When Silva Mello was a medical student and a young doctor in European hospitals, he often noticed that little Mediterranean-type men had the advantage in this matter over Scandinavian and German giants. He later learned that the difference was "not only anatomical, but principally functional." His Brazilian student friends seemed real athletes to German girls, and German students would come in flocks to admire the collection of African penises in the Berlin Anatomical Institute, which remained in permanent erection because of the preservative injected into them. "Because of all this,

---

[2] Gunnar Myrdal, *An American Dilemma: The Negro Problem and Modern Democracy,* New York, 1944, pp. 140 and 1213.

[3] *Coleçao Documentos Brasileiros,* Vol. 73, Rio de Janeiro, 1953, pp. 297–299.

how can we refrain from classifying the masculine sex organ, both anatomically and functionally, as the most important for social and anthropological values?"

As far as I know, an anthropometric study to settle this vexed question has still not been made. It would be excessively simple, and one can only suppose that it is the general fuzz surrounding sex in our culture, and particularly the fear of seeming ridiculous, which has prevented it. In the meantime, one can only note the three attitudes: (1) (White view) Negroes are different from us, therefore they must fuck more, and have bigger pricks, (2) (White view) Negroes are no different from us, therefore it is illiberal and racist to suppose they have bigger pricks, (3) (Black view) White men are different from us, therefore they must fuck less and have smaller pricks.

Famous people come in for as much projection as foreign people. There is a series of obscene prints showing all Napoleon's marshals hard at it in the countries they had conquered, and single prints of Napoleon himself, and the Pompadour, and Byron, and Aaron Burr. In America, though not in England, there is a flourishing trade in booklets of obscene comic strips showing the famous; you have not arrived in the hall of fame until you have had one about you. Often there is a little-man's-revenge flavor to them; the big boxer will have a tiny prick, the famous bit of beefcake will come too early, while the little man will show himself a perfect paragon. Libel does not arise, since the things are illegal as pornography anyhow. They are so widespread that some sociologists believe they are the chief way American boys are informed on the actual basic look and facts of sex.

Clerics have always attracted projection. A belief in their dissolute ways was one of the reasons for the abolition of the monasteries and of clerical celibacy in northern Europe. In countless pornographic novels the hero is an abbot or a bishop; orgy scenes are more often than not set in convents. There even exists a *Bibliographie Clérico-Galante*. Here the need to project onto an unfamiliar class of persons coincides with and is reinforced by the pleasure of exposing hypocrisy, and of imagining someone doing something which he doesn't look as though he ever would. Also the automatic need to invert the elements of a cult; if the cult rests on chastity, it will be bound to give rise to a counter-cult, whether in literature or life, based on promiscuity. In French pornographic novels, English *milords* run abbots a close second.

Foreigners, people of another race, famous people, clerics, lords, anybody different will do. But pornography is made by men, and there is one class of people who are under men's eyes all the time, and are yet visibly different: women. It seems to me that an amazing amount of what men in our society think about women is folklore tinged with projection mechanism. Very often, in the Christian erotic tradition, they appear to be simply foreign men; creatures superficially like us but underneath it all tremendously addicted to fucking, far more than we could ever be. We have already mentioned the tradition of Lesbian art, and remarked how these were not really pictures of Lesbians but of two heterosexual women, such as the artist knew, doing together the things that he had seen them doing with him. There is another tradition too, that of the women's bath pictures. The most famous is Ingres' "Bain Turc." An earlier one, and more specific in the message, is a print of the Fontainebleau school. Behind this too there lies a shadowy medieval tradition of public bath pictures. The feeling is; when a lot of women get together with no clothes on, this is bound to be what happens. Of course it is not what happens when a lot of men get together with no clothes on, but it is what I would like to happen if I got together with a lot of women with no clothes on, therefore it must be what happens. Where's my pencil?

Formerly, and the topic is bound up with the whole history of embryology and genetics, women were thought to *spend* just like men. *Spend* is the old English word for come; women were thought to diffuse an actual fecund fluid at the moment of orgasm exactly as men ejaculated.

The old erotic books are full of descriptions of the mingling of these vital fluids. Man does this at the moment of pleasure, so presumably that little passive counterpart of himself which is his woman does exactly the same. We wonder now how this can ever have been believed, but it may be that we shall soon look back on the Freudian concept of "penis envy" with equal wonder; man has one of those, and the lesser creature must envy him the main respect in which he differs from her.

The projection toward women often uses one or the other of two physical stepping stones, two mediations in matter: the dildo and the clitoris. The frequency with which the dildo crops up in the corpus of erotic art and literature teaches us a lot about that male-conditioned world. The things themselves are rare; they exist in all cultures and at all times, but in very small numbers. It appears from the Kinsey Report that Lesbians do not, or hardly ever, use dildoes, and it must also appear, to anybody who is more concerned with what really happens than with the joys of projection, that they would not. Masturbation for a woman consists of tickling her clitoris, not of plunging a great hard piece of machinery in and out of herself. Likewise, love-making between two Lesbians, as between a man and woman, consists of using what they have, not on manufactured hardware. What one loves about someone else, whether the beloved is of the same or the opposite sex, is herself (or himself). And yet in pictures and erotic stories by men, one comes again and again on the dildo. It is a refusal to accept the difference of women, a projection onto them of the need to use and the need to experience what the man has and the woman has not. It is also an excellent emblem of lust itself, of using the body as a thing. It stands in for the body; it is haptism in an extreme form. Nothing else matters, only the local, concrete, reproducible, purchaseable organ.

The clitoris gives a justification in the flesh for the feeling that women are really just the same as men. Look, they have pricks, too! Of course they are only little pricks, but then women are only little men. The corpus of erotic art and literature in Christendom is full of curious clitoris-lore. The Marquis de Sade conceived of a heroine with a clitoris so large she could get it into her girl friend's cunt, just like a man. I mentioned earlier a recent Roman Catholic manual for confessors which recommended the excision of the clitoris as a cure for Lesbianism, and here is an opinion of the nineteenth-century Italian anthropologist Sonnini, which is quoted in a respectable little book of hearsay anthropology called *The Masculine Cross*. (This latter was published anonymously in 1891, and is still in the Private Case at the British Museum because it holds that the symbol of the cross does not draw all its force from what happened on it at Golgotha, but draws some also from an older phallic tradition.) Sonnini describes female circumcision among African tribes, and continues: "It is very probable that these operations have been performed not only in Egypt but in several other countries in the East, where the heat of the climate and other causes may produce too luxuriant a growth of those parts."

The sentence sums up masculine projection feelings about the clitoris in our culture. These operations happen in hot climates, namely climates different from ours. Such climates produce an excessive or "luxuriant" growth of the principle of all lechery, and cutting it out is quite justifiable in order to reduce the incentives to said lechery. Here the man first sets up the woman as a sort of little man, and next cuts her back so that she shall be a better or more unfucking sort of man.

Lexicographers derive the word clitoris from the Greek *kleiein*, to shut, as I mentioned earlier. At that point I jokingly preferred to derive it from *kleitos*, renowned, famous, excellent. But perhaps not so jokingly. What sort of temperament will consider the clitoris as something which shuts? It could not possibly be so considered by anyone on speaking terms with reality. The wish to force such a derivation can itself only derive from a wish that the vagina *should* be shut or barred. The derivation is a bit of square, scholastic Manicheism.

Too luxuriant? Sentry? The battle is still on, in rather

different terms. According to Freud and the psychoanalysts, the immature girl or woman is likely to have experienced, or to desire, clitoridean orgasms, caused by stimulation of the clitoris without penetration of the vagina. The mature woman, on the other hand, is supposed to negotiate this half-hatched pattern of sensuality and to rest secure in the greater and more fecund pleasure of the vaginal orgasm. There are thus two sorts of orgasm: the clitoridean, which is bad, or "immature," and the vaginal, which is good, or "mature."

Kinsey,[4] on the other hand, has set out all the different parts of the body which play a part in orgasm, and drawn the conclusion that there is one sort of orgasm only and that different people on different occasions will do different things on the way to it. Some psychoanalysts have come back in defense of the Freudian picture, with all its overtones of *ought*; women, this attitude presupposes, are in danger of remaining what they really are, namely little men depending on their little pricks, unless they engage in an important and rewarding process of maturing. A woman is something a woman has to work hard to become; femininity is an acquired characteristic.

Kinsey has it. People come all over; love contributes to it, or liking; so does the clitoris; so does the cunt and the prick and the hands and the mouth and the arms and the understanding and the thighs and the eyes and the cultural tradition and the warmth of the room and the breasts and the past and the children or their absence and just about everything you can think of.

We imagine that women feel and fuck like men, we imagine that the ancients fucked more than we do, and that foreigners and animals still do. That which we deny and distrust in ourselves, we have to place somewhere. We know well enough that there is sex, lots of it, going on, but it can't be us who are doing it. We take the sexuality

---

[4] *Sexual Behavior in the Human Female*, Philadelphia and London, 1953, chapter 14.

that is in us and we extrude it from ourselves and constitute it as an autonomous balloon. But action means agent; who shall be agent? Anybody will do: animals, foreigners, ancients, women. "Please sir," we say to the jealous God who still lives so strongly in us, "it wasn't us. It was them."

But it wasn't them; it was us. And only when we face the fact that it was us can we go on to face the more interesting facts, so unbearable before we have faced them, so obvious after, that nobody blames us, and that the pleasure comes from the pleasure, not from breaking a taboo.

PART VIII

INCLUSION

Chapter 28

The Religious View

There are, it seems to me, two views of love and fucking which are very nearly untainted by the wish to deny a part of life and a part of the body; I call them the religious view, and *carpe diem*. By the religious view I mean the reverse of the view held by Manichean and Augustinian Christianity; I mean the view which binds all love to the general flow of things as an equal part of what is whole, and thus of what is good. To a greater or less extent it may actually make fucking an emblem of religion, of binding in. The notion is not wholly absent in Christianity; it was identifiably present in the baroque age, and an extremely dilute version of it can be found in the conception of the sacrament of marriage at most times in Christian history.

By *carpe diem* I mean the approach of take what you can get and enjoy it.

Both of these are an improvement on anything we have considered so far, but neither, it seems to me, will quite fill the bill because both feel that it is necessary to do something special about fucking. One makes it a specially hallowed emblem of the whole and the good, the other wishes to gather it with tremendous energy, with conscious complaisance and delight. In the last resort, it is better not to do anything special about any of our natural pleasures and functions; it is better to let them operate, as they will do very nicely if we let them.

But first let us consider these two views in more detail. There is a sexologist's chestnut about a monk who used to masturbate. After that he would flagellate to punish himself for yielding to the temptation. Flagellating made him come again, so he had it both ways.

Now that is only funny as long as we confine ourselves to the orthodox view that religion and orgasm are incompatible. At that level, the story suggests that it is vain to seek to do without pleasure; pleasure will reassert itself even in the midst of penance. We laugh because human nature overcomes an absurd asceticism. But if we consider the possibility that religion and orgasm need not be at loggerheads at all, the story becomes richly symbolic. And then look how God rewarded him! Religion and orgasm simply are not separable.

In the person of this monk, one of the battlefields of Europe is summed up. When Christianity severed and excluded fucking from the rest of man, we have seen in how many sad little forms it cropped up: pornography, rakery, and so on. These were anti-religious or irreligious forms. It also continued in a religious form as witchcraft, or "the old religion"; and that meant war. The churches won, and burned the documents. But there is little doubt from the few which remain that European and American witchcraft were partly survivals of pre-Christian religion, of the sort of polytheism which gave birth to the great literate civilization of ancient Greece. They were survivals of only a part of the old religion, the fertility rites. The rest could be and was absorbed into Christianity. It is a tenable view that the "old religion" of Europe, which presumably persisted throughout the Middle Ages, and of whose suppression such plentiful records remain from the sixteenth and seventeenth centuries, was a structure, if that is not too formal a word, of reactions to repression built on a foundation of the continuing, but starved, human wish to celebrate fucking and increase.

Like other social expressions of persecuted people or persecuted strands in human nature (like Mau Mau) it had its atrocities. It adopted the polarity of Christian theology, and put itself under the banner of Satan, of whom Christianity had taught it. It blackened the Mass. It invaded the churches and monasteries. But underlying all the tit for tat reversal mechanisms there seems to have been in the "old religion" a foundation of feeling and procedure which is common to all or most religious ritual. There was a priesthood, there were eating and drinking rites, there were feast days, and there was probably even a victim-God symbolizing the death and rebirth of the year, of animals, of people, of hope. The God was the dismembered Osiris, Attis, Dionysus; only just not the spreadeagled Christ. Above all there was rapture, and there was faith unto death. The repression was reinforced with the full fury of the projection mechanisms we examined in an earlier chapter; incubi, succubi, broomsticks, the evil eye, and probably 99 per cent of the human sacrifice grew up in the churchmen's imaginations and were promptly pinned on the already residual survivals of the old religion.

It could not have been otherwise. Religion is real; the wish to hallow one's whole life, to consider and make sense of it, to relate it to all that lies outside it, to feel a right and proper part of all that one knows, is real and is good. Fucking and increase are real. The wish to rejoice in the body of the beloved and in one's own, to beget and bear children and to cherish them as they grow, and the wish to love where love is, not only where it is directed by ceremony or oath, are real and good. How can religion and fucking be kept apart? By bloodshed, yes; and we have had the bloodshed. But by no other means, and now that we have decided against bloodshed in this field, they are perhaps coming together again.

The battle was never entirely one-sided; in the last five hundred years a few inroads have been made by naked human love and joy-in-increase into the true body of Christianity, as distinct from the pathetic looting of Christian paraphernalia which we mentioned above. In the work of the late nineteenth-century Belgian "pornographic" illustrator Félicien Rops, for instance, it is hard to say which is the dominant feeling, Christianity or sexuality. When I say that he drew a detumescent phallus on a crucifix with an exhausted Magdalene prostrate before it, the reader may exclaim, "What an extraordinary thing to put on a crucifix." But he could equally exclaim: "What an extraordinary place to put a phallus." The blasphemy seems total, but what is blasphemy? It is a truism that only a religious man is capable of blasphemy. Would it have been less or more blasphemous if Rops had put a cap and bells on the cross, or a rotten cabbage?

Consider also the bodily grief of Rodin's study of the Magdalene and the crucified Christ. We are moved by, for instance, Michael Flanders' ballad *Drummer Boy*; we find it proper and touching that the little boy should beat his drum for his savior. It is his way of doing him honor; the pathos lies in its being all he can do. And the Magdalene?

In one of his sonnets, Giorgio Baffo, who called himself on the title page of his book (1771) "Patrician of Venice," and wrote usually like a silly dragoon, hit off the point we are considering with a nice gusto.[1]

> Le mie meditazion le xè in pensar
> Che gusto possa aver i santi in cielo,
> Quando no i ghà cogioni, e no i ghà oselo,
> E che no i ghà una mona da chiavar.
> Senza el gran godimento del sborar,
> Che no sò veder, che ghe sia el più belo,
> Che a sol pensarghe se me rizza el pelo

[1] *Le Poesie di Giorgio Baffo, Patrizio Veneto*, London 1789 (earlier ed: 1771), Sonnet 157.

Eternamente come porli star?
Ma mi co el mio pensar vago piu avanti,
E digo, Dio xè el mondo, e de sto Dio
Una parte nù semo tutti quanti.
Donca quando che fotte el cazzo mio,
E che continuamente fotte tanti,
Anca Dio fotte, e i santi ghe va drio.[2]

Again, Richard Payne Knight, an eighteenth-century nu-
mismatist, wrote:

Enthusiasm on one subject naturally produces enthusiasm
on another; for the human passions, like the strings of an
instrument, vibrate to the motions of each other; hence parox-
ysms of love and devotion have oftentimes so exactly ac-
corded, as not to have been distinguished by the very persons
whom they agitated.[3]

This is a precise summary of the baroque sensibility.
As baroque architects delighted in placing the visitor or
the worshiper in a block of space which could be felt
either as one part of the building which was by tradition
distinct, or as another; as baroque composers delighted in
giving the listener a line which could be heard either as
a melody or as a voice in a polyphony, and as baroque
poets delighted in the conceit which presented one image
for two thoughts, so did all the artists and, one must assume,

---

[2] My meditation turns to thinking
How the saints in heaven can have any fun
When they've got no balls and no pricks
And not a cunt to fuck.
How can they get through eternity
Without the great pleasure of coming,
Which I can't see how anything can be lovelier than,
So that my hair stands on end when I just think of it?
But I go further in my thought,
And I say: God is the world, and of this God
We are each one of us a part.
So when my prick fucks,
As it so often does,
God fucks too, and the saints who are with him.
[3] *A Discourse on the Worship of Priapus*, 1786.

many of the consumers of art of the baroque age delight in the reconciliation of human and divine love, in puns where God fucks and the lover prays to his mistress. Rubens used a live whore as the model for his Saint Domitilla in the Chiesa Nuova in Rome, and Caravaggio a drowned one fished out of the Tiber for his "Death of the Virgin." Both were blamed by their elders.

St. Theresa of Avila wrote how an angel came to her in a vision bearing a long golden spear with a fiery tip and several times "plunged it into my deepest inward. When he drew it out, I thought my entrails would have been torn out too, and when he left me I glowed in the hot fire of love for God. The pain was so strong, and the sweetness thereof was so passing great that no one could wish ever to lose it."[4] How Bernini caught and externalized this moment in marble, the young angel with his spear poised, the saint in orgasm, the spectators in their boxes with their opera glasses and programs, is one of the extreme points of the history of European art, and of Christian feeling too. In the church of Santa Maria della Vittoria in Rome, the one moment when humanity, wearing only light disguise, stormed and captured the heart of orthodoxy, still stands in glowing and obvious white.

The baroque age saw sexual union as half a pun or conceit or oxymoron, the other half being the love of God. They reverted to the Greek image of the hermaphrodite, they dwelt on the *concordia discors* and the *discordia concors,* the reconciliation of opposites. But usually, I think, of two opposites only, and it was into this general dingdong (or, as E. H. Gombrich would say, ping pong) that they brought fucking both as the union of the opposites, man and woman, and as one term in the antinomy of human and divine love.

In the early Renaissance things had been more complicated. Then, the habit of thought and feeling was not

---

[4] *Experience,* 1550's. Autobiography posthumously published 1587. Canonized 1622.

to reconcile two in one, but many in One. The work of Marsilio Ficino and Pico della Mirandola on the Orphic mysteries was in essence a revival of what Christian scholars have tended to call the "Oriental" strands in Plato.[5] The One, expressed in myth perhaps by Osiris, perhaps by Attis, perhaps by Brahman as Purusa, of which more below, somehow got divided up and reduced by a sacrificial agony into the many. Virtue and religion lies in the constructive work of putting the One together again; hence, incidentally, the unforgettableness of the story of Humpty Dumpty, a legend of cosmic despair. The recollection or resurrection of the One from the shattered many was, in fifteenth-century Florence in one sense, in first-century Palestine in another, and in India at any time in a third, religion itself. Recollection and resurrection are homonyms for religion, for tying in, binding in, binding up, healing, atonement, reunification, *Wiedervereinigung* (evil is that which parts, is power politics), reconciliation, union, meeting, fusion, repair. Whence life renewed.

Thus Botticelli painted the naked Venus or Aphrodite, ("foam-born") arising from the foam which was the semen of her castrated father Uranus. From the sacrificial scattering of seed arises love, to reunite all that is severed. Thus Pico della Mirandola had a medal cast in the image of the classical Three Graces and they were called Beauty, Love and Pleasure; which is to say, the possibility of union (or religion), the desire for union (or religion), the act of union (or religion). The girl he loved, Giovanna degli Albizzi, had one cast from the same matrix, but she named them Chastity, Beauty, Love. She, being married to another man, neatly set the whole series back one along the line. But it was the same line, the same progression.

Thus again Pico; love is blind because pleasure is greater than understanding. Sight and understanding are no more than limitations which must be transcended on the way to

---

[5] It is recounted in that prodigiously thoughtful book by Edgar Wind, *Pagan Mysteries in the Renaissance*, London and New Haven, 1958.

pleasure. God is to be experienced only in the ecstasy of
direct union. Or, as the inscription on the temple at Delphi
had it: "Moderation in all things—Know thyself—Oh!"

It is Diotima's ladder; but where Plato held that the soul
mounting to God must discard each rung as it climbed, the
Renaissance seized an another strand in Greek philosophy,
not absent from Plato either, which held that each rung
prefigures and remains present in the succeeding one, and
each can stand for all.

The union and repair of the many in the one is present
in the architecture of Giulio Romano which we discussed
above, and the little incipient orgy scenes of Francesco
del Cossa and the Master of the Die. The presiding deity
of the Cossa fresco was, as one would expect, Venus,
and, as was usual, Mars is with her, in unwarlike mood.
The subjugation of Mars to Venus is usually indicated by his being asleep, and by Venus' *amorini* playing
with his helmet and spear. But this was not enough for
Cossa; he chained Mars to Venus' throne. Discord must be
chained to concord, strife must become the slave of unity
and love. And indeed fifteenth-century Italy was not a time
of war. "Wars" were fought by handfuls of mercenaries
for causes unknown to the people and often to the mercenaries themselves. Ordinary life went on undisturbed,
and the violence of the age expressed itself in murder,
treachery and more or less political street brawls. When
Mars is chained to Venus, men fight alone, not in battles.

We said a moment ago that early Renaissance feeling
about human and divine love rested on the "Oriental" elements in Greek teaching. The word Krishna itself, the
name of the Hindu god of peace and joy, means precisely
"he who has left the battle." It is easy for us in our Atlantic
corners to see the cultural continuum which binds us in
space and time to the classical age of Athens; there our
vision tends to stop. But there is an equally strong cultural
continuum binding Greece with India. Four hundred years
before Christian monotheism came to Greece and a thousand years before Muslim monotheism came to India,

Alexander the Great set up Greek kingdoms in India. The contact did not begin then, and it continued long after through the mediacy of the Persian and Syrian empires. Monotheism and the conflict between monotheisms were superimposed late in the day on a fairly unitary structure of religion and feeling, which held that the many were made one again in the healing of love, and which honored fucking as an emblem of this binding in.

In considering the cult of Krishna, the Westerner has a big backlog of Christian horror to write off before he can see straight. Take for instance this, from Sir Charles Lyall's article "Hindostani Literature" in the eleventh edition of the *Encyclopaedia Britannica* (1910). The cult of Krishna "had for its basis the legendary career of a less estimable human hero (than Rama), whose exploits are marked by a kind of elfish and fantastic wantonness; it has more and more spent its energy in developing that side of devotion which is perilously near to sensual thought, and has allowed the imagination and ingenuity of poets to dwell on things unfit for verse or even speech." Or this, from Julius Eggeling's article on Hinduism in the same: "This survey of the Indian sects will have shown how little the character of their divine objects of worship is calculated to exert that elevating and spiritualising influence, so characteristic of true religious devotion. . . . Religious fervour is all too apt to degenerate into that very state of sexual excitation which devotional exercises should surely tend to repress." One could quote for pages from English writing on India, about vile practices, degrading cults hardly calculated, unhealthy influences, etc. The Manicheism of anti-life had entered so far into the souls of these ancestors of ours that even in an age when objectivity and accurate information were highly prized, the writers could write and the editors could publish as anthropology and history what were in fact no more than sectarian diatribes.

Such has been the effect of the Western scholarly tradition on Indian life, and such anyhow is the lack of historical records in India, that it is very hard to give an account of the true nature of erotic religious art in India. The Krishna stories, mainly the one of how he came down and fucked a whole lot of little cowgirls, gave rise to many stories and pictures. The feeling is simply one of pleasure in pleasure, of fun for fun's sake. Krishna is the god of relaxation.

The erotic temple sculptures[6] seem to reflect a different and more arduous tradition, though there are those who hold that all this is imagined back into them later, and they too are simply fun for fun's sake. If there is a philosophical meaning, it is perhaps this. Brahman, the One, desired. He said: "Let there be many, that creation may be." There were many, and the many came together in love to make One again, and also to increase, to make more many to do the same another day. Texts survive which show that the temples of Orissa (around 1000 A.D.) were built in two sections. The bottom part, the Bhadra, was simply the terraced pyramid which survives in so many examples. The top part, the Rekha, does not always survive, and was sometimes not even built, owing to the excessive largeness of the design. The Rekha was a tower-like structure, and had parts called shin, trunk, neck, skull, etc. It was an image of Brahman as Purusa: Purusa was the cosmic man, created by Brahman in his self-division, and designed to achieve the experience of desire. The architecture is humanistic.

All over some of these temples there remain reliefs of people fucking. There are texts from about the correct time and place which describe rites of initiation and celebration that may have been connected with these temples, or may not. It is hard to say precisely what they do describe, let alone whether Konarak and Khajuraho and such places are where whatever it was went on. All that is certain is that these are temples, and the temple images are of fucking. The thing can perhaps best be expressed by saying that the

---

[6] See Chapter 7.

experience of physical union, which man shares with the animals, gave rise to the myths of division and religion (rebinding) and was again taken to be emblematic of the myth it had itself given rise to.

I love. Love loves in me. God is love. God loves in me. I will worship God. How? By loving.

Another progression: Pure act. Spirit of act. Act as emblem of spirit.

The chicken and egg problem is only as serious as the generation cycle of the chicken is long. Speed up the cycle, speed it up farther, speed it up till there is an instantaneous chicken-and-egg, and there is no problem. Turn the colored wheel fast enough and it is white. Religion is the realm where problems are seen not to exist.

Chapter 29

Carpe Diem

The best *carpe diem* poem after Horace's comes from that same fifteenth-century Florence we were talking about in the last chapter. Lorenzo the Magnificent, the Duke of Florence and head of the writers as well as of the state, put it thus:

> Chi vuol essere lieto, sia.
> Di doman non c' è certezza.[1]

It has been pointed out that this was not only a poetic proclamation, but also an objective political statement. There was indeed no knowing about tomorrow in Lorenzo de' Medici's Florence; he saw to that himself, being just as likely to hang you and pauperize your family, as to delight you with his ballads. Mars was chained to Venus, wars were small things for professionals, murder was bread and butter, the many were being reconciled in the one, and *chi vuol essere lieto, sia.* Thus poets less platonized than

---

[1] If you want to be happy, be happy.
There's no knowing about tomorrow.

Pico wandered eternally through those flowery meadows, always finding a girl and always fucking her. The popular culture was based on the *prato fiorito* with a *donzella* in it, ready and willing. No need to look farther than the flowers and the girl.

While the more serious characters of the Renaissance took human as an emblem of divine love, others were bringing heaven firmly down to earth in an impatient Zen-like short cut. Thus Luigi Tansillo, military governor of Gaeta, writing in the early 1530's and addressing pious young women:

> Si mentre il corpo è vivo non godete,
> Sperate di goder, quando egli è morto?
> Quel paradiso, onde voi tanto ardete,
> Che pensate che sia, altro che un'Horto?
> E se quest'horto in grembo a voi tenete,
> A che cercate altrove ir'a diporto?[2]

Carpe diem as a spirit and a way of looking at things is so familiar to all of us that I will confine myself in this chapter to quoting some good examples which may not be too well known to the reader. I have purposely chosen those which do not dwell too much upon the *duty* of enjoying oneself, but tend more to a simple acceptance of loving and fucking as it comes along.

Here is a translation of a Venetian dialect poem[3] by Maffio Venier, the son of the Lorenzo Venier whose deplorable poem *la Puttana Errante* we noticed in Chapter 8 above. Maffio Venier was a very different poet. He lived from 1550 to 1586, lost the use of his legs in youth, and became Archbishop of Corfu. He wrote romantic Petrar-

---

[2] If you don't enjoy yourselves when the body is alive,
Do you hope to do so when it is dead?
That paradise which you so long for,
What do you think it is but a garden?
And if you have this garden in your lap,
Why try to go elsewhere for pleasure?

[3] I am indebted to Dr. Gaetano Cozzi for help in the translation.

chan yearnings in Italian, and chose the Venetian to express the very opposite pole of love, simple contentment. The original is at Appendix 6.

The Ragged Girl

Here we are, my love, between the cat and the hearth (but you don't seem to mind) where the bread and the lamp are all mixed up with the distaff, the clothes, the wine, the old lady and the firewood, the children and the hens, and the bed's halfway up the chimney. Hung on a hook like a trophy there's the frying pan, a hat and a hod, a hollow gourd with vinegar in it, and a couple of baskets. The bed's made of seaweed and tow; it's so bumpy the fleas fall over.

Instead of a parrot we keep a goose, instead of a dog a sweet little pig who kisses one on the mouth, sexy little thing. Sweet company, gentle concert; the goose and the cat and all, the old lady, the pig and the children; and my love beneath the roof, which is open in a hundred places so that the sun and the moon can make the house happier and lighter. Just as niggard nature hides a jewel under the doormat or a pearl in the sweepings; infinite beauty in a thousand rags!

The pastryboard closes a balcony with no shutters or glass; everyone eats with their fingers like the hawk, with no table or plates; the whole family stands round the pot to see when it's ready, everyone drinks from one glass and pulls bits off a pennyworth of greens. Real life, and blessed; one sheet does for six and gets black with smoke from one day to the next; hands, arms, heads and feet all mixed up in a heap, making its own grotesque hierarchy of people, and animals, and bits and pieces.

In our house the bedroom's the living room and the living room's the cellar. There's only one bed, under the stairs, where I pass nights full of sweetness in the arms of my love, even if the wind and the rain come in sometimes, and freshen love up from behind. Dear nights of peace, dear place of love, heavenly beauty in sackcloth! Take away that pompous bed, and the Gabrina[4] in it; old grampus-face there looks like a dirty magpie in a fine cage. But in this blessed and shining house lives the beloved of my heart, beautiful and ragged.

---

[4] A Beauty from Ariosto.

Richly ragged, since the more rags and the less clothes she has on, the more her white and rosy flanks show through; so the day is better with less clouds. Think of a too rich costume covering pearls and rubies, covering a beauty above all others! Hemmed in between two chimneys you can see the moon shining; that's how the face and the eyes of this girl shine from between rag and rag.

Such beauty ought to go in rags; you can't shut it in. You cover carrion with clothes, when you retch to look at it. But her body shines without art or care, firm in every part, so that coverings and veils could never dispute her beauty. White stupendous flesh, naked and uncovered to the sky; poor women, go open like this in the pomp of nature! O neck, O shoulders, O breasts; one only cuts a glove to show the ring because it's the prettier thing.

What clothes, even of gold, would not seem dung on a jewel, if they obscured such colors? Go so, then; that lowness raises you. Go so, proud pauper, go barefoot, for you are more beautful the less shoe you have. As the sky makes me jump with its extreme beauty, so in a house where there are not two halfpence to rub together: supreme providence of the heavens and the stars! which went out and brought together two scattered things, your rags and my verses.

Dear rags to which I have turned my heart, sweet lovely rags, windows of grace, eyes of love, rags lined with roses which you can see open and bloom between one rag and the next, and through the rents a handsbreadth of flank gleaming fit to blind you. My girl, anyone who's not seen you is a man half alive, and anyone who sees you and doesn't die on the spot is a dead stump already. And I who describe you, I know I do you wrong; I tax your glory and defraud you, and foul your good name more than I praise it.

I wish I could have more tongues on loan, even at the price of my life, because mine alone is not much for an infinite beauty, and I know I'm saying nothing compared with what I leave unsaid; but what little I can, I measure and comprehend as one measures the sky with a pair of compasses. In this beauty I lead my life contented, finding a sure faith in torn garments; I have no one who torments me either day or night. We have one will and one soul in two breasts, a thing you don't often find in most beds. Ladies, try if you like to muster lakes of tears and rivers of sighs and always to have armies of lovers before you; invent new martyrdoms if you like. Nourish a hundred devils in your eyes to tempt contrite hearts, try to have a hundred afflicted souls on their knees before you. But love, if you ever find me in doubt again, you can fry me; oil and flour provided. This is my woman; she wants me and I want her. I've nothing here to be angry or frightened about; he who wants war of love, let him arm.

And now, my patched-up song, if you are spoken ill of, speak ill of him who says it; show that you know what you're talking about, and say that if you have no velvet gown, then he who is the god of love goes naked too.

And here is Jan Everaerts, known as Johannes Secundus, because he was the second John born to his parents, the first having died in infancy. He was born at The Hague in 1511, was appointed secretary to the Emperor Charles V at the age of twenty-five, and died before he could take up his post. His main work is a series of poems called *Basia,* "the Kisses," written to a Spanish girl whom he called Neaera. Here is his fifth Kiss (the Latin is at Appendix 7).

While you press and clip me here and here with your soft caresses and lean above me with all your breast and neck and your smooth face, Neaera, and bring down your shoulders and place your lips on mine, and while I bite you and you bite me and moan again and shake your quick tongue here and there and suck my tongue here and there till it hurts, and breathe the soft moist breath of your sweet soul in to nourish my poor life, Neaera, and while you drain my soul, falling and burning, cooked in the great steam of love, cooked in the cauldron of my impatient breast, you play with my flames, Neaera, and with the panting of my empty breast; joyful breath of my own desire! Then I say: "Love is the god of gods, and no god is greater than love. Yet if there is any one greater than love, it is you, you, Neaera; you are greater than love to me."

There's humanism in a nutshell; the girl is greater than the god, the particular than the general.

And here is *The Perfect Enjoyment,* which is probably by George Villiers, second Duke of Buckingham, the B in the Cabal, politician, rake, playwright, racing man, wit and cynosure.[5]

The Perfect Enjoyment

Since now my Silvia is as kind as fair,
Let wit and joy succeed my dull despair.
O what a night of pleasure was the last!
A full reward for all my troubles past;
And on my head if future mischief fall
This happy night shall make amends for all.
Nay, though my Silvia's love should turn to hate,
I'll think of this, and die contented with my fate.
Twelve was the lucky minute when we met,
And on her bed were close together set;
Though listening spies might be perhaps too near,
Love filled our hearts; there was no room for fear.
Now whilst I strive her melting heart to move
With all the powerful eloquence of love,
In her fair face I saw the colour rise
And an unusual softness in her eyes.
Gently they look, and I with joy adore
That only charm they never had before.
The wounds they made, her tongue was used to heal,
And now the gentle enemies reveal
A secret which that friend would still conceal.
My eyes transported too with amorous rage
Seem fierce with expectation to engage.
But fast she holds my hands, and close her thighs,
And what she longs to do with frowns denies;
A strange effect on foolish women wrought,
Bred in disguises, and by custom taught;
Custom, which wisdom sometimes overrules,

---

[5] The poem is printed in more than one eighteenth-century edition of Rochester's works—e.g. the edition of 1721—with a footnote saying the Duke of Buckingham admitted having written it. These editions of the "Works of the Earls of Rochester, Roscommon and Dorset" etc., are full of extraneous matter, sometimes distinguished as such, sometimes not. The title, *The Perfect Enjoyment*, is presumably a swipe at Rochester's two poems called *The Imperfect Enjoyment*, one of which was quoted on p. 232 above. The contrast is a valid one.

But serves instead of reason to the fools;
Custom, which all the world to slavery brings,
The dull excuse for doing silly things.
She by this method of her foolish sex
Is forced a while me and herself to vex.
But now when thus we had been struggling long
Her limbs grow weak and her desires grow strong.
How can she hold to let the hero in?
He storms without, and love betrays within.
Her hands at last, to hide her blushes, leave
The fort unguarded, willing to receive
My fierce assault, made with a lover's haste,
Like lightning piercing, and as quickly past.
Thus does fond nature with her children play;
Just shows us joy, then snatches it away.
'Tis not the excess of pleasure makes it short;
The pain of love's as raging as the sport;
And yet, alas, that lasts; we sigh all night
With grief, but scarce one moment with delight.
Some little pain may check her kind desire,
But not enough to make her once retire;
Maids wounds for pleasure bear, as men for praise.
Here honour heals, there love the smart allays;
The world, if just, would harmful courage blame,
And this more innocent reward with fame.
Now she her well-contented thoughts employs
On her past fears, and on her future joys,
Whose harbinger did roughly all remove,
Then make fit room for great Luxurious Love.
Fond of the welcome guest, her arms embrace
My body, and her hands a better place,
Which with one touch so pleased and proud does grow
It swells beyond the grasp that made it so,
Confinement scorns in any straiter walls
Than those of love, where it contented falls.
Though twice o'er thrown, he more inflamed does rise
And will to the last drop fight out love's prize.
She like some Amazon in story proves,
That overcomes the hero whom she loves.
In the close strife she takes so much delight
She then can think of nothing but the fight.
With joy she lays him panting at her feet,

But with more joy does his recovery meet.
Her trembling hands first gently raise his head;
She almost dies for fear that he is dead;
Then binds his wounds up with a busy hand
And with that balm enables him to stand,
Till by her eyes she conquers him once more,
And wounds him deeper than she did before.
Though fallen from the top of pleasure's hill,
With longing eyes we look up thither still:
Still thither our unwearied wishes tend,
Till we that height of happiness ascend
By gentle steps. The ascent itself exceeds
All joys but that alone to which it leads.
First, then, so long and lovingly we kiss
As if like doves we knew no dearer bliss.
Still in one mouth our tongues together play,
While groping hands are no less pleased than they,
Thus clinged together now a while we rest
Breathing our souls into each other's breast,
Then give a general kiss of all our parts
Whilst this best way we make exchange of hearts.
Here would my praise as well as pleasure dwell;
Enjoyment's self I scarcely like so well;
The little this comes short in rage and strength
Is largely recompensed with endless length.
This is a joy would last, if we could stay;
But love's too eager to admit delay
And hurries us along so smooth a way.
Now wanton with delight we nimbly move
Our pliant limbs in all the shapes of love,
Our motions not like those of gamesome fools
Whose active bodies show their heavy souls,
But sports of love, in which a willing mind
Makes us as able as our hearts are kind.
At length all languishing and out of breath,
Panting as in the agonies of death,
We lie entranced, till one provoking kiss
Transports our ravished souls to paradise.
O heaven of love, thou moment of delight!
Wronged by my words; my fancy does thee right!
Methinks I lie all melting in her charms
And fast locked up within her legs and arms;

Bent are our minds, and all our thoughts on fire,
Just labouring in the pangs of fierce desire,
At once like misers wallowing in their store,
In full possession, yet desiring more.
Thus with repeated pleasures while we waste
Our happy hours, that like short minutes passed,
To such a sum of bliss our joys amount
The number now becomes too great to count.
Silent as night are all sincerest joys,
Like waters deepest running with least noise.
But now at last, for want of further force,
From deeds, alas, we fall into discourse;
A fall which each of us in vain bemoans,
A greater fall than that of kings from thrones.
The tide of pleasure flowing now no more,
We lie like fish left gasping on the shore.
And now, as after fighting, wounds appear
Which we in heat did neither feel nor fear.
She for her sake entreats me to give o'er,
And yet for mine would gladly suffer more.
Her words are coy, while all her motions woo;
And when she asks me if it please me too,
I rage to show how well; but 'twill not do.
Thus would hot love run itself out of breath
And, wanting rest, find it too soon in death,
Did not wise nature with a gentle force
Refrain its rage, and stop its headlong course.
Indulgently severe, she well does spare
This child of hers, which most deserves her care.

This modest poem, so far from both romantic swooning
and death-seeking remorse, speaks with the voice of that
simple humanity which we can bind and lacerate if we will,
but can always find again.

Chapter 30

Conclusion

So much for the heritage. What of the present?

Some books about love end by distributing different sorts of feeling to different parts of the personality; body, spirit, soul, make their appearance, and eros, philia, agape, etc., are dished out one to each, like biscuits to school children in a line. Others end with a polysyllabic and carefully God-avoiding restatement of orthodox Christian ethics; marriage is permissible, but otherwise total continence. The word "mature" plays the part formerly played by "God-fearing." Others again end with evocations of this or that culture or myth where they order these things differently, thus implying an exhortation to do likewise, or with broadsides of pellets fired against "conventional morality" and judges and bishops (1920's more than now) or even with the mere assertion that, whatever happens, the human race will go on all right (pre-1945).

It is a hard thing to wind up a book about love between the sexes. I cannot end up this one by talking about eros and agape; the scheme of the Greeks proved capable of lasting a good long time, but this is not the moment to talk about mind and soul and spirit and those things. New plains of knowledge about human consciousness are coming over the horizon and it is very doubtful if the traditional concepts will be able to cope with them. Nor do I believe it is any longer interesting to relay the orthodox Christian view, whether in traditional form or dressed up as "psychological maturity." It doesn't work, and most people are not interested in trying to make it work. Meanwhile, children grow up and are handed a scheme for their sex lives which doesn't take account of what happens, only of what is said ought to happen. To praise other systems at the expense of our own is an easy out, and to decry our own *tout court* an even easier one.

There are great, creaking anachronisms at large in our sexual morality today; injunctions and prohibitions which once had meaning and function, but are now left without, high and dry, and generate resentment and depression: these are the dead shreds of Manicheism and libertinism which I called the Cheshire scowl and the Cheshire leer. The former is the stronger. They generate resentment and depression by themselves, since the religious struggles which created them and gave them meaning are now over. But more that that there have been changes in the structure of society in this century, and in industrial technology, which make these anachronisms doubly hurtful; not only have they no meaning any longer, they are bedeviling a kind of people who did not formerly exist at all.

We have in the economically forward countries now a new class of people and it is not an accident that we have found a new word to describe them—"teenager." We used to call people of that age adolescents, and language has not changed capriciously: it has only followed the fact. People of that age are now adults; they mature physically two years before their parents did. And how they worry us! What serious and sympathetic probes on television, what column miles in the newspapers, what letters lashing out, what articles gently admonishing, what resolutions calling for much flogging, what governmental and non-governmental reports, trusts, sponsored schemes, unsponsored schemes, martial exhortation, episcopal solicitude, wardens (one letter away from *warder*), counselors, leaders; much that is good in all that: much that even a society which liked its young people would do.

But our society does not like them; it keeps a nice little cautery stuck into their vitals. They must not fuck, which is as much as to say that they must not be what they are. We feed them well with one hand and make them healthy; with the other we block them off from the waist down. We show them movies in which people kiss and kiss and kiss, and never move their pelvises. We make great proclamations about the deep and satisfying fidelities which some of us are lucky enough to wake up one day when we are about forty and find are what we turn out to have, but to young people it only means: "Don't." We tell the boy: "Respect your girl"; she weeps. We tell the girl: "Your boy will respect you if you say no." He turns away sneering. Hope wilts, and love is stillborn.

"Premarital promiscuity," as moralizing psychologists call it (John Donne and William Blake called it something else) tends to be followed by good marriages and more of them. This is one way of expressing Kinsey's findings that no fucking before marriage leads to little and poor in marriage, and you stay married. A certain amount of fucking before marriage leads to more and better fucking in marriage, but a higher chance of divorce on the ground of adultery. Naturally; it would be very odd if it were not so. Like life itself, because of life itself, fucking is something you either have a taste for or not, and if you do have a taste for it, there is no doubt you will be inclined at least to think of fucking more than one person a year and if you don't have a taste for it, you will be less inclined to think of that. Some people have a built-in indifference to all fucking, but nobody has a selective indifference to adultery.

The boy who has observed the present official morality

of England or America and has exchanged two chaste kisses with the girl he then marries will be a spiritless and inert husband and spend his life in a flabby domesticity, oppressed by the essential savorlessness of things. The same for the girl and the wife. Conversely, the boy or girl who has had a certain number of affairs before marriage will find it hard to stop having them afterward, and must either put up with the tensions of adultery or else consciously find a means of avoiding it.

There is a simple continuum from one extreme pattern of life to the other; it is obvious to the naked eye, it is confirmed by statistical sociology, it is readily comprehensible by a child of ten, and it has been a commonplace observation at least since Milton formulated it more than three hundred years ago.[1] "They who have lived most loosely by reason of their bold accustoming, prove most successful in their matches, because, their wild affections unsettling at will, have been as so many divorces to teach them experience." This is what does happen, and if we prefer to tell young people something else, namely what we think ought to happen, we are bigots. To urge someone younger or simpler than oneself, though of reasonable age, to behave in a certain way without laying the full facts before him is something we may find necessary in an emergency. It is how wars are fought, how any operation which depends on speed or discipline may properly be carried out by a battalion or a team. But life does not depend on speed or discipline, and it is not like a war. On the contrary, it depends on knowledge and freedom and peace. In these circumstances, a regard for young people dictates that we most carefully let them know the true facts about sex and love, which are as we noted above. If we inform them of the continuum and the way it works, we shall then be justified in urging them to place themselves at one point or another along it, and they will be able to form their own judgment of the reasons we give them.

---

[1] John Milton: *The Doctrine and Discipline of Divorce*, 1, III.

If we urge them to place themselves at the extreme point of total continence before marriage, we shall presumably base our arguments either on the reward to be reaped in an after life, or the satisfaction to be reaped in this life from conformity to a moral injunction. The danger is that they may identify this reasoning for what it is, namely an appeal to rewards and satisfactions which have many things in their favor, but are not related to those of love. To regulate one's sex life by reference to extraneous matters is something we sharply blame in other contexts, as for instance when a prostitute regulates her sex life by reference to money.

At present our society does, broadly speaking, trick teenagers in this way. If they fuck casually in doorways and in cars it is because we take good care they shall have nowhere else. If they go to twenty-dollar abortionists it is because we keep contraceptives from them, especially from the girls. If in their general attitudes they seem set against society it is because society is so set against them. We work off our guilts on them, just as we do on the prostitute. The prostitute exists for sex, and carries on her back a good part of our conviction that sex is a bad thing. Young people, whether they are married or not, are more sexually active than the middle-aged and carry the rest.

If fucking is a bad thing then so are we; there is no hope, because what makes us bad is what makes us. It is a closed circle of despair. If we are bad, can we not get better? No, because evil lurks in the manufacturing process itself. It is little reduction of the condemnation to say that there is no evil when children are intentionally begotten in wedlock, or that what evil there is can be partly washed away at the font; what is held to be bad except under certain conditions is held to be bad in general.

The closed circle of despair determines all our culture. In it, good and evil are not felt to be things which arise and continue as a result of our own actions, not felt to be judgments which we may make, according to our changing ideas and conditions, within the experience of humanity itself, but on the contrary to be absolutes one of which, evil, is inextricably built into us by the way we are physically made. Every Christian and neo-Christian scheme of redemption is only a mitigation of the original premise that we need redeeming.

There is no original sin except as we shroud ourselves in it. We need no redemption except as we decide we do. Man is not born under the star of evil; he is not born under any star at all. He is just born, and may or may not later allot himself stars. There is no worm in the bud, no fatality, no taint, no flaw.

It is not easy in this culture of ours to face the fact that we are self-constructing constructs. There are so many ways of shuffling off responsibility, and most of them come to roost in the bed of our parents. But though it is not easy, it is possible. I think that anyone who has once broken out of the circle of despair, out of the permanent cower, can never again fall back into it for good. He or she may fall back into it again from time to time; environment may reassert itself, but when the way out has been found once, it can be found again. The way out is to accept the condition of man in its totality; whoever does this will not be tempted to seek beyond. And the action which expresses this condition better than any other is fucking in love and in the wish to beget a child. The roots of our language know it: "to build, to enjoy, to bear." The stuff of our bodies knows it. Our dreams know it. Our consciousness knows it. Our history knows it, and our future pulls us on.

Put like that, it sounds simple and secure. But it is not; it is something easy to impair, even to deny. The way in which it is denied to many people here and now is the ceaseless reiteration of the orthodox Christian doctrine that the action itself, fucking, is only good on condition. I do not mean to argue that it is always good without condition. But the official morality of our culture, however we may laugh at it, patronize it, aim off for individual needs and natures, speaks loud, and loudest to the young. It does not say "fucking is good except . . ." it says: "fucking is bad except. . . ." It speaks of it with bated breath; warning, delimiting, stammering, solemn. It says: "Er . . ." It should speak clearly; celebrating, describing, proclaiming, cheerful. It should say: "Aha." It could then tell young people that there are exceptions to the general rule of pleasure and value; the exceptions of furtiveness, grabbing, venality, and so on. It should present fucking as a joy and a good which may be spoiled, not as a dirt and a danger which may be made antiseptic. And it should make clear that, whichever way you look at it, marriage is not the magic condition; neither the small good area beyond which lies spoiling, nor the small condition which may override the general evil. Love is that area, and it is large. Love is achieved through fucking. Fucking is a condition of love, not the other way round. Without orgasm in intercourse, there is only the arbitrary tension of romantic passion. With it, there may arise love, or there may not.

This brings us back to our earlier distinction between romantic and eirenic love. If the affection which may link a virgin boy and girl is love, what can we call the affection which may link a man and woman who live together, fuck together, come together, and have children? If the lesser is love, there is no name left for the greater. If on the other hand we regard them both as valid and valuable conditions, the lesser of which may or may not lead to the greater, then we shall not be denying human nature and common experience.

The proclaimed and deep misgiving about fucking which is so central to our society not only makes a niggling desert of individuals' lives, it also erects the closed circle of despair into a general philosophical and social principle. There was a time when those who chose to live within this circle were simply those who chose to live within this circle. Others did not; the two sorts of people recognized and avoided one another. Despair could be practiced relatively harmlessly in corners.

No longer. These two attitudes, the despairing and the hopeful, the deathly and the lively, the romantic and the

eirenic, coexist in our society and in all societies, in all
minds and in each mind. It will be the task of the next two
or three generations to make sure that the hopeful, lively
and eirenic strand predominates, and that the despairing,
deathly and romantic strand is kept down. Because those
who believe there is something wrong about the way people are made are bound to believe there is something right
about the way they are unmade.

Appendix 1

Pornography: The Trade

In discussions of obscenity at the moment it is usual to distinguish between, on one hand, "real" or "out-and-out" or "hard core" pornography, "dirt for dirt's sake," and, on the other, things with a claim to artistic merit; to condemn the former without discussion, to allow that overt erotic description must not be the excuse for suppressing the latter, and to admit that there is a difficult borderland between the two. These were the preconceptions which underlay both the long campaign for the passing of the Obscene Publications Act in Britain in 1959, and the first big prosecution brought under it, that of Penguin Books for publishing *Lady Chatterley's Lover,* in 1960.

It is hardly necessary to give an account of the works claiming literary or artistic merit which have been banned as obscene at one time or another.[1] But it may be helpful to give some idea of the "hard core," "dirt for dirt's sake" material which circulates under the counter in English cities at the moment. It comes in three mediums: films, still photographs, and stories or short novels. The pornographic film—"blue film" in England, "stag movie" in America—is usually about twenty minutes long, or less. The earlier ones often had some sort of a plot, based on a casual encounter; a salesman calling at the door was a typical one. Since the Second World War, they have mostly dispensed with even that much story line, and are completely de-socialized. Typically, about one-third of the time is spent in undressing. There is almost always a close-up of penetration to show there's no deception, and often the man pulls out and comes ouside, to show there's no deception there either and you're getting your money's worth. There are more likely to be dike trimmings than faggot. In America, perhaps one in twenty show black and white together, and this is fifty-fifty white man and black woman and black man and white woman. In America these films are typically shown in the course of business and political conventions. In England it is probably more often at parties.

Still photographs cover a much wider range of "per-versions" and oddities; perhaps because it is not worth showing a film without a dozen people present and a dozen people means half a dozen without any odd tastes—whereas the photographs are for solitary perusal, and you buy what you want. They come in cellophane packets of five; prices are roughly a pound a packet for breast-kneading, flagella-tion, and Lesbian scenes, and 25 shillings for straight fucking or male homosexuals. Both films and photographs are made with whores, and layabouts for men. In the films, the whores do not come, they "jive," or assume what passes on the game for a look of pleasure.

The novels and stories, sometimes printed abroad, some-

---

[1] This has been well done by Gilbert Armitage in *Banned in England*, 1932, and Alec Craig in *The Banned Books of England*, 1937. An account of the law before the Jenkins Act is in St. John Stevas' *Obscenity and the Law*, London, 1956.

times mimeographed at home, being for solitary consumption, also cater to all tastes. They, like the photographs, are often obtainable for rental as well as purchase. Many of them are sado-masochistic, since those who have that taste find their satisfactions harder to come by in real life than those who are more fortunate. I never saw a "hard core" periodical.

Here is part of the circular of a dealer in pornographic photographs which gives some impression of the hermetic world of guilty delight in which the people who depend on these things live.

STRICTLY PRIVATE
YOUR DISCRETION EXPECTED.
Dear Mr. Sir   Your Ref. No. 7789   Date Oct 14
Thank your for your enquiry. We feel confident you are not interested in the Sterile type of Childish Pin-up Photos which are flooding the market at the moment. The collections listed below are *ALL HAND PRINTED POSTCARD ENLARGEMENTS*, taken from Negatives which have come into our possession from the Libraries of *PRIVATE COLLECTORS POSSESSION*. Many originate from *FRANCE* and other less Orthodox Cities in EUROPE. They are intended for and CAN ONLY BE SOLD TO RESPONSIBLE PERSONS WHO ARE PREPARED TO USE THE UTMOST DISCRETION WITH THEIR USE. They come to you exactly as the lens of the Camera recorded the INTIMATE DETAIL —COMPLETELY UNMUTILATED. The ages of the Models vary from Teen-age to young Adults, and as you will see below, include both Sexes. All are calculated to REVEAL MAXIMUM INTIMATE ANATOMICAL DETAIL!!!!!!!

You must RETURN THIS COMPLETE LIST WITH YOUR ORDER addressed to (name and address). PLEASE SUPPLY by return post under extra strong PLAIN SEALED COVER
Collections No. . . . . I enclose remittance of £ . . . . . s . . . . d. Payment may be made by INTERNATIONAL MONEY ORDER, BRITISH POSTAL ORDERS, or CASH. Do you wish FUTURE CONFIDENTIAL LISTS SENT

(YES) (NO). If no, all correspondence is destroyed upon completion of your order.

COLLECTION No. 1 TEN FABULOUS POSTCARD ENLARGEMENTS OF TEEN-AGE GIRLS . . . with Fantastic measurements. Photographed by concealed Cameras that fully REVEAL their WONDERFUL ANATOMY from STARTLINGLY EXCITING and *NEW ANGLES!!!* Recommended for the AVID STUDENT OF THE UNUSUAL IN INTIMATE FEMALE ANATOMY 40/-d

---

COLLECTION No. 2 A SENSATIONAL AND FRENZIED COLLECTION OF CONTINENTAL LOVELIES IN TEN AMAZING AND THRILLING CONTORTION STUDIES that will have even the Experienced Adult Connoisseur astounded. UNBELIEVABLE POSTURES with VIVID and SUBTLE MIRROR DETAIL!!!! Posed by these RAVISHING GIRLS FOR YOUR BREATHLESS VIEWING!!!!   TERRIFIC!!!! and STIMULATING!!!!
. . . . 45/-d.

COLLECTION No. 4 TEN STUDIES. GENUINE FOREIGN COLLECTORS ITEMS for the Adult keen on UNUSUAL SEMI-DRAPED STUDIES . . . Various Lovely Girls in Items of INTIMATE DRESS that are arranged to REVEAL, INTRIGUING AND VERY SUBTLE!!!! . . . AMAZING CAMERA ANGLES!!!! . . . A DARING FEAST OF PROVOCATIVE ARTISTRY!!!! . . . . 40/-d.

IMPORTANT!!!! ALL THE ABOVE FOUR WONDERFUL COLLECTIONS COMPLETE FOR £5. 15. 0d. YOU SAVE £3 !!!!

ALSO AVAILABLE . . . RARE CONTINENTAL ALL MALE SETS . . . No Pouces. COMPLETELY UNDRAPED! VIRILE HANDSOME YOUTHS and YOUNG EXCITING ADULT MALE PHYSIQUES . . . in DUO and SINGLE STUDIES . . . UNMUTILATED . . . STRAIGHTFORWARD VISUAL EXCITEMENT for the STUDENT OF THE MALE NUDE!!!! WONDERFUL PIN SHARP DETAIL!!!! SETS OF TEN MIXED SINGLES AND DUO. POSTCARD SIZE.
40/-

ALL ORDERS ARE SENT BY RETURN POST!!!!

IT WILL HELP US TO SUPPLY YOU WITH WHAT
YOU WANT, IF WHEN ORDERING YOU WILL MEN-
TION YOUR FUTURE SPECIAL INTERESTS, to EN-
ABLE US TO FORWARD YOU THE APPROPRIATE
DETAILS ONLY . . . THANK YOU

Dear Sir . . . . I SHOULD LIKE YOU TO SEND
ME DETAILS OF . . . .
. . . .
*(THIS ONLY APPLIES TO CLIENTS ORDERING FROM
THESE LISTS.)*

It is men who consume hard core pornography, not
women. The stock explanation of this at the moment rests
on the two assertions that men are visual about sex and
women are tactile, and that men like to imagine it more
often and more intensely than women. I do not know what
the justification for the first assertion is; there is a certain
amount about it in Kinsey, but nothing that seems very
conclusive. The second on the other hand seems at least
meaningful, because of the usual procedure in adolescence.
If a girl never imagines fucking, someone will nevertheless
come along and want to fuck her; the possibility will be
forced on her notice by boys. But if a boy never imagines
it, nobody is going to force it on his notice, and he may
never get around to it at all. He has to have a blueprint
in his mind of what he wants to do, and a girl doesn't,
because the convention is that the boy takes the initiative.
If custom had thus really brought it about that boys did
more imagining about sex than girls did, this would be
some explanation of why men respond more to "pornography."

But it is not at all certain that this is what does happen,
and it may be that the whole fact of women being "the
second sex" has more to do with it. Women in bed, according to the custom of our society like what their first
man likes them to like and, roughly speaking, they like
it ever after. Not all men like pornography, fewer actually
use it, fewer still would like their women to like it, and

quite few teach their women to like it. The women who really do like it are often those who have been taught to like it by their men. It is a question of "we like it."

The assertion: "Men like it; women don't" is only partly a statement of what happens; it is also partly a statement of what is supposed to happen. To judge by the literature, it was supposed to be the other way round in the eighteenth century; women were supposed to like it, if anything, more than men.

Here are some accounts of men with pornographic books. The first is from Pepys, the archetype of the *homme moyen sensuel*. "And I to my chamber where I did read through *l'Escholle des Filles*,[2] a lewd book, but what do no wrong once to read for information sake. . . . And after I had done it, I burned it, that it might not be among my books to my shame, and so at night to supper and to bed."[3] That is probably still the commonest attitude today; either burn it or put it in the bottom drawer.

The nineteenth-century French publisher of erotica, Gay, described the people who collected the books he published thus: "The specialists who seek them out and collect them are generally extremely reserved persons, extremely discreet, and of a most exemplary conduct."[4]

And here is a description of a British collector of erotica in the Victorian age called "James Campbell."[5] He "read with ease Latin, French and Italian, and, although not familiar with German, few erotic books in that language were unknown to him. So thorough indeed was his knowledge of this particular branch, that hardly an obscene book in any language had escaped his attention. His industry was unflagging. Each book, or different edition, as he acquired

---

[2] See p. 94.

[3] 9th Feb. 1668.

[4] Quoted in "Rolf S. Reade," *Registrum Librorum Prohibitorum*, 192.

[5] [C. R. Ashbee], "Pisanus Fraxi," *Catena Librorum Tacendorum*, 187. He was really called James Campbell Reddie, a schoolmaster.

it, was at one collated, confronted with every available authority upon it, and compared page by page, word by word, with any other procurable issue of the same work. Of very scarce books, which he might not be able to procure, he frequently made copies with his own hand. . . . By this it may be judged how exact and thorough he was, and how completely he had mastered his subject. James Campbell viewed erotic literature from a philosophical point of view—as illustrating more clearly than any other human nature and its attendant foibles."

There is also an interesting and full account in *Monckton Milnes: The Flight of Youth,* by James Pope Hennessy, of a Victorian collector called Frederick Hankey, who lived on and for the trade in erotic and sadistic books and pictures.[6]

---

[6] London, 1951, pp. 117-122.

Appendix 2

The Later History of the Giulio-Aretino Works

The Giulio Romano prints have fared badly in later centuries.[1] Our knowledge of them comes from three main sources: (1) a collection of one complete original print and nine fragments of others in the British Museum; (2) a book published in Venice in the second quarter of the sixteenth century, and (3) a series of copies made about a hundred years ago by Friedrich von Waldeck.

(1) The British Museum Collection:

The one whole print in comparison with other work of Marcantonio Raimondi shows beyond reasonable doubt that it is either from his hand or a very good contemporary copy. The nine fragments belonged at one time to Sir Thomas Lawrence.

(2) The Venetian book:

Perhaps about 1550, a book was published in Venice

---

[1] For a full bibliographical account, which corrects many errors current until now, see David Foxon, *Libertine Literature in England, 1660-1745*, II, in *The Book Collector*, London, Summer, 1963.

containing some of Aretino's verse, and some other verse attributed to him. The *Sonnetti Lussuriosi* formed part of it. They were illustrated by woodcuts taken from the Giulio-Marcantonio prints. These woodcuts are of course pretty good—Venice was a good place for book production in those years—but a woodcut must always be a coarse affair compared with a copper engraving. Most of them are reduced from the Marcantonio prints, that is to say the background is cut down to concentrate on the figures. Two or three of them are evidently not from Giulio's drawings at all; they are out-of-door scenes (whereas all those in group three below are indoors), and the distribution of the weight is all wrong. The Giulio prints showed real mortals in possible places, with the weight naturally disposed. Some of these added figures have no visible means of support. Then too there are a couple of sonnets added at the end which suddenly turn round and kick the reader in the teeth for being such a degraded lecher as to have enjoyed the others. It is not impossible that they should be by Aretino—it is not impossible that anything should be by Aretino— but they are certainly not by the same Aretino that wrote the main series of sonnets. They are as far removed as could be from the straight, exuberant enjoyment of the other sonnets, and I incline to think they must be by another hand. The only copy of this book known to me is in the possession of Mr. Walter Toscanini of New York; he has deposited a microfilm of it in the British Museum. Dismembered cuts from another copy were changing hands in Rome in the 1930's.[2]

(3) The third source of knowledge is a series of copies made by Count Friedrich von Waldeck, a Bohemian artist and traveler who lived mainly in Paris. In 1865, when he was ninety-nine years old, he wrote in French a manuscript account of his copies; lithographed reproductions of it are in several public collections. He claimed that he had found

---

[2] Information from Dr. Donati of the Vatican Library.

a complete run of the Marcantonio prints in a convent in Mexico City, where he had traveled thirty years earlier in order to record and describe Amerindian antiquities.[3] These copies, which look like lithographs but reveal themselves as drawings under the magnifying glass, agree perfectly with the one whole surviving print and with the nine fragments, as well as with most of the Venetian woodcuts of group (2) above. The best way of deducing what the originals were like is to get a triangular fix from the Venetian woodcut and the Waldeck copy on the Rosetta Stone of the one surviving print, and use that to translate back from the other copies to their lost originals. The Waldeck drawings are on the whole true copies, that is to say, the disposition of the people, the composition, and the backgrounds are the same. But apart from that, almost every detail has gone wrong that could go wrong. Waldeck was working from the nineteenth-century feeling about these things, from guilty delight and secret, punishable indulgence. Moreover, even if he made his copies at the time he was in Mexico, he was more than twice as old as Giulio, and if he made them at the time he wrote his account of them, he was more than three times as old. (He died at the age of 109.) The eyes and expressions of Giulio's rather noble and open-looking couple are made bestial and leering and small, like a Charles Addams person. The flesh is softened and weakened, the fingers and toes are straightened and enfeebled; the life has gone out and leer come in. Moreover, the true feeling of the weight and balance of the body, the foundation on which all the achievements of Renaissance drawing were built, has quite gone. A fold in a curtain will show clear beside a head instead of being cut by it, a head or a foot turned two degrees this way or that will destroy the whole composition, and in one of

---

[3] The obituary of Waldeck in *The Illustrated London News* says that many of his papers were confiscated by the dictator Santa Anna before Waldeck left Mexico. I have caused inquiries to be made among historians and archivists in Mexico City, but none knows of these confiscated papers.

his copies Waldeck has even changed the lighting from right to left.

In the Cabinet des Estampes at the Bibliothèque Nationale in Paris there is a run of early nineteenth-century erotic prints, some of which are based on the Giulio Romano designs, and some on the erotic prints of Agostino Carracci. In both cases the backgrounds are brought up to date.

As I said earlier, many sets of erotic prints are attributed to Giulio Romano, but those described above are the only ones which really bear any reference to his own. There is a series reproduced in Kary von Karwath's *Die Erotik in der Kunst* under the title of *Mythologisches Kabinett,* without any further explanation, which corresponds to those in a book of early nineteenth-century engravings which bear in the British Museum copy an attribution to Giulio Romano, and the name of an engraver "Pirolli." These engravings have no backgrounds, whereas the *Mythologisches Kabinett* ones do. They are not bad, being open, sane in feeling, though a couple of times the boy is wagging his finger at the girl in a coy and minatory manner. One of them shows a girl being lowered in a basket with a hole in the bottom onto a boy's prick; he is holding the rope which runs up over a pulley and down to the basket. In Aretino's *Discussions,* a nun is looking at a book of erotic pictures, and one of them is described as showing this scene. The series in any case has nothing to do with Giulio Romano, and I only mention it because it is rather better than most of those which use his name.

Some of the Waldeck copies are reproduced in Eduard Fuchs, *Geschichte der Erotischen Kunst,* in his *Grossen Meister der Erotik,* and in Fernando Henriques' *Love in Action,* London, 1960.

Marcantonio Raimondi also engraved other erotic subjects; many printrooms have examples of these separate prints, which have survived better than the Giulio Romano series. There is one in the Cabinet des Estampes of the Bibliothèque Nationale, of a standing girl just putting a dildo into herself; it has a Raphaelesque lilt about the hips.

The Aretino sonnets on the other hand have been fairly often reprinted; the most easily accessible edition is that published in Paris in 1882 by Isidore Liseux. It contains a good French translation.

An edition exists with an English translation alleged to be by Oscar Wilde. It could not possibly, I think, really be by Wilde, it is so wholly without either his felicity or his occasional turn of melancholy and ornamental grandeur. The translator, whoever he was, missed the point of the sonnets badly enough to put all the speaking into the man's mouth; presumably he was writing out of the Victorian tradition that women don't enjoy sex, or at any rate would not say so if they did. Here is an example. The ending of the sonnet I quote above on p. 91 comes out like this.

> Of nothing my lewd senses now deprive,
> Dart all thy tongue between my lips apace,
> And suck until we faint of thirst—and strive
> To clutch at passion's core; but half alive
> We swoon and drop.—O God in heaven, dost see
> Our souls exhale and melt in ecstasy?

Apart from the more obvious horrors like "lewd" and "apace," there are some points here which are quite instructive for an understanding of the difference between the Renaissance approach and that of the nineteenth century. "Strive to clutch at passion's core." Every word here is romantic through and through. If there was one feeling more strikingly absent from Aretino than striving, it was clutching. The word *core* brings up the same picture: things in the Renaissance didn't have cores which you had to clutch at, elusive, secret hearts which were likely to escape you unless you sweated and strove to seize them. And the use of the word *passion* shows a sublime indifference to the whole history of philosophy and poetry in Europe. Passion, what is undergone, is the romantic word *par excellence*. Aretino's poems are all action. And lastly the pompous and exhibitionistic invitation to God to take note of the proceedings—what is God supposed to answer? Wait while I get my telescope? If he doesn't answer, are they going to shout louder about it?

The second volume of Samuel Putnam's *The Works of Aretino* (New York, 1926) also contains what purport to be translations of the sonnets, but are really independent inventions. They are so coy, guilty, timid and periphrastic that the eye involuntarily erases them from the page and leaves a sonnet-shaped blank there and in the memory.

Appendix 3

Arnaud Daniel: Caras Rimas

> L'aur amara
> Fa'ls Bruoills brancutz
> Clarzir
> que'l doutz espeissa ab fuoills,
> El's lets
> becs
> dels auzels ramencs
> Ten balps e muts,
> pars
> e non pars;
> Per queu m'esfortz
> de far e dir
> Plasers
> A mains per liei
> que m'a virat bas d'aut,
> Don tem morir,
> si'ls afans no m'asoma.
>
> Tant fo clara
> ma prima lutz
> D'eslir
> lieis, don cre'l cors los huoills,

Non pretz
necs
mans dos aigonencs,
D'autra s'eslutz
rars
mos preiars;
Pero deportz
m'es e d'auzir
volers
Bos motz ses grei,
de liei don tant m'azaut
qu'al sieu servir
sui del pe tro c'al coma.

Amors gara!
Sui ben vengutz?
C'auzir
tem far, si m'dezacuoills,
Tals detz
pecs
que t'es mieills que t'trencs;
Qu'ieu soi fis drutz
cars
e non vars;
Ma l'cors ferms fortz
mi fa cobrir
mains vers
Qu'ab tot lo mal
m'agr'ops un bais al chaut
Cor refrezir,
que no i val autra goma.

Si m'ampara
cill que m'tralutz
D'aizir
Si qu'es de pretz capduoills,
Del quetz
Precs,
c'ai dedins a rencs,
L'er for rendutz
clars

mos pensars:
Qu'eu fora mortz;
mas fa m'sofrir
l'espers
Que'ill prec que m'brei,
c'aisso m'ten let e haut,
Que d'als jauzir
no m'val jois una poma.

Appendix 4

Choderlos de Laclos:
On the Education of Women[1]

Draw near, women, and hear what I have to say. Turn your curiosity for once toward useful objects, and consider the advantages which nature gave you and society ravished away. Come and learn how you were born the companion of man and became his slave; how you grew to like that condition and to think it natural; and finally how the long habituation of slavery so degraded you that you preferred of freedom and repute. If the picture I shall paint leaves its sapping but convenient vices to the more difficult virtues you in command of yourselves, if you can contemplate it without emotion, then go back to your futile pastimes; "there is no remedy; the vices have become the custom."[2]

But if the tale of your sorrow and your loss makes you blush with shame and rage, if tears of indignation start to your eyes, if you burn with the noble ambition to win back

[1] Written in 1783, this was first published in 1903. This translation is made from the *Oeuvres Complètes*, NRF, Paris, 1951.
[2] Seneca.

your natural advantages, and to return to the fullness of your being, allow yourselves to be abused no more by deceitful promises, and hope nothing from the help of men, for they are the authors of your ills. They have neither the will nor the power to end them; how could they consent to form a woman before whom they would be forced to blush? Learn then that the only escape from slavery is by a great revolution. Is such a revolution possible? It is for you alone to say, for it depends on your courage. . . .

[There follows an account of Natural Woman as Laclos imagined her in a Rousseau-like state of nature. Here is the child.]

Twenty times, a hundred times over, she has seen the act of generation take place before her; she has not blushed, she has not fled, she has gone on her way indifferent, without casting so much as a furtive look behind her. She has seen with the eyes of the body, not the eyes of the imagination. Her senses are still asleep; they await the call of nature for their awakening. . . .

[The adolescent.]

Already her form is rounding, her breasts grow sensibly, the generative parts are protected and covered by newborn hair. Often, before that time, our young girl has found herself among men in the hunt, or on some other occasion, without either feeling or inspiring the least sensation. Some new chance now takes her there again, and no sooner does she touch the hand of one of them than a sweet trembling spreads through all her body. Involuntarily, her hand withdraws; she blushes; not with shame, but with desire. She would go to him again, but fears to, and this unknown feeling wholly occupies her being. Now she seeks solitude and in some sort folds herself in. For the first time she is concerned with her own thoughts. Bleak apathy and vague unrest trouble her by turns; a slight numbness in the groin, an almost painful sensitiveness in the joints make her plight yet more distressing. She tires easily on journeys, and stays behind, but without repose. Soon she feels a heaviness in the head, and the signs of ripeness in her breasts and in all the parts which have to do with generation. Thus she remains until the first menstrual flow, which comes both to relieve her and to prepare the workshop of nature. No doubt at this time the natural girl thinks herself ill; not that she can possess the concept of illness as we see it, but she knows she suffers, and that a change is happening in her. Meanwhile these symptoms pass, but they leave behind them the devouring fire which nature lights and only pleasure can quench. She is the victim of an unknown need, and a secret ardor consumes her; unquiet days are followed by nights more troubled still; the first light of dawn finds her no longer in the arms of sleep; no longer does she enjoy the refreshing rest of the morning. Everything round her is asleep; she alone of all nature is awake. As soon as the first faint light distinguishes one thing from another she wanders abroad with her trouble. She runs to the nearest stream and hopes the water will put out the fire which burns her; the first rays of the sun fall on her as she bathes. Vain remedy; she climbs out and burns again. All round her she casts her ardent and troubled glances. And soon they come to rest, enchanted by the beauty of the morning. She has felt the first fires of love, nature is coming to life for her; the sweet smell of the flowers prepares her for pleasure; the chorus of the birds is no longer an empty noise; it is a moving harmony which answers her own heart, and their repeated caresses affect her yet more strongly. With raised hands, with parted lips and shining eyes she gazes, and fears to disturb them; her short and hurried breathing, the precipitate movement of her breast, everything shows clearly the desire of her soul.

And then, a little way off, she sees a man. A powerful instinct, an involuntary movement, makes her run toward him. Close to, she is timid; she stops. But carried forward again she goes to him, she clasps him in her arms. . . . Delightful consummation, who dare ever describe thee?

[The grown woman.]

Her ornament is her flowing hair, her perfume is a bath of clear water. This is the condition, we dare to assert, which is, of all conditions, the most favorable to pleasure. But, one may say, what is consummation without love? Sensitive souls, we agree with you. Love is the consolation of society. Social man has redeemed this good alone of all those which natural man possessed. . . . But must we believe that natural woman is without love? We agree that there could be no continuing passion between two beings who join together without ever having seen each other before, and who the next moment will part and never recognize each other again. But this moment is not indivisible and, if we look closely, we can see in it all the gradations of sentiment. To them, the first caresses are the declaration; the woman retreats and provokes by turns; so grows desire; which, seen at its height, brings on ecstasy, expressed not in elegant phrases, but in shining looks and burning sighs, which are common to all languages. This language they know well enough to come at the same time. And, which perhaps distinguishes them most from us, they part without disgust.

Why should we fear to say it? Women of integrity, it is you we ask. Is there one among you who has consistently come without fear, without jealousy, without remorse, and without the distressing boredom of duty or conformity? You do not answer; but have the courage to examine your hearts and judge from yourselves. In vain would pride pity the natural woman; she has strength, health, beauty and love. What is lacking for her happiness?

Let us invent of our free will a perfectly happy woman, or at least as much of one as humanity is capable of encompassing. This will be one who, born of a tender mother, has not been delivered at birth to the cares of a hired nurse, one who has later been brought up under the eye of a teacher equally indulgent, wise and enlightened, so that without ever constraining her or boring her with lessons, he will have imparted to her every useful skill and will have removed her from all prejudice. Arrived at the age of pleasure, she will find for her husband a man who is always new, loving but not jealous, assiduous but not importunate. She will taste the joys of maternal love without feeling its perpetual worries, so often followed by frightful despair. Her wise imagination will see her happy youth depart without regrets. And, as she ages, she will know how to avoid both sickness and ridicule; so contemplating death without fear, she will fall peacefully into the last sleep. . . .

[And now here is the picture of the enslavement of women.]

Lacking strength, they could not defend and preserve their civil rights; companions in name, they soon become slaves in fact, and miserable slaves. Their lot can hardly have been better than that of the blacks in our colonies. . . .

Thus we still see them today in the canoes of Greenland, rowing like our convicts, and subjected to the same treatment; among the Kalmuks ceasing at the age of forty to be the companions of their husbands and becoming the servants of the house and of the younger women who succeed them; among the Koreans treated as slaves and often driven away with their children for trivial faults; on Mount Lebanon corrected with severity and made the slaves not only of their husbands but of their male children too; burdened in the Congo with all the heavy work, serving their husbands and daring neither to eat with them nor to sit in their presence; and thus too the Hottentots, though they are brought up by their mothers, make it a point of honor to despise them and even strike them when they reach the age of nineteen and are counted among the men. . . .

This situation endured in full vigor until the experience of a long train of centuries taught women to substitute cunning for strength. They felt at last that the only resource of the weak was to seduce; they learned that if they were dependent on men because of their weakness, they could make these same men dependent on them by pleasure. Less fortunate than men, they had to think and reflect the more. They it was who first knew that pleasure never comes so high as the idea one may form of it, and that imagination goes farther than nature. With these prime truths in hand, they learned first to veil their charms and arouse curiosity. They practiced the painful art of refusal, even when they wished to consent: with that they discovered how to fire the imagination of men, how to call forth and direct desire. And thus beauty and love were born.[3] From then on, the lot of women softened. Not that they had entirely succeeded in freeing themselves from the state of oppression to which their weakness had condemned them; but, in the state of perpetual war which subsists between them and men, they can be seen for ever fighting, with the help of the caresses they have invented sometimes winning, and often cleverly turning to advantage the very forces which are directed against them. Sometimes, too, men have turned against women the arms which the women had forged to fight men, and then the slavery of women is more abject than ever.

From beauty and love, jealousy was born. These three illusions have entirely changed the relative condition of men and women; they have become the charter and the guarantee of all the contracts which are made between them. They are infinitely varied in their forms, and no less so in their effects; today they are the only source of our passions. . . .

[On beauty.]

In our view, beauty is simply that appearance which is most favorable to pleasure; it is the manner of being which arouses hope of the most delightful orgasm. . . .

Man perceived that, when he came, his pleasure was not always equally great. A thousand reasons could combine to produce this inequality, but he ignored those which lay within him, since these he could not even know, and sought those which seemed to lie in external objects. The woman who procured him the most lively pleasure became pre-

---

[3] So that the inattentive reader should not accuse us of contradicting here what we said above about the natural woman, we must inform him that we are here speaking of beauty *as choice*, and of *exclusive* love. (Laclos' footnote.)

cious to him; he sought her again and, if he could not find her, he chose the one likest to her. He must have made mistakes, but there, he examined, he knew, or thought he knew, he got used to preferring, in short he found in time that a soft and fine skin stretched over firm and elastic flesh, the exclusive perquisite of freshness and the ordinary concomitant of youth, was more agreeable to touch and led to sweeter rest. Therefore he desired freshness. He found that a big woman multiplied his sensations by touching him at more points; therefore he desired a substantial figure. He found that it was not enough to embrace the object of his pleasure closely unless he too experienced a delightful embrace. Therefore he desired strength. . . .

Man only knows things by the impression he receives from them. Beauty only acts on him through memory; it does not exist for a man who has no idea of coming. And that, incidentally, is why an older man or woman who still wishes to please, even in decay, will seek out people who are too young to have been able to compare ideas of pleasure. They know that youth cannot yet know beauty, and they hope to profit by the first dawn of natural desire, before unwelcome comparisons shall have made their own aspect enough to extinguish it. But it is otherwise with the man of some experience. Lineaments which nature produces but rarely, whatever form they may have, awake no memories in him and thus no hope; consequently they are not beautiful in his eyes. Indeed if they are too foreign, or too like those of childhood or old age, when pleasure does not yet exist or has already ceased, if they carry him too far, whatever may be the reason, from that idea of coming which is never absent from him during his inspection, in that case, far from being attracted to them, he will repulse them. It is this association of lineaments which he calls ugliness. On the other hand those which he is most used to see, which most easily recall to him the idea of pleasure, to those he gives the name of beauty. And in fact, if we examine the rules which artists prescribe for the proportion of features . . . [etc.].

[On dress and conduct.]

. . . Without freshness, no beauty. Therefore avoid above all useless late nights; rest suits you better than the deceitful light of candles. . . . The nights which you deny to your amusements will make more precious those which you devote to your pleasures. . . . You are young and strong; what need have you of strong liquor? It is love must make you drunk. . . . Never let yourself be ruled by resentment; this inward state shows outwardly as well, and no one will trouble to please her who is not afraid of displeasing others.

Appendix 5

The Cazzaria and the Libro del Perchè

Nothing is known of Antonio Vignale but his name and his academic pseudonym. By the first half of the sixteenth century, almost every city in Italy had an Academy where the intellectuals of the town would meet to dine and talk about the new learning. The movement gave rise to the academies of sciences and arts and music and letters which still fill the world and continue largely as teaching, examining and administrative bodies. But at this time they were hardly more than discussion groups or dining clubs, and it was in this way that they served as the main means of diffusion for the new ideas. These academies often took whimsical names, such as the Academy of the Idle, the Sleepy, the Muddled, the Frozen, the Unstable, and the Thirsty at Bologna; of the Wet at Florence; the Insensate at Pistoia; the Shady at Ferrara; the Petrified at Turin; the Doubtful at Venice; the Motionless at Alessandria; the Excited at Este; the Infatuated at Mantua; the Ethereal at Padua, and the Reinvigorated at Foligno. One of the academies in Siena was called the *Accademia degli Intronati*, the Academy of the Enthroned Ones. It was al-

ready going in 1460. Each member of it called himself the
Something-or-Other Enthroned One. Vignale's academic
name was Arsiccio Intronato, which is hard to translate; it
really means the Rather Broiled-looking Enthroned One,
or perhaps the Slightly Toasted Enthroned One. *Arsiccio* is
the usual adjective, for instance, for the brown grass in
summer. His *Cazzaria* is in the form of a dialogue between
himself and some of his fellow academicians. It is the
wildest and most hilarious mixture of political philosophy,
crazy mythical anatomy, and general bawdy backchat, all
based on the Golden Age and its loss. He leads off the
dialogue in his own person with a resounding paean to
womanhood. ". . . And from this it follows that for the
great resemblance there is between Nature and the cunt we
sometimes, when we wish to speak correctly, call a woman's
cunt her *nature*[1] as being a thing of equal perfection and
capacity, whence, since a knowledge of the secrets of
nature is glory, honor and repute, so also should seeking
out the secrets of the cunt be glory and worship, and the
more so considering that wise nature has much to do
therein making within it the form and habitation of so
noble an animal as man."

But this is too solemn to let pass, so he has himself interrupted by his fellow academician, Sodo Intronato, the Solid
Enthroned One, whose real name was Marcantonio Piccolomini. "But wait, Rather Broiled One," he says, "I want
to prove to you that you don't know everything, and that
the cunt is not perfect. On the contrary, it suffers from a
very grave lack. . . . Nature should have given it buttons,
so that according as the prick was a little smaller or a little
larger, it could be buttoned up or unbuttoned." The Solid
One goes on to say that he had heard this complaint voiced
by a learned friar, and this provokes the Rather Broiled
One to an anticlerical tirade. "Those pigs would even pass
remarks about the cunt, and accuse nature of not having

[1] See C. S. Lewis' admirable essay on "Nature" in *Studies in
Words,* Cambridge, 1960.

made it to the measure of their pricks, as if they were not bursting with plenty and idleness and had nothing to think of all day, but . . . ," etc., etc.

Later Vignale takes up the question of language in this sort of writing; his approach to it is more subtle than his contemporary Aretino's absolute zeal for colloquial clarity. With a characteristic rueful twist he says in one place that it would probably have been better to write in Latin all along, as we in the twentieth century often still do when we come to this topic. "When they see *vulva* and *cunnus* written, they do not know that they are reading about cunts, and so they keep quiet. Besides, even if the work treats of pricks and cunts and asses, it may yet treat them in a pleasant way, so that everyone can understand it and take pleasure in it. So the delight would be all the reader's, and all that would be left to me would be the blame and the insults arising from it." Later he expresses in an obscure but rather moving passage the doubts and difficulties which beset anyone who tries to write in this way. "Nor, even if they wanted to, could anyone get prick or cunt or anything else that is less than natural or honest out of my book but I should tear it up, since I have here charged that it should sooner be burned and torn in pieces than that I should in any way whatsoever give to others what I have written in it, and that whether it be bad or good. But yet let him read it who will; there is nothing to be got from it, and if anyone is to be blamed, let it be nature, who has given us pricks and cunts and asses, and has taught us the other things which are spoken ill of and then, so that all should see them, has made us naked." The swing in feeling from the extreme of cautious retention to that of a careless communicativeness worthy of Aretino himself is quite striking. It is the same swing that affects all Western literature; here we see it one paragraph.

The book is full of little stories and jokes and sudden insights. For example, Vignale takes up the Greek legend of how men and women came to be differently made, and adds a vividly Italian detail to it. When God made the first two men of clay, he stood them up against each other for length, and when he parted them a bit of one came away and stuck to the other; that is why men have pricks and women have cunts, and why they desire to fit the one into the other, since that was where it first came from. So much is Greek. Vignale added that when he saw what had happened, God decided to make the best of it and taking the new appendage between his thumb and his first two fingers he gently pressed it home to make sure it would not fall off, and that is why it is the shape it is. Meanwhile, he inadvertently left the second man, who was now a woman, standing up. But since she was still soft, she settled a little, and that is why women are shorter than men, and broader in the lower half.

When Vignale is well into his stride he feels that he could go on forever, and promises the reader a future work in three volumes, to be entitled respectively: Of the Ancestry and Baptism of the Prick; Of the Nativity and Works of the Cunt; and Of the Life and Passion of the Ass, the whole to be subsequently reissued in one volume under the general title of *Lumen Pudendorum*.

There are little flashes of poetry, such as when he describes kissing as the tongues binding one another to secrecy, and occasionally of a sort of inverse vision oddly like the Zen technique of trying a proposition the other way round, as when he tells of two women passing the fishmarket at San Martino in Siena and saying: "Strong smell of us."

His anatomy is—I was going to say fantastic, but perhaps unbridled would be a better word. How deep is the cunt? What is at the inner end? The hand you are holding over her mouth to stop her waking the neighbors. That is why you kiss her, to see if your prick has arrived. Then some women have a pair of balls hidden away inside them, which makes them proud and quarrelsome. It also blocks the internal passage leading from the asshole to the cunt, which is why proud women's cunts don't smell. Again, why aren't women's asses hairy? Because they aren't real assholes at all, but "*di specie pottesca*," they are of a cuntish species, and women have them so that when they're pregnant you can use that instead, and thus avoid "casting seed on seed" which would lead to the birth of two-headed monsters. And so on and so on.

The bulk of the work is taken up with political allegory in sexual terms, based on the myth of the Golden Age and its loss, the myth common to Genesis and Rousseau, to Ovid and Karl Marx. Many writers have used political symbols to describe love-making, but none that I know of except Vignale and a later writer who derived from him have used sexual symbols to describe politics. You occasionally find love used in a vague way to symbolize the relationship between a ruler and his people—Claudel was given to that. But this is something much more elaborate and concrete and, of course, funny.

The allegory is one of justified revolution, leading to results other than those desired. In this primitive community of free organs, there arose a situation of economic injustice; the big pricks captured all the pretty cunts and kept them to themselves. In time the little pricks and the ugly cunts began to murmur together. A conspiracy was laid, and meetings were held. The leading spirit among the little pricks agreed with the leading spirit among the ugly cunts that "he should speak to one or two other pricks about it, and likewise she should speak to one or two other cunts." And so the plot spread until the forces were assembled to do battle. Meanwhile the balls and the assholes, aware of what was afoot, decided to stand aside and let their betters fight it out. They were the artisan and laboring classes in this allegory of a Guelf-and-Ghibelline-type squabble. Each class is carefully characterized. "The assholes," for instance "were a most proud and magnanimous people"; it is the language of Herodotus, or of the fifteenth-century chroniclers.

The battle was terrible and terribly confused. Treachery abounded, there were sieges and sacks, pillaging and parleys, ambuscades and embassies. At the end of it all a working agreement was reached on a new order, on a new balance of forces between the classes of this polis. The rather subjective complexity of Vignale's mind makes it impossible to unravel precisely what it was, but the sort of thing that happened is that the balls, as so often befalls the patient and unassuming classes, got the worst of it and were sentenced to live ever after in pairs in a sack. At heart, Vignale was a pessimistic radical. It is easy to see from the outline of his history, and from various concerns he mentions in passing, that he identified himself with the little pricks, and thus to guess at the genesis of his compensating wit.

Vignale's joke was taken up shortly afterward by the writer, whose identity is unknown, of a narrative poem called *Il Libro del Perchè*, "the Book of Wherefore." This writer, more pedantic and more dilute than Vignale, though not without a turn of phrase, sets the fancy even more severely into the framework of the history of philosophy; there is something definitely donnish about him. He traces the legend of the age of unrelated organs back through Aristotle to the Egyptians, or Preadamites, who, he says, distinguished between two images of primeval chaos. One was that of the four elements, earth, air, fire and water, and the other was the less familiar one of these *membrae disjectae*, disjointed members, which later coalesced to form men and women. He identifies the *membrae* with the particles of Anaxagoras, the seeds of Epicurus and Democritus, the ideas of Plato, and the forms of Aristotle. He sets the scene, the Golden Age before the fall, in this stanza:

> In quei tempi felici, in quel principio
> Incognita era ancora la malizia.
> Tutti s'amavan con amor reciproco:
> Gli occhi amorosamente riguardavano,
> Sinceramente le braccia abbracciavano,
> Teneramente le bocche baciavano,
> E senza complimenti, e cerimonia,
> Senza chieder licenza, e senza regole,

Per tutto i cazzi a lor piacer entravano,
E questa potea dirsi, a ben riflettere,
Che fu del secol d'or la prima imagine.

In those happy times, in that beginning/malice was still unknown;/All loved one another with a reciprocal love[2]/ Eyes looked lovingly/Arms embraced sincerely,/Mouths kissed tenderly,/And without standing upon ceremony,/ without asking leave, and without rules/pricks entered everywhere at their pleasure,/And this, if you come to think about it, you could describe/as the first image of the Golden Age.

---

[2] Cf. Theocritus.

Appendix 6

Maffio Venier: La Strazzosa

Amor vivemo trà la Gatta, e i Stizzi
Int'una Cà à pè pian
E non vedo però che ti t' agrizzi,
Dove la Lume, e'l Pan
Stà tutti in t'un, la Rocca, i Drappi, e'l Vin,
La Vecchia, e le Fascine,
I Putti, e le Galline,
E mezo el Cavezal sotto'l Camin,
Dove taccà à un'anzin
Ghe in muodo de trofeo
La Ferzora, una Scufia, e la Graela
Do candelle de Seo
Un Cesto, e la Sportella,
E'l letto fatto d' Alega, e de Stoppa.
Cosi a valio ch' pulesi s'intoppa.
In pe d'un Papago s'allieva un' Oca,
In pe d'un Cagnolatto
Ghe un Porchetto zentil, che basa in boca.
Lascivo animaletto
Suave compagnia dolce concerto,
L'Oca, la Gatta, e tutti.

La Vecchia, e'l Porco, e i Putti,
La Gallina, e'l mio amor sotto un coverto,
Ma in cento parte averto
Dove la Luna, e'l Sol
Fà tanto piu la casa alliegra, e chiara.
Come sotto un Storiol
Sconde fortuna avara,
Una Zogia, una Perla in le scoazze
Infinita bellezza in mille strazze.
E'l Concolo dal pan stroppa un Balcon,
Che n'ha Scuri, ne Veri
Magna in tel pugno ogn'un co fà i Falcon
Senza Tola, ò Tagieri,
Stà la Famegia intorno a la Pignata,
A aspettar che sia cotto,
Ogn'un beve in t'un Gotto,
E tutti aguazza à un bezzo de Salata
Vita vera, a beata,
Un Lenzuol fa per sie,
Che da un di all' altro amarizà dal fumo
Man, Brazzi, Teste, e Pie
Sta in t'un, tutti in t'un grumo
Onde se vede un' ordene à grottesche
De Persone, de Bestie, e de Baltresche.
In casa, chi ze in Camera ze in Sala,
Chi è in Sala, e in Magezen
Ghe nome un letto in t' una sotto Scala,
Ove il brazzo al mio ben
Passo le notte de dolcezza piene
Se ben la pioza, e'l vento
Ne vien tal volta drento
A rinfrescar l'amor su per le rene
Notte care, e serene,
Caro liogo amoroso,
Beltà celeste in povera schiavina,
Toggia un letto pomposo,
C'hà dentro una Gabrina,
Che fa lù quel effetto un viso d'Orca,
Che in bella cheba una Gazzalo sporca.
In sta Cà benedetta, e luminosa
Vive poveramente

Sta mia cara d'amor bella, e strazzosa,
Strazzosa riccamente,
Che con più strazze, e manco drappi intorno
Più se discovre i bianchi
E verzelai fianchi
Com'è più bel con manco niole il zorno
Habito troppo addorno,
Sora perle, e rubini,
Sora beltà, che supera ciascuna
Qual ze frà due camini,
S' imbavara la Luna,
Che lusa in mezo, tal splende la fazza,
E i razi di costia frà strazza, e strazza.
A sta beltà ste strazze ghe bisogna,
Che non se die stropparla,
S'hà da covrir de drapi una carogna,
Che stomega à vardarla,
Ma quella vita in st'habito risplende
Senza industria, e senz'arte
Massizza in ogni parte,
Che ne cassi, ne veli il bel contende,
Carne bianche, e stupende
Al ciel nude, e scoverte,
Per pompa de natura poverette
Ande à sto muodo averte
O collo, ò spalle, ò tette,
Che non se tagia un vanto ov' l'anello
Se non perche è piu bel questo de quello?
Che drappi porìa mai s'io fossi d'oro
Covrir si bei colori
Che non fusse un leame in t'un tesoro,
Un fango sovra i fiori,
Và pur cosi che st'humiltà t'inalza,
Và povereta altiera
Cosi co'pie per terra
Che ti è piu bella quanto più descalza,
Come'l ciel me strabalza
A una belleza estrema
In t'una casa, che no ghe do scuelle
Providenza suprema
Del Cielo, e de le Stelle,
Che ze andà a catar fuora do despersi

Per unir le to strazze co'me versi.
Strazze mie care ond'ho rivolto il cuor
Dolce strazze amorose,
Fenestre della gratia, occhi d' Amor.
Strazze fodrae de ruose,
Che se vede a spontar fra lista, e lista
Fuor a de quei sbregoni
Quattro dea de galoni
Che traze lampi, che te tiol la vista
Fia mia chi no t'ha vista
E un'huomo mezo vivo
Chi te vede e no muor, è un Zoco morto,
E mi che te descrivo
So che te fazo torto,
Che te taso la gloria, e te defraudo,
E te stronzo l'honor pi che te laudo.
Podessio pur con dar de la mia vita,
Trovar piu lengue à usura,
Che la mia sola a una beltà infinita.
E piccola mesura,
Sò, che non digo niente à quel che lasso
Ma quel puoco ch'intendo
E'l mesuro, e comprendo.
Co se mesura el Ciel con un compasso,
In sta bellezza passo
La mia vita contenta,
Che trova salda fede in veste rotte,
Non hò chi me tormenta
Ne il zorno, ne la notte
Ghe ze un voler, un'anima in do petti
Cose che ghe n'è puoche in molti letti.
Perche donne d'haver laghi de pianti,
Rivoli di sospiri,
E sempre inanti esserciti d'amanti,
Formè nuovi martiri.
Nutrive cento diavoli in te i occhi,
Che tenta i cuor contriti,
Cerchè che mille afflitti
Ve se vegna à butar morti in zenocchi,
Amor sti me in fenocchi,
Mai piu frizzeme all'hora,
Che te aparecchio la farina, e l' ogio

Questa è la mia Signora,
La me vuol, mi la vogio,
Non hò qua d'arabbiar, ne da instizarme
Chi vuol guerra d'amor se metta in arme.
Canzon mia repezzà
Sti e per sorte represa, e ti reprendi
Chi te reprenderà,
Mostra, chè te l'intendi,
E dì che ti m'he drappi de Velvo,
Che quel ch'e Dio d'Amor và sempre nuo.

Johannes Secundus: Basium 5

Dum me mollibus hinc et hinc lacertis[1]
Adstrictum premis imminensque toto
Collo, pectore lubricoque vultu
Dependes umeris, Neaera, nostris
Componensque meis labella labris
Et morsu petis et gemis remorsa
Et linguam tremulam hinc et inde vibras
Et linguam querulam hinc et inde sugis,
Adspirans animae suavis auram
Mollem, dulcisonam, humidam measque
Altricem miserae, Neaera, vitae;
Hauriens animam meam caducam,
Flagrantem, nimis vapore coctam,
Coctam pectoris impotentis aestu,
Eludisque meas, Neaera, flammas
Flabro pectoris haurientis aestum—
O iucunda mei caloris aura!

---

[1] After Virgil's tremendous lines (*Aeneid*, VIII, 387): Dixerat, et niveis hinc atque hinc diva lacertis Cunctantem amplexu molle fovet.

Tunc dico: Deus est Amoris maior,
Si quisquam tamen est Amore maior,
Tu, tu sola mihi es, Neaera, maior!

Appendix 8

Freud Today

The reader may have noticed the absence of references to Freud in this book, although its field is one in which his influence is very strong. This is not because I am ignorant of Freud, still less because I believe his work was wrong or foolish, but because I believe much of it has been inflated and mummified by foolish "Freudians" and has now come to the end of its immediate relevance. Freud was a great innovating thinker in that he enabled individuals to remember what they had forgotten, and did so with such efficiency that he also enabled one very influential section of our culture to remember what it had forgotten; the section of educated Protestantism and Jewry. It so happened that the classes and countries he addressed at the turn of the century had forgotten that there is physical affection between mother and son as well as between lovers, and that children as well as adults are made of flesh and blood. The real wonder is not that Freud reminded them of this, but that they had ever forgotten it. Other classes and cultures had not; as Freud himself was the first to admit, he uncovered nothing which had been unknown to the Greeks and in the Renaissance. But there; they had forgotten it, they were suffering from their forgetfulness, and Freud's work was necessary and admirable. His contribution to knowledge lay not so much in what he uncovered, as in the way he uncovered it. He was a wonderful remover of man-hole lids. What happened to be festering in the sewers then was sex. It is not now; what is festering there now is probably money. But latter-day Freudians are still busy unearthing the unearthed; they are hung up with the over-exploited first fruit of the method, and neglect to apply it to other fields.

Freud was himself a product of the age he changed, and the way he felt and thought about sexuality is not an appropriate guide for this age. That it is not is largely his own merit. Let us take two examples. He used to describe the sexuality or "libido" of young children as "polymorphously perverse." By this he meant that they feel physical pleasure in many different parts of their bodies: genital organs, anus, mouth, etc. To a pre-Victorian or, equally, to a post-Freudian, the choice of the word "perverse" is capricious. It seems to refer to the Krafft-Ebing—Magnus Hirschfeld tradition, according to which the attachment of "libido" to anything except the genital organs themselves is wrong, dangerous, abnormal, psychopathic. To feel that a young child is perverse, whether polymorphously or monomorphously or even protomorphously, seems to accept the doctrine of original sin and the works of the devil.

Secondly: "The genitals themselves have not undergone the development of the rest of the human form in the direction of beauty; they have retained their animal cast; and so even today love, too, is in essence as animal as it ever was."[1] And again: "It is remarkable that the

---

[1] *Collected Papers,* Rivière and Strachey, eds., London, 1950, Vol. IV, p. 215; Ernest Jones, ed., New York, 1959.

genitals themselves, the sight of which is always exciting, are hardly ever regarded as beautiful. . . ."[2]

The exclusion and contempt of the sexual organs here is striking. Freud felt that we carry a bit of the animal realm around with us between our legs; a feeling which can be traced throughout the history of Manichee morality, and even in Rabelais. I doubt if a biologist would hold that our pricks and cunts are more like those of, say, monkeys, than our teeth or ears are. And when he speaks of the "tendency towards beauty" he is of course saying no more than that he himself didn't like the look of the things much. He can never be a satisfying guide to those who do.

There are many other flaws. To enumerate briefly: the map of the sexuality of women is terribly man-centered. I can hardly believe that even then little girls went round feeling jealous because they didn't have pricks; I'm quite sure they don't now. The alleged two types of orgasm we have discussed already; one for when a woman is behaving like a man, one for when she's helping a man to behave like a man. (Instead of one general type for when she's behaving like a woman.) The Oedipus complex, which sometimes seems to be the main motivation of all human activity, applies to half mankind only; the Daughters-of-Lot complex figures almost nowhere.

To Freud, honor where honor is due, and that is for the method. For the psychopathology of everyday life, for the analysis of certain dreams in terms of what tended to be in the subconscious of upper middle-class Viennese in 1900, for the analysis of the causation of certain neurotic syndromes in the same terms. Not for the attempts to re-assess human nature in general in the light of what, by chance, the method turned up at that time and in that place.

To his followers, little honor. None for perpetuating a mummified version of Freud's local reassessment of human nature. Less than none for the psychoanalytical school of

[2] *Civilisation and its Discontents,* translated by Joan Rivière, London, 1930, p. 39.

biography, proving that Beethoven "was" his nephew's mother, or the White Knight "was" Lewis Carroll's penis.

Then there is the Freudian so-called psychotherapy. Freud had many interests, and in his day statistics were not a very highly developed implement; he can be forgiven for claiming in the euphoria of intellectual construction that psychoanalysis had a therapeutic value. But sixty years have gone by, and, as I write, the assertions of Eysenck and others that psychotherapy of the general type initiated by Freud cures neurosis no quicker or better than the passage of time stands uncontradicted. "A psychoanalysis" is not a medical procedure at all, but a religious one. It is often observed that psychoanalysis only flourishes in Protestant countries and presumably fills the same need as confession does in Catholic countries. But there are other resemblances. The fee fulfills the function of the tithe, the transference of the repentance, the long, long schedule of visits, of penance, and the reintegration of personality fulfills the same function as the absolution. The training analysis, where a fledgling psychoanalyst is analyzed by a fully qualified one, corresponds to the laying on of hands in ordination.